The Plays of Thomas Kilroy

ALSO BY THIERRY DUBOST

Struggle, Defeat or Rebirth: Eugene O'Neill's Vision of Humanity (McFarland, 1997; paperback 2005)

The Plays of Thomas Kilroy

A Critical Study

THIERRY DUBOST

McFarland & Company, Inc., Publishers
Jefferson, North Carolina, and London

LIBRARY OF CONGRESS CATALOGUING-IN-PUBLICATION DATA

Dubost, Thierry, 1958–
    The plays of Thomas Kilroy : a critical study / Thierry Dubost.
       p.   cm.
    Includes bibliographical references and index.

    ISBN-13: 978-0-7864-2797-0
    (softcover : 50# alkaline paper) ∞

    1. Kilroy, Thomas — Criticism and interpretation. 2. English drama — Irish authors. 3. English drama — 20th century.
4. Ireland in literature. I. Title.
PR6061.I38Z65   2007
822'.914 — dc22   2007001152

British Library cataloguing data are available

©2007 Thierry Dubost. All rights reserved

No part of this book may be reproduced or transmitted in any form or by any means, electronic or mechanical, including photocopying or recording, or by any information storage and retrieval system, without permission in writing from the publisher.

On the cover: Stephen Rea in *Double Cross,* Field Day Theatre Company, Derry, 1991 *(courtesy Field Day)*

Manufactured in the United States of America

McFarland & Company, Inc., Publishers
  Box 611, Jefferson, North Carolina 28640
    www.mcfarlandpub.com

To my parents

Acknowledgments

I should like to thank people who helped me continue my work on the theatre of Thomas Kilroy. First among them is Rosalind Dilys, the translator of the six chapters I had initially written in French. Rosalind's dedication to her work and her wonderful sense of humor made her an exceptional working companion. She died while this book was in progress, but she is not forgotten. I am grateful to Eric Bollengier, Olivier Cosme, Philippe Collaintier, and Caroline Ni Eili for their help. My sincere thanks go to Jeremy Malim and Valérie Burling, who read the manuscript and eradicated a number of infelicities of style. I am grateful to Suellen Fitzsimmons, Phil Pavely, and Tom Lawlor for giving me permission to use their photos. I owe thanks to many theatre companies, among which are the Abbey Theatre, Field Day, Rough Magic, and Pittsburgh Irish and Classical Theatre. I would like to acknowledge the help of Mairead Delanay, Cormac Deane, Loughlin Deegan, Claire O'Neill and Michelle Zinger, who helped me gain access to precious archives. I wish to thank Caen University Press for allowing me to translate and publish six chapters of my French book, *Le Théâtre de Thomas Kilroy*. I am also grateful to Peter Lang for allowing me to reprint the chapter "Irish Disconnections with the Former British Empire: Thomas Kilroy's Adaptation of *The Seagull*," initially published in *Crucible of Cultures*. I also thank *Etudes Irlandaises* for allowing the reproduction of "New Voices in Irish Theatre: An Interview with Tom Kilroy" (XXVI, Spring 2001). I owe thanks to Peter Fallon for his support, and for giving me permission to quote from the plays published by the Gallery Press. I am also very grateful to Lynne Parker, Max Stafford-Clark, Patrick Mason and Andrew S. Paul, for sparing the time for interviews and for their support of the project. I also wish to express my gratitude to Thomas Kilroy for agreeing to be interviewed and for giving me access to unpublished material.

Contents

Acknowledgments	vii
List of Abbreviations and Dates of Publication of the Plays	xi
Preface	1

Part I: The Plays

1. *The O'Neill*: An Early View of Irish Identity	7
2. Encounters in *The Madame MacAdam Travelling Theatre* and *The Death and Resurrection of Mr. Roche*	20
3. Comic Variations in *Tea and Sex and Shakespeare*	33
4. Space in *Talbot's Box*	44
5. *Double Cross*: The Faces of Betrayal	57
6. Lighting Up the Masks: *The Secret Fall of Constance Wilde*	69
7. Skywork for a Symphonic Theatre: Scenic Images in *Blake*	81
8. *The Shape of Metal*: Portrait of a Successful Artist	98
9. Irish Disconnections with the Former British Empire: Thomas Kilroy's Adaptation of *The Seagull*	108
10. Conclusion	118

Part II: Interviews

11. An Interview with Thomas Kilroy, 2001
 by *Paul Brennan and Thierry Dubost* — 125
12. An Interview with Thomas Kilroy, March 8, 2004 — 137
13. An Interview with Lynne Parker, Dublin, October 30, 2003: On *The Shape of Metal* — 155
14. A Telephone Interview with Max Stafford-Clark, June 3, 2004: On *Tea and Sex and Shakespeare* and *The Seagull* — 161
15. A Telephone Interview with Patrick Mason, September 27, 2004: On *Talbot's Box, The Secret Fall of Constance Wilde,* and the First Irish Production of *The Seagull* — 164
16. An Email Interview with Andrew S. Paul, December 2005: On *The Seagull* and *Henry* — 174

Appendix: Premières of Thomas Kilroy's Plays and Adaptations — 181
Chapter Notes — 185
Bibliography — 193
Index — 201

List of Abbreviations and Dates of Publication of the Plays

Note: (date of first performance); [date of first publication].

BL	*Blake.* Unpublished
DC	*Double Cross.* (1986) [1986]
DRMR	*The Death and Resurrection of Mr. Roche.* (1968) [1969]
MMTT	*The Madame MacAdam Travelling Theatre.* (1991) [1991]
MSL	*My Scandalous Life.* (2000) [2004]
ON	*The O'Neill.* (1969) [1995]
SFCW	*The Secret Fall of Constance Wilde.* (1997) [1997]
SM	*The Shape of Metal.* (2003) [2003]
TB	*Talbot's Box.* (1977) [1979]
TSS	*Tea and Sex and Shakespeare.* (1976) [1998]

Adaptations

EC	*Enrico Cuatro. (Henry)* (2005). From Pirandello (unpublished play)
GH	*Ghosts.* (1989) [2002]. From Ibsen
SA	*Spring Awakening.* From Wedekind (unpublished play)
SCSA	*Six Characters in Search of an Author.* (1996). From Pirandello (unpublished play)
SEA	*The Seagull.* (1981) [1981]. From Chekhov

Preface

Thomas Kilroy was born in Ireland, in 1934, at Callan, County Kilkenny. He began his schooling with the Christian Brothers, then went to St. Kieran's College and finally entered University College Dublin (UCD) in 1953 to study arts and complete an education degree, after which he became a teacher, then a headmaster. In 1965, he was appointed to a senior lectureship at UCD where he lectured mainly on English and Anglo-Irish drama, more specifically eighteenth-century drama. In the course of his years as senior lecturer at UCD, he also taught as a visiting professor in several American universities. In 1973, following the success of his novel *The Big Chapel*, he took a break from his university career. In 1979, however, he resumed his former activities, and was appointed to a professorship at the National University of Ireland, Galway. As a member of the Royal Society for Literature and of the Irish Academy of Letters, Thomas Kilroy has also been very active in the field of drama, since he worked with avant-garde Irish and English companies such as the Royal Court in London and Field Day in Derry.

His first play, *The O'Neill*, was performed after *The Death and Resurrection of Mr. Roche*, even though it was written at an earlier date. It tells, from a human point of view, the story of Hugh O'Neill, Earl of Tyrone, who was beaten by the English in 1601 at the Battle of Kinsale, one of the major episodes in Irish colonial history. His next work was *The Death and Resurrection of Mr. Roche*, in which a group of inebriated men mistakenly imagine they have brought about the death of a homosexual. The social and moral background of Ireland weighs heavily on the characters' lives in this play, which has many points in common with *The Playboy of the Western World*.

A sense of humor, never totally absent in any of the plays, comes to the fore in *Tea and Sex and Shakespeare*. This comedy, which one might almost qualify as burlesque, gives a festive touch to the depiction of a writer in quest of inspiration. It has something of the surrealistic in its handling of the playwright coming to grips with writing, in an environment in which the ordinary interacts with less predictable elements. With *Talbot's Box*, Kilroy explores the idea of sainthood, and the moral solitude to which some spiritual pathways lead in modern society. As in his other plays, he is careful to remain at a certain distance from his subject. He breaks through the limits of dramatic form so as to widen the scope of his central theme.

Before writing his next play, *Double Cross*, Kilroy adapted *The Seagull* from Chekhov. *Double Cross* (like *The Madame MacAdam Travelling Theatre*) was a Field Day play. These plays were intended to be part of the debate taking place in Northern Ireland, and to address the major political issues of the time. In *Double Cross*, the playwright examines the question of identity and of the interaction between man and history from an Irish point of view. Two historic characters, Brendan Bracken and William Joyce, who, during World War II chose to side, one with the English, the other with the Germans, find themselves placed at the center of a debate which is all the more disconcerting for its refusal of any form of Manichaeism. The main feature of *Double Cross* is the subversion of the nationalist ideology, showing its absurdity through the two figures of Joyce and Bracken, who are grotesque versions of loyalty and betrayal.

Kilroy adapted a second play, *Ghosts*, from Ibsen, then returned to his reflection on the theatre with *The Madame MacAdam Travelling Theatre*, which portrays a theatre company who have arrived by chance in Eire. The various interactions and the resulting encounters between the villagers and the troupe are so many ways of looking at life, in which the banal mingles with the extraordinary. Still focused on the staging of what takes place on stage, Kilroy then adapted Pirandello's *Six Characters in Search of an Author*, which was performed at the Abbey Theatre, Dublin, in 1996.

The Secret Fall of Constance Wilde illustrates a gradual shift in Kilroy's approach to historical reality, which he still uses as a starting point for his plays, while adapting its content with ever-increasing freedom. This play tells the story — in an adapted form — of the unfortunate destiny of the wife of Oscar Wilde, laying particular emphasis on the relation between womanhood and society. Constance is depicted as the victim of indecent assault, forced, because she is a woman, to wear a mask that exemplifies her stifled existence.

In *Blake*, Thomas Kilroy continues his dramatic quest for new means of expressing his dramatic talent. Inventing an episode in the biography of William Blake, turning the poet into a socially defined madman, he interweaves a love story with a stage expression of his reflection on art. To do so, he creates new forms of staging, in which images and music indirectly echo the inner journey of the character. Wondering where the borderline between madness and genius lies, he sets the play in an asylum, which enables him to probe into the nature of staging, while reminding the audience that they are watching a performance.

The Shape of Metal portrays a sculptress in her last years pondering the intensity of her personal and artistic failures, both as an artist and a mother. After the death of her father, Judith confronts her mother, Nell, and forces her to explain why her elder daughter vanished. Thanks to their conversations, the playwright combines the gradual revelation of a past tragedy with a reflection on art and its future. Contrary to *Blake*, in which music and languages others than speech proved especially important, *The Shape of Metal* relies heavily on the power of language, and with a measure of success, even if the move toward a storytelling tradition from which Kilroy's other works break away is far less convincing.

As had been the case for *Ghosts*, *Six Characters in Search of an Author* or *The Seagull*, Kilroy's latest work, his second adaptation of a Pirandello play, *Henry (Enrico Cuatro)*, is a reflection on both masks and theatre, through which he resumes his multiple questionings of human existence.

As for critical perspectives, to date, individual articles published in theatre journals and the special issue of the *Irish University Review* can help readers grasp obscure aspects of the plays. However, the theatre of Thomas Kilroy — as opposed to that of other major contemporary Irish playwrights — has not yet given rise to a general appraisal of the extensive scope of his works. The complexity of the plays, which intellectually challenge both audiences and critics, cannot solely explain the limited interest in the playwright. The unfamiliar alliance between a serious theatrical complexity and varied but demanding forms of comedy may also account for this resistance. While the vision behind some plays is essentially comic, it is impossible to equate them with shallow forms of entertainment, which might draw more immediate interest. However, this deficit of popular support is counterbalanced by academic respect, hopefully announcing future national and international successes.

Thomas Kilroy's play-writing reflects his analysis of the essence of theatre intertwined with his meditations on humanity, which sometimes lead him to refer to an ambiguous background of Irish history. Kilroy's plays are indeed rich and frequently so disconcerting for the spectator that I have chosen — in the limited scope of this book — to present a separate chapter for each play, rather than undertake a synthetic and comprehensive study of all his dramatic works. The order in which the plays are presented corresponds to the order in which they were completed, sometimes at a much earlier date — especially for the plays written in his youth — rather than that of their first performance. The combined chapter on *The Death and Resurrection of Mr. Roche* and *The Madame MacAdam Travelling Theatre* is however an exception. Although these two comedies differ greatly in both the temporal setting and the content, I have attempted to give the reader a glimpse of some common themes which may not immediately catch the eye.

The consistency underlying Thomas Kilroy's dramatic production as a whole finds an echo in the correlation between the themes chosen for each individual study of the plays. These themes — among others of course — could be starting points for readers who wish to pursue their own investigations. In this respect, the exploration of the theatre of Thomas Kilroy is rather traditional, but I tried to give a wider scope to this study by including photos of staged plays, and by interviewing stage directors and the playwright himself. I felt it was essential to bring readers closer to the performance of the plays. I am convinced that interviews with the author expressing himself on his work and, on the other hand, interviews with people who collaborated with him in the staging of the plays, will prove helpful. Behind this attempt at forming a critical triptych lies the hope that, in meeting a variety of perspectives on the works of a major playwright, readers of this book — a reflection on his theatre — will be encouraged to go further in their discovery of Thomas Kilroy's often exceptional plays.

Part I
The Plays

1

The O'Neill:
An Early View of Irish Identity

The driving force behind literary creation is all the more mysterious and inscrutable as the writers under study often pursue a course with hidden motivations. Critics are thus led to make various conjectures — vain ones, some might say — which are nevertheless often a necessary element in the analysis of the writers' trajectories. Indeed, the beginnings of any literary career are always significant, whether they portend the essence of a work to come, or merely hint at the author's future field of investigation. Each piece of writing comes to center on a time-sphere and a set of places, and personal experience gradually ripples into the texts as the author expresses his perception of the world. In the present case, these initial reflections on Thomas Kilroy's early play-writing appear necessary in order to clarify the author's position regarding the significance of the subject matter of his first play. In spite of the uncertainty which arises each time a hidden facet of a writer comes to light, it is possible to identify a number of questions that have consistently attracted the author's curiosity. So, when Thomas Kilroy decides to begin his career as a playwright with an analysis of the story of Hugh O'Neill, one may infer that the question of Irish identity holds a special place among the areas he wishes to explore. In its subject matter, *The O'Neill* reflects a deliberate and potent choice, given the fact that the play's most characteristic feature is its reference to a painful episode in Irish history.

Tom Kilroy's theatre is extremely complex. His plays draw their substance from the author's reflection on the condition of humankind faced with the difficulties of life and the suffering they bring, including renewed self-definitions springing from life's vicissitudes. The concern for Ireland's past and the focus on a major historical character are expressed as an initial approach to ontological questions. Far from being contingent, these harbingers of Kilroy's later works trigger a reflection process which heralds future investigations staged in more contemporary environments. The very title of the play, *The O'Neill*, takes us back in time, as it reverts to an archaic way of naming people. The absence of the plural morpheme underscores the unicity of the referent, whereas an "s" added to the surname would have widened the reference to a lineage and would have meant a different approach to history, less centered on one person and more suggestive of a clan. Moreover, the absence of a Christian name lays greater emphasis on the man as the bearer of a name or of a title, making him stand as a figure of exception. Whatever personal qualities were his, Hugh O'Neill is mainly characterized by his social function — his personality playing a secondary role. The choice of such a title for his first play shows Thomas Kilroy's desire to offer a new approach to an episode of ancient history whose contemporary relevance heightens — in the pain which it reflects — the dramatic potential of the misfortunes to be narrated. The first scenes of Act One center on the latent conflict between the English and the Irish, against a background of sentimental transgression which at the beginning seems to be a reference to Romeo and Juliet's amorous misconduct. However, contrary to the force of love expressed in the Elizabethan drama and epitomized in the association of the two names, Hugh and Mabel would be quite incapable of assuming the role suggested by a title such as this. In fact, as opposed to what happens in Shakespeare's tragedy, the passing of time only magnifies the obstacles which the lovers had believed they could overcome. The title *The O'Neill* thus leads us to expect a reevaluation of the past,[1] while also suggesting the extinction of a human being. In this respect, the first words Kilroy addresses to the spectator, via the title, set the scene for a play on false pretences and doubt, for the words on the bill lead one to think that the plot is to revolve around the historical figure, rather than around the man.[2] According to the title, it would appear that the main character of the drama is not to be staged as an individual grappling with his destiny and whatever private concerns it may hold, but as an emblematic figure of Irish history.

Any play which projects the spectator into an alien time-sphere sets up a particular type of dialogue between the audience and the time-sphere referred to, and runs the risk of meeting a lack of response to bygone situations. Nevertheless, Irish spectators, alas, have no difficulty in relating to Hugh O'Neill as the main character, since in spite of the passing of time, tensions between parties resulting from differences of opinion on religious and social questions are still part of their everyday environment. Kilroy's play is therefore quite devoid of any nostalgia for folklore. The issue is rather one of a playwright approaching the past from a different viewpoint. Conversely, in the background behind the study of the relationship between man and history — Irish history of course — looms the question of Irishness.[3]

From a literary point of view, the choice of the stage rather than the novel to tell the story of Hugh O'Neill's life implies using techniques which are closer to the epic construction than to drama, which tends to reduce the time-scope to the narrow frame of the instant. Accordingly, one may observe that the opening scene stages two refurbished versions of the ancient chorus, which enable the playwright to provide the audience with facts about the situation as it stands at that point in time (the triumph displayed by Hugh O'Neill and his men after the victory of Yellow Ford).

> O'NEILL: Read out our claims now, Master Mountfort, so that everyone may know what Ireland demands.
> MOUNTFORT: The claims of O'Neill, Prince of Ulster, given out at the Yellow Ford in the heat of this great victory over the English [*ON*. 11].

In this apparently classical opening scene, the playwright announces the general nature of the issues to be addressed in the play. The demands formulated by one people against another place the speech within the context of conflict, albeit conflict in its final stage, if one is to trust this opening declaration. Mountfort, in his role as a narrator, carries out the function of the ancient chorus, sharing with the audience a foresight into future action. He gives voice to the Irish demands before victorious soldiers, which precludes any intimate presentation of the conflict. In his very first speech, Mountfort's role is closer to that of the narrator than to that of the classical confidant — whose presence tends to emphasize the private side of conflicts — and his reading on the battlefield clearly refers to a historical event of major importance. Interestingly, his contemporary embodiment of the ancient chorus proves ephemeral, and other characters are to fulfil this role in the rest of the play. Although this dramatic function of his is short-lived, Mountfort is nevertheless invested in the eyes of the spectator with a role and a function which place the play firmly among works of serious drama, the subject matter being a major event in the history of Ireland. It is noteworthy, however, that his speech is interrupted by an

Englishman, whose intrusion among the soldiers eventually undermines Mountfort's reading as a historical act. It soon becomes clear that Cecil's entry and his determination to curtail the triumphant declamation of the enemy are more far-reaching than the primary reaction of an invader confronted with words which incriminate him. The real issue has to do with the status of the narrator, who is treated more as a character than as a historical figure.

After a few exchanges, another Englishman, Mountjoy, delegated to quash the Irish rebellion, demands further explanations so as to better assess the difficulties to which his situation exposes him. Cecil's words, and more especially the reactions of the other characters ("Let us begin at the beginning once more, please. Everybody now. [*There is a disgruntled murmur from all present*]" [*ON.* 12]) fundamentally undermine the initial historical presentation. To an even greater extent than Cecil's untimely entry, the disgruntled attitude of the other characters can be interpreted as a reference to an on-stage atmosphere and to the work of actors as they rehearse. This skilfully handled turnaround in the drama confronts the audience with their own capacity to be misled and taken in. The sudden return to reality in all of its theatrical artificiality brings to a halt the historical adventure to which the spectators seemed to have been bidden. Although they recover the freedom to adhere once again to illusion as the performance goes on, the fact remains that this partial invalidation of a certain type of historical speech, achieved through the introduction of the play within the play, is highly significant. Beyond the obvious reference to Brecht's distancing, the real issue at stake is the meaning of this reversal of perspective. Through this questioning of the status of reality as he has presented it, which is to say in a way acceptable to the audience, Kilroy insinuates doubt just where the spectator was about to forget it. What should one take for granted as reality—as it is revealed through the coding of the theatre—but also as reality through its everyday occurrences, in forms one accepts as established? Disorder gives rise to double-talk, making it clear firstly that the situation is nothing but a theatre play and therefore a convention, but also that every historical presentation is fraught with referential fragility. This distancing from a pointillistic approach to history, which one understands to be deceptively realistic, opens the possibility of exploring new areas in which the lack of tangible anchorage points no longer seems to be scandalous. While maintaining the focus on Hugh O'Neill as a historical character, Thomas Kilroy, drawing on his powers of invention, is now free to handle his character as a man with a private life and not only, as the title seemed to announce, as a triumphant, then defeated, historical hero figure.

Before telling the story of Hugh O'Neill's life, the playwright adds a finishing touch to his presentation by summoning three Irish spies working for the Crown. This ultimate embodiment of the chorus — which in the course of the play comments on the victories and defeats of both parties — serves to heighten the distancing effect intended by the author. The way Cecil introduces the spies emphasizes the artificiality of the performance, but Hugh's reaction at the mention of the traitors reveals just how disconcerting their very existence turns out to be. Indeed, each of them introduces himself as an ordinary person, using speech full of commonplaces with which many other Irishmen would be able to identify. Thomas Kilroy refuses to ascribe to them the specific status which their lack of dignity might seem to deserve, and in doing so, shapes their very ordinariness into a defining characteristic. This has the effect of invalidating any kind of Manichaeist perspective, leading on the contrary to a discussion on double-talk and duality just where one would have expected to see duality disappear, when an individual sacrifices his own side to join enemy ranks.

Before entering into the question of Irish identity as portrayed in the life of Hugh O'Neill, it may now be expedient to say a few words about the structure of the play, while bearing in mind the way the opening scene defines the mode of a historical approach with all its implications. Knowing how Thomas Kilroy longed to discuss the history of Ireland and its people, one might have expected him to choose Easter 1916 and tell the story of these events in an exclusively dramatic and highly realistic way, bringing the spectator right into the heart of the uprising such as it was experienced by the fighters in the General Post Office. With *The O'Neill*, Kilroy resorts to an epic approach, built on a longer time scale and raising questions on the meaning and interpretation of historical events. Accordingly, a study of the structure of the play will enable us to raise a few more questions. The drama opens with a victory and closes with a defeat — seen from the Irish side — but the same doubt can be thrown on the accuracy of the hindsight analysis as on the time of the action, where live perception can be likened to blinding. In other words, the initial questions challenging historical representation also challenge the certainty surrounding the real status of Hugh O'Neill's defeat when, in the last scene, he repents of his rebellious activities. At a far remove from the initial clamor, the murmuring of his name is a prompt for the spectator to reflect on the meaning of this ultimate invocation of his patriarchal name, which is a reference to the tensions about identity presented in the course of the play, and to which we shall now direct our attention.

In the opening scene the Irish, following their victory, give voice to their demands, and refer to the enemy in terms of nationality. Two sides, two worlds, Irish and English, define each other in terms of what opposes them. The conflict generates primary definitions of identity, as it serves to designate the Other as the enemy, precluding any apprehension of individual features, hence reassuring Manichaean visions which shut out any disquieting queries. Thus Cecil, draped in his invader's self-importance, applies himself to the drawing-up of a typology of the Irish, basing his views on so-called scientific evidence:

> CECIL: You see an Irishman's blood is not like ours, my lord. It is fat with unnatural substances which break out like boils in fierce passion and temper [*ON.* 14].

The grotesqueness of these words may bring a smile to a contemporary audience — all the more so if they are Irish — but it would be a mistake to view this extract as sheer entertainment. In the staging of this woolly demonstration, the playwright underscores the apparent, almost scientific rationality of words which generate exclusion. By contrast, Cecil defines himself as an Englishman, and explains the difference by means of a speech in which the main thread of the argument rests solely on the use of abusive items. By means of this mask which he places on the Other — the enemy — he is able to qualify the Irish as barbarians. The insistence on the difference, on features non-standard in the sense that they are almost monstrous, enables him to paint a simplistic picture of an otherness reduced to the opposition between two ethnic communities. If we were to adhere to this definition, the case of Hugh O'Neill would be extremely simple: he would be defined as a member of a barbarian group, without any further queries about his own individual personality.

Reality turns out to be more complex. Apart from the curtailed vision of the Other, corresponding to a definition of the enemy — simplistic in its very essence — Irish identity, such as it may be apprehended from without, is composed of a somewhat rigid set of structures, which partly explains the logic of an analysis founded on surface elements.

> CECIL: His people, their customs, their ignorance, their pettiness will destroy O'Neill for you. You have only to use them [*ON.* 16].

In the preceding definition Cecil had sketched a typology of the Irish as they appeared to him in their near-animal dimension, the grotesque character of his representation being the result of a phantasmagorical vision fueled by his self-assurance as a conqueror. However, when he directs his attention to the political dimension of the conflict, his analysis is somewhat subtler, and helps us to appreciate the difficulties encountered by Hugh O'Neill concerning the definition of his own identity. Furthermore, Cecil's simplistic dualism, which restricts his vision to primary oppositions, seems to be shared by his enemies, who seek to confine Hugh O'Neill to a rather narrow piece of territory. As an enemy, the English expect him to appear with the features predefined by his condition as a non-native opponent, but then a similar attitude appears within the very community into which Hugh O'Neill was born. This is why his clemency in battle and his affair with a woman from the opposite side cause ill-feeling among his fellow warriors. The young woman, whose family and cultural ties differ from those of the O'Neill clan, arouses ill-concealed disapproval, for Hugh's choice is an outright flouting of his community's expectations. One notes that the power of the clan is thwarted with regard to their transgression, in that clan members fail to prevent the union of the two lovers. Conversely, the early disappointment experienced by the newly wed couple can be accounted for by the clan members' continuous challenging of Mabel's legitimacy as Hugh's wife. The deterioration of the love relationship which follows bears witness to the painful transition from private intimacy to a destructive confrontation with the community. It becomes clear that the absence of outside interference was doomed to come to an end, with the community rejecting the lovers' transgression.

Mabel, aware of this danger and sensing the oppositions to come, had considered eloping with Hugh, as she was conscious of the degree to which space anchors people — in spite of themselves — to a cultural environment whose expectations shape their individual identity. Failing this change of spatial environment, the lovers can no longer live out the identities which they had defined for themselves in their private life, for the twofold identity of Hugh as the husband of Mabel and the chief of an Irish clan generates insurmountable tensions. Should they decide to give priority to the love relationship and override the expectations of the clan, this would indeed help the marriage to survive, but this remains impossible because of the denial of identity which this entails for an O'Neill. Their non-standard union catalyzes oppositions, which bring out the practical difficulty of cohabitation. Although it stages a love relationship against a background of social conflict, the construction of the play, a reversal of that of *Romeo and Juliet,* suggests a different mode of approach to drama. This perspective, no less tragic in its portrayal of the impossibility for individuals to attain common fulfilment, differs from Shakespeare's drama in that it draws attention to the ordinariness of divisions. In *The O'Neill,* Kilroy refrains from a paroxysmal handling of the struggle between love and society so as to draw attention, through the question of identity, to what ultimately turns out to be just as important: ordinariness as an indication of human misfortune.

The love relationship staged in the first act as a transition from clandestine love to a marriage disapproved of by enemy groups, followed by separation, provides an overview of the community problem to be developed in the rest of the play. Hugh's cross-boundary love relationship appears as a way of asserting his identity, given that the community had itself defined *a priori* the sentimental latitude which it granted to him. Hugh is too lucid to take any pride in this, as he knows just how much his clan membership stands in the way of true emancipation, and Mabel's speech of loving protest brings him no help. Paying the price of the love he feels for his wife by cutting himself off from his very roots would be to him a form of alienation which he strongly rejects. Moreover, each time a domestic argument occurs, he reasserts his membership in the O'Neill clan. Mabel, on the contrary, launches scathing attacks on the forms of identity-centered oppression which her husband accepts, likening his lack of resistance to a surrender of his private life. Hugh, in his refusal to adhere to a single-track representation, attempts to formulate his own perspective, in which he includes antagonistic worlds. However, his two-sided identity, as the chief of an Irish clan and the husband of a woman born on the opposite side and faithful to her origins, leads to an insurmountable crisis. Indeed, each attempt to draw closer to one side distances him from the other, and the day-to-day antagonisms eventually lead to the breakup of the couple.

Implicitly, the aim of the marriage had been to build a causeway between two worlds, but Hugh finds himself faced with several possible options, each incompatible with the others: flight, fruitless confrontation or self-denial. The failure of the love relationship due to intercommunity tension prefigures a broader context, that of the armed conflict which opposes the English and the Irish, staged in the second act. Act One might almost be considered as a play within the play: while announcing the tragedies to come, it is also a near-autonomous summary of the essence of a conflict, focusing on two figures who represent the future tensions. If one bears in mind the semantic impact (achieved by the distancing effect of the opening scene) of the breakup which had been predictable right from the start, one may also suggest that the failure of Hugh and Mabel's marriage heightens the bleakness of the vision concerning the Irish question as presented in Act Two, since the intensity of the differences finally overcomes the strength of love.

In the case of Hugh O'Neill, marital tensions bring to light a typically Irish dimension of identity which is, as he sees it himself, the clan. This special anchorage point provides him with an intellectual yardstick, but the pervasive influence of the community's lifestyles and thought patterns leads him to an inner conflict between his personality as he would like to define it and what he actually is by virtue of his name and the social expectations which center upon it.

> O'NEILL: I will not wear my family's past on my back like a bag. It will drag me down because it has the weight of the dead. Let the glorious past take care of itself [*ON*. 21].

Here, Hugh is mapping out the limits of the unacceptable concerning the influence of traditions on his behavior. The exaggerated reverence of his fellow warriors for feats of the past rendered glorious by the passage of time ends up as an ossifying vision of society. His non-standard marriage is proof that transgression is possible, notwithstanding the fact that the community applies itself to annihilating the origins of whatever differs from the habits and customs of the day. Tension mounts between the Irishman as defined by the clan and the self-proclaimed human being embodied by Hugh who, in spite of his eminent social function, refuses to pledge total allegiance to the community's diktat. As either a refuge or a prison, Irish identity is at the heart of a quest which makes of Hugh either a human being in his own right, or the object of forces which he does not master. Full of misgivings about his own identity and what it consists of, Hugh asks Roisin to help him define himself:

> O'NEILL: What in God's name am I at all?
> ROISIN: You are Hugh, son of Ferdorcha, son of Con Bacah, son of Henry, son of Owen — [*ON*, 31].

The formulation, biblical in its phraseology and content, refers O'Neill back to his ancestors in an archetypal way. Roisin here voices the point of view of the clan, which considers the individual as nothing more than a link in the male chain, and implicitly defines descendants as beings bearing the stamp of all the preceding generations, as is underscored by the rigidity of the enumeration in which they are listed. The lineage and the name appear both as titles of glory and *lettres de cachet*. It seems impossible to extricate oneself from the course of history, and if the issues at stake were not so serious, this image of a clockwork mechanism applied to an animate being would bring a touch of the grotesque. Faced with the uncertainty of a mode of existence over which nobody can gain control, Hugh finds himself endowed with the destiny of his clan, which his fellow warriors expect him to accept. Some judge that his partial refusal of Irish identity as defined in the course of the centuries is akin, if not to treason, at least to betrayal. This is why the poet refuses to sing Hugh's praises, for he feels the foreign influence creeping in through their chief, and fears that it may be harmful to the community as a whole.

> O'NEILL: Am I to be the first of the Irish with an English britches and an English tongue? Or the last of the O'Neills? Answer me that. Or am I just something torn apart at the crotch between the two? [*ON.* 31].

The threat which Hugh's fellow warriors detect turns out to be founded; O'Neill is being torn apart by a heritage from which he does not wish to break away completely, yet which he feels is being challenged by another cultural anchorage point. Indeed, unlike his friends, Hugh was brought up in England and suffers from the resulting discrepancy when he converses with the members of his clan. According to the English representatives of the Crown, the opposition between the English and the Irish lifestyles boils down to a conflict between the ancient and the modern, but these oversimplified contrasts turn out to be artificial. Hugh rebels against the way people around him continually refer to the past, not only because he considers that Irish culture must evolve, but also because of the abusive use they make of the past as a mode of interpretation for the present. Modernity, scorned by some, is seen as a threat by many because of the doubt it introduces into a community, who are left at a loss as to how to react. The possible modes of evolution include the threat of betrayal, hence the rising tension between Hugh, who is in favor of change, and his fellows, who view these cultural upheavals as disastrous. In this respect, the challenge from within turns out to be more formidable than the enemy, who, through their Manichaean images, actually consolidate the clan-based identity undermined by Hugh O'Neill's uncertainties.

1. The O'Neill   17

> O'NEILL: You are Irish. I am Irish. Madam, we are only separated by time, blood, religion. These are small things. History will not be able to tell the difference between us.
> MABEL: I should certainly hope not. If people have sense.
> O'NEILL: On the other hand, you will never be Irish because you do not have the weight of time on your back [*ON.* 23].

The dramatic irony of "these are small things" does not slip the notice of the audience who will probably detect a passing commentary on the absurdity of persistent and murderous warfare. In the course of this exchange, O'Neill grants Mabel the rank of an Irishwoman, only to go back on his words. He eventually underlines the incompleteness of her status as, unlike himself, she does not meet all the criteria which would make a true Irishwoman of her. The failure to recognize a person's identity obviously raises the problem as to which authorities have the power to confirm or invalidate an individual's membership of a community. In the present case, Hugh does not seem to be endowed with the legal authority one might expect, as he is himself a prey to doubt. His misgivings concerning his own Irish roots and his need for reassurance about them throw some discredit on his critical assessment of Mabel's case. The chorus, which stands for the people, cannot be taken as a reference either. It is composed of spies, individuals who introduce themselves as being Irish, knowing all the while that their treason in favor of the English Crown makes corrupted beings of them, not only on the financial level, but also toward an unspoken, indisputable concept of Irishness. The gradual invalidation of arguments resting on a unique definition of Irish identity, and likewise of a procedure for ascribing Irishness which would exclude part of the people born on Irish soil, weakens the claims of the self-proclaimed holders of ethnic identity. As one scene succeeds another, the audience becomes aware of the wavering of certainties. The rampart formed by the Other as being different, therefore a catalyst for the identity of the opposite side, simply crumbles away as one discerns certain overlappings which empty of all their substance any arguments founded on excluding outsiders. The myth of the pure and the impure caves in when masked similarities appear. The unique becomes double, and the two sides are brought together both by their blindness and by their presumption in thinking they possessed the ultimate truth. This recurrent reappraisal is not accidental, for at each point the convergences are underlined, even in the fratricidal struggles in which the two parties appeal to outside forces. The question is then raised as to the reason behind these conflicts which center upon an indefinable Irishness, behind these murderous antagonisms whose very meaning is a problem because of their internal contradictions.

Although he is at the center of the conflict, Hugh O'Neill remains at arm's length from the warlike speeches of his comrades. His position is thus implicitly Kilroy's own in its tacit condemnation of total commitment when either side is seeking to annihilate the other. Hugh's extreme reserve is a strategy used by the playwright to insinuate that the spectators are like the characters in that they unwittingly fall into the trap of identifying with a cause. They are then better able to measure the consequences of an outlook which excludes any possibility of mutual understanding. However, there is no simple way out, and the drama unfolds in all of its human complexity. As an O'Neill, Hugh crystallizes a vision according to which the individual's freedom is restricted by something which is nevertheless an integral part of his being — that is, his name. In this respect, he symbolizes Irish people whose identity stirs up tensions between contradictory forces. Being rooted in a community enables them to live their lives, but it also turns out to be destructive because it cultivates the refusal of the Other. For "Ire-land," land of ire and land of tumult, whose history is orchestrated in the counterpoint of hatred, Kilroy finds a fitting mode of representation in the theatre. The characters are at once free individuals and puppets on strings, as they build up a drama whose tragic impact springs from intricate and primitive links between the logic of certain cultural precepts and the absurdity of certain presuppositions. This is why Thomas Kilroy, in the face of insoluble contradictions, lists failure among the very terms of the conflict, at the same time setting aside the naive Manichaean alternatives which would inevitably slump into the failures denounced in the course of the play. To break off would mean to lose oneself, but to live implies that one should try to destroy the Other, whose victories merely portend his downfall. When he is defeated, however, he is reborn thanks to an inner force which enables him to survive the harshness of his Irish destiny.

> O'NEILL: I'll leave you my lord. I'll go back to my kinsmen. They'll need me, you know. I'm still O'Neill, am I not? My name has not been taken from me. I may not have two spears to support me but even in poverty I am still their Prince. (*Whisper*). O'Neill [*ON*. 74].

The defeated man still possesses the most important thing, a name which proves he belongs to Ireland, for whom he has fought on the battlefield, but the final tableau, like an echo of the battle presented in the opening scene, is a reference to a disaster suffered by both sides. The future, briefly mentioned in the course of the play, now looms in the form of fresh battles, rallied around a name, emblem of an identity ready to rebel against any hint of English domination. From a military point of view, this defeat is by no means the last, and the moans are fleeting echoes of victory cries, before the roles are reversed. From this point of view, it bears hope for some, but the playwright's message is exactly the opposite, underlining the insaneness of xenophobic visions. The viewing of this episode from Ireland's past arouses a very real fear, that of seeing battle upon battle resulting from the urge of one group to appropriate Irish identity at the expense of the other. Hugh O'Neill, a historical character portrayed in the grips of a challenge consisting in overcoming uniqueness and accepting the Other, embodies a disaster sinister in its relevance today. He is an Irishman who either self-destructs or only succeeds in asserting himself by mutilating others, and whose shadow cast over a tragic present calls into question the heinous doctrines under the burden of which the people of Northern Ireland were still staggering at the end of the twentieth century.

2

Encounters in *The Madame MacAdam Travelling Theatre* and *The Death and Resurrection of Mr. Roche*

It is difficult to make a global historical study of the way theater techniques evolve, given the ephemeral nature of each performance. One should take into account the fact that each new period either continues, transforms or invalidates the conventions instituted by the preceding generations, and bear in mind that an assessment of the various transformations in dramatic art would surely provide us with a more accurate view of the in-depth meaning of theatricality. Failing an intellectual vantage point such as this, if we look merely at the preliminaries of the performance (narrowing our vision, for instance, to the twentieth century in France), we note that the replacement of the three knocks by a specific lighting effect constitutes a technical mutation, but the in-depth meaning remains unchanged, as both procedures invite the audience to silence. Today's custom then, although likely to undergo further evolution, requires that the house and the stage should be darkened until a more intense lighting effect enables the audience to discern the first elements of the play. This mutation affecting the preliminaries, whereby the signal to the spectator is declined in several different modes, clearly dissociates before our eyes two essential phases of the performance, the relevance of which transcends the French frame previously mentioned: on the one hand the invitation to silence and, on the other, the first instant of the performance, which one might refer to as an encounter.

With the scenery and perhaps with a few actors before his eyes, the spectator now beholds the birth of drama. An emotional trajectory begins to unfold; words are added to the visual; the performance stamps its rhythm on the audience, and as act succeeds act, multifarious encounters are staged. The essence of the theatre which, owing to the many and various aspects of theatricality, obviously cannot be reduced to the simple concept of the encounter, nevertheless remains very strongly characterized by the numerous interactions, whether these concern the characters among themselves, the actors, the audience or the individual with himself. Furthermore, Thomas Kilroy, whose playwriting invariably includes some reflection on the staging of plays, chooses to head *The Madame MacAdam Travelling Theatre* with an inaugural *mise en abîme* effect illustrating this interest. He pursues his deep-seated preoccupation with the encounter in several other works, hence the choice of a combined study on *The Madame MacAdam Travelling Theatre* and *The Death and Resurrection of Mr. Roche*. A twenty-three-year interval separates the two works, but the passing of time has no hold over the lives of the main protagonists, whose pathways converge upon the same questions. Both plays stage a mingling of the contradictory aspects of absence, desire or fear of the encounter, together with moments when the characters define the closeness of their relations, both in terms of their material reality and of their immediate or long-term consequences.

> MADAME: You may well ask how I, Madame MacAdam, am so reduced? To tell you the truth, m'dears, from the moment we set out on this dreadful tour we have been beset by malignant deities.... The other question, of course, is this: What on earth are we doing here? Do you know, I believe we simply reached a crossroads somewhere in Ulster. Someone mentioned the Free State. The name beckoned. So here we are! [*MMTT*. 1–2].

The account of the misfortunes met by Madame MacAdam's company on their tour enables Kilroy to begin his play with an opening scene in which the heroine muses upon the reasons which led to her arrival in a foreign country.

The *mise en abîme*, which consists in visibly incorporating technical conventions into the text itself, underlines the artificial character of the performance. Behind the jesting allusion — not unusual in Kilroy's writing — one discerns two searching questions. The first concerns the origins of the theatrical arts; the second, expressed by Madame MacAdam's musing on the whys and wherefores of the place and of meeting the audience, is more like a questioning of fate. The arrival in Eire serves as a starting point for Madame MacAdam's contradictory theories: is the present situ-

1991 FIELD DAY TOUR

SEPTEMBER

9-14	DERRY: Guildhall
16-21	GALWAY: An Taibhdhearc
23	TULLAMORE: Social Centre
24	CLAREMORRIS: Town Hall
25	CAVAN: Town Hall
26-28	SLIGO: Hawk's Well Theatre
30	COOKSTOWN: Town Hall

OCTOBER

1-2	ARMAGH: St. Patrick's Hall
3-5	ENNISKILLEN: Ardhowen Theatre
7	OMAGH: Town Hall
8	ANDERSONSTOWN: St. Agnes' Parish Centre
9	DOWNPATRICK: Down Leisure Centre
10-11	COLERAINE: Riverside Theatre
12	NEWRY: Town Hall
14-26	DUBLIN THEATRE FESTIVAL: Gaiety Theatre
28-2 Nov	BELFAST: Lyric Players Theatre

NOVEMBER

4	CALLAN: St. Brigid's College
5-9	CORK: Opera House
11	ENNIS: Holy Family Hall
12-16	LIMERICK: Belltable Arts Centre

The Madame MacAdam Travelling Theatre will run at the Royal Court Theatre, London from 3rd to 21st December 1991.

Field Day Theatre Company, Foyle Arts Centre, Old Foyle College, Lawrence Hill, Derry, BT48 7NJ, N. Ireland.

Cartoons from "Dublin Opinion" magazine 1939 - 1945. Illustration of the Madame MacAdam Lorry by OCTOBER STONE DESIGN LIMITED. Design by OCTOBER STONE DESIGN LIMITED. Printing by Nicholson and Bass Ltd.

Program Book of *The Madame MacAdam Travelling Theatre*. Field Day Theatre Company, 1991 (courtesy of Field Day).

ation an inexplicable coincidence or, on the contrary, are the misfortunes attending the tour the work of malignant deities? In spite of the philosophical musing which opens the play, our first observation is that the encounter is above all a part of everyday life, whether in *The Madame MacAdam Travelling Theatre* or *The Death and Resurrection of Mr. Roche*. In both comedies, the events related (especially when the resurrected Mr. Roche calls himself Lazarus) lead us to reflect on the real status to be ascribed to the encounter. Indeed, its origins and its consequences raise the question of a fate — governed or not by divine forces — which would surpass the understanding of the characters involved.

Although the very nature of the encounter in its fundamental aspects is at the heart of Madame MacAdam's musings, its actual existence, in spite of its apparent banality, is far from self-evident. Indeed, personal exchanges presuppose a mode of social organization; they also depend on material possibilities and individual abilities to establish contacts with others — as many delicate points on display in *The Death and Resurrection of Mr. Roche* and *The Madame MacAdam Travelling Theatre*. The traumatizing absence of links with other human beings and the solitude this brings kindle a desire for the encounter which social customs occasionally appease, some of them offering fake fellowship and short-lived oblivion of the impression of isolation which afflicts individuals. The bacchic rites of the weekend, staged in *The Death and Resurrection of Mr. Roche,* demonstrate the fleeting character of this relief. Kelly entertains no illusions as to the depth of the friendship which links him and his drinking-mates of an evening, but he nevertheless invites them to pursue their libations after Mass, so as to push back the excruciating moment when he will find himself faced with the moral desert of his bachelor's life.[1]

Jo, Kelly's female alter ego, encounters similar difficulties; she attempts to solve them, but her response takes her to extremes.

> JO: The little Lannigan girl they're all looking for. It was me that took her. I just wanted to love her, y'know. I just took her for one night. And then she disappeared again. I'm near frantic with worry — what'll I do? [*MMTT.* 23].

Unlike Marie-Thérèse, who hopes to break her solitude by eloping with an actor, Jo does not fill her head with wild dreams. Her immediate need for affection is so intense that it leads her to commit a socially and humanly unacceptable act, for the unrealistic hope of sharing feelings had seemed to be within her reach in the shape of a rebirth which she would build around a particular relationship with the Other, in the

The Death and Resurrection of Mr. Roche. Photograph by Fergus Bourke. From left to right, Jonathan Ryan, Clive Geraghty. Abbey Theatre, Dublin, 1989 (courtesy of The Abbey Theatre Archive).

The Death and Resurrection of Mr. Roche. Photograph by Fergus Bourke. From left to right, Joe Dowling, Michael O'hAonghusa. Abbey Theatre, Dublin, 1973 (courtesy of The Abbey Theatre Archive).

present case, a child. As we noted in Kelly's case, Jo's uneasiness has nothing unique about it. The kidnapping of "the little Lannigan girl" is the result of loneliness and suffering, leading to dramatic consequences, and affecting, to various degrees, the characters which Kilroy gathers in his Irish frescoes.

The outstretched hand reaching towards the Other (both a stranger and an image of the self) appears, sometimes metaphorically, on several levels in the plays. Paradoxically — for the issues at stake seem to belong only to the order of sentiment — the musing on the theme of the encounter is a perfect corollary to the author's critical reflection on the nature of theatre. Thus, in *The Madame MacAdam Travelling Theatre,* the art of staging a dramatic work is linked up with this theme by a mirror effect, and invites us to reflect on the place of the spectator within the performance.[2] The extract chosen by Kilroy develops its full meaning in the sense that it interacts on several different levels. The audience attend a performance in which an encounter is reenacted on the stage for an Irish audience, who in turn become the object of observation for the spectators whose own mode of interaction with the playwright and his art is a fresh subject for analysis. The author brings back to life an episode of Irish history, and demonstrates how involved the audience become as they recognize their own experience in the story of resistance to the invader, which is bound to undergo some form of mental updating. The audience quiver, but their involvement in the performance does not arise out of superficial enjoyment, which would confine this encounter to the order of contingencies. On the other hand materiality — in its artificial aspects — is transcended, thus bringing the artificial closer to the real, and drama closer to real life. The interaction of the audience with the text spoken by the actors belongs to an emotional register which is not very different from that which Jo had shown concerning the kidnapping of the child. As one act succeeds another, the spectators set up a special relationship with a dramatic situation, which throws back to them an indirect image of themselves. The encounter as experienced in the form of a performance is sought after insofar as the description of oneself has a structuring dimension, and fulfils the audience's desire to see themselves on stage. Accordingly, beyond the material aspects, the audience seek to gain access to existence by discovering themselves as they contemplate the figures on the stage offered to their emotion.

To gain access to existence by establishing a relationship with the Other — such had been Jo's secret desire. Once again, the boundary which separates the theatre and real life becomes blurred, as on the occasion of an encounter both through and with the theatre (a process of self-definition through confrontation or interaction), the spectator includes himself in a process very close to his daily experience. This phenomenon is not limited to the audience, or even to the characters whose life stories are reenacted on the stage. It also affects the actors, who face similar challenges. The anxiety which grips them as they go on stage ("LYLE JONES: Mumsie, I am so very frightened. Look at my hands how they shake!" [*MMTT.* 14]) is not only due to the stage fright which attends the entry on stage of the actor as an artiste. It includes a fundamental ontological dimension which explains why the idea of the encounter arouses both hope and fear, while at the same imposing itself as a necessity.

> LYLE JONES: But, my dear boy, we actors are the creation of our audiences. They create us nightly. We exist only in their imaginations. When they walk out of the theatre we cease to exist. We become nonentities once more. Just like everyone else [*MMTT.* 17].

The provocative nature of Lyle Jones' speech about shared nonexistence is in perfect keeping with the author's creed. Several times in his plays Kilroy insists on the fact that to exist is to act — one or several roles — thus ascribing to all and sundry, at least potentially, the role of an amateur actor. Following such principles, one understands why the playwright pays such keen attention to the relation between the actor and his audience. The close bond between the theatre and real life, emphasized in various registers to the point sometimes of giving the impression of a blending of two usually dissociated worlds, emerges with particular clarity through the concept of the encounter as means of gaining access to existence.

The desire for exchange is naturally associated with fear. Among the risks run, the inability to communicate, the verbal confrontation between two individuals holding antagonistic positions and the difficulty in defining boundaries between private and public space are several potential pitfalls. In its representation on stage, the relationship with the Other ranges from an almost complete vacuum to a close-knit bond embodied in sex, the climax of the encounter in *The Madame MacAdam Travelling Theatre* and in *The Death and Resurrection of Mr. Roche.* In both plays, the background of Irish culture holds an important place, and it is made clear that any sexual contact implies the taking into account of social codes, since carnal relations acquire a permanent intellectual value once the protagonists have measured them with the yardstick of collective rules. In the relation which the main characters entertain with sex — this applies both to Jo and to Kelly — the carnal act constitutes a departure from accepted standards. Kelly, for his homosexuality, feels the weight of the community's opprobrium haunting his mind, while Jo suffers condemnation by Marie-Thérèse and Bourke because of her extramarital heterosexual relation. Bearing in mind the restrictive social context described above, one understands that the only love encounter which can conceivably be performed before the audience's eyes is the romance between Jo and Rabe — the visual representation of Kelly's homosexual escapade would probably have overstepped the limits of provocation admitted on the stage.[3] This being so, the Irish spectator in his own social dimension predictably detects a hint of transgression when foreplay is performed on the stage:

He embraces her and they begin to make love. Lights down [*MMTT*.48].

Jo: I heard nothing — Rabe. Don't touch me. I'm sorry. I should never have brought you into this — [*MMTT*. 49].

The naked bodies and limbs entwined are a concrete expression of the bond between Jo and Rabe, and at this very special moment the disagreements described above seem to fade away.

The amorous embrace is a sign not only of the short-lived victory of unity over destructive loneliness, but also of the fact that the basic difficulty in relating to the Other, the struggle to be recognized as a person, has been overcome. However, this relational windfall quickly turns out to be nothing more than a flash in the pan, and after the love-making, the congruity of the bodies disappears, and distance — that insuperable expression of forbidden closeness — comes back to them, bringing with it all of the unappeased yearnings which Kilroy stages in his plays. Jo tries in vain to make their relationship last, but Rabe shakes off his role as a lover, and the arrival of Bourke turns him into a Jew being collected by Nazi militiamen. Whether or not love is shared, the physical relationship between the characters is all-important. The carnal union and the sharing it brings provides a pathway to the Other but also to oneself, in the sense that the encounter, both as an element of self-definition and as a means of attaining a form of being, develops its full significance.

SEAMUS (*Alarmed*): What are you talking about?
KELLY (*Head bowed*): God forgive me. I let him handle me —
    (*There is a long pause.*) [*DRMR*.60].

Whatever he may do or say, his carnal misfortune classifies him among those he has been scorning all evening: homosexuals. After making a vain attempt to broach this delicate question with a priest, Kelly reveals his disgrace to Seamus, whom he sees as his last chance of salvation. His body language and words take the form of a confession ritual which, he hopes, will give him the strength to face — or better still to erase — a traumatizing experience. This admission corresponds to a moment of total uncertainty, as the likelihood of meeting and relating with the Other hangs on Seamus' reply. Either he will embrace the total solitude attending the human condition, or he will be able to establish a relationship — albeit imperfect — with the Other, which will enable him to combat the shame he feels. Jo's sexual initiation, necessarily different — mechanical according to Rabe's reasoning — entails discovering her partner's body, but goes beyond the physical aspects. As opposed to Kelly, and in spite of the public humiliation which has surrounded her carnal relation with Rabe, Jo asserts it for what it is: a metamorphosis. It becomes clear that in her eyes the pleasures of the flesh transcend the hedonistic frame to which the militiamen confine it. Through this special encounter Jo becomes a woman, thus putting an end to the anxiety of loneliness experienced as a lack of recognition of herself as a person.

Carnal union — even short-lived — whether hoisted aloft like a flag or masked like a shameful disease, leads to a deep reflection about the stakes of existence. Although Jo's and Kelly's behavior patterns differ regarding this intimate question, both come to redefine their identity after their sexual experience. Whether expressed or not by physical contact between the actors, the existence of intimate relations between two characters — an ultimate form of encounter — plays a major role in the construction of their identity. The absence of a link or of some way of drawing closer to another person makes characters feel that something is lacking — perhaps even their very existence, as each person seems to need to build up a strong relationship with someone outside of himself, whether a deity or an individual. This relationship also serves as a catalyst which, apparently creating disorder, in fact reveals unknown facts to the person. When confronted with a new situation, the individual discovers his difficulty in coping with it. Kelly thus finds himself in a delicate position as he has to recognize, in spite of all the denials reiterated in the course of the play, that he has made a choice, of which he was perhaps not fully aware, but which nevertheless grew out of a repressed desire.

In his direct approach to sexuality, Kilroy places himself and his writing on the fringe of what is tolerated by self-righteous morals. The way he voices his projects shows that the provocations — genuine or fake — consisting in putting sexual questions in the limelight, are a means of bringing his medium of expression into keeping with the content.

> RABE: What I want, more than anything, is a theatre which can hold — danger. You see what I mean? Where danger can detonate upon a stage. You see, I believe if theatre can do that, there will be less — danger left in the world. Our only hope is that art transform the human animal. Nothing else has worked [*MMTT.* 24].

The danger Rabe is talking about might at first sight appear subversive, as is the case in Jean Genet's plays, but for Kilroy sexuality gives substance to another cardinal dimension, and ties up, in its depth, with the essential concerns of the French playwright. It would thus be a mistake to focus merely on vaguely indecorous appearances which, fundamentally, express the intensity of the playwright's expectations toward his art. In his quest for a mirror able to reflect the core issues of theatrical art, Kilroy associates the encounter — central to the very idea of representation on the stage — with the perils of existence.

On the social level the encounter — viewed alternatively as something lacking or as a fulfilment — holds a place of prime importance in each of these diametrically opposed positions. Between the two, the mundanity of the exchange is blended almost imperceptibly into the works, without the void which one sometimes detects in the ordinary words of the characters opening the way to metaphysical reflection. Sex, on the other hand, is the culminating point of the protagonists' unions, and gives all their meaning to encounters as modes of creation and of access to existence for individuals hitherto kept aside from maturing processes. Whether experienced as an illumination, as a happy metamorphosis or as an inner shipwreck, intimate relationships considered in their consequences have a positive outcome in that they lead to the dropping of masks. The discrepancy between the playwright's views on theatrical art and his reflection on sex as the supreme mode of encounter gradually disappears. Indeed, the type of encounter which the playwright wishes to bring about is voiced in Rabe's words and anticipated in the scene about Irish history. According to Kilroy's manifesto — issued in the form of an indirect address to the spectator — the performance, like sex, should help everybody to experience strong feelings which should contain within themselves the possibility of metamorphoses. These are the grounds on which Kilroy voices his ambitious project for the theatrical arts. He offers the spectator a process of intimate self-exploration, enabling him to perceive an image of himself as appearances fade away and individual truths emerge. Having discovered his path at the outcome of a perilous encounter, each person is able to put an end to the non-existence resulting from a carefully assembled patchwork of fake images passing for an identity. Freed at last from the faded finery of appearance — albeit for a fleeting moment — the spectator will finally gain access to existence, the first and foremost step toward the recognition of his humanity.

3

Comic Variations in *Tea and Sex and Shakespeare*

The transition from a patriarchal name to a complex noun phrase constructed around the name of a writer is in itself a recognition of a highly personal style which encompasses the themes addressed and the way in which they are handled. To date, Thomas Kilroy has not yet received the glorious distinction of antonomasia, and short of bestowing upon him such an honor by entering into an exhaustive and meticulous definition of "the Kilroy style," we shall content ourselves with shedding some light on one aspect of his writing: his approach to the comic and the comedy in *Tea and Sex and Shakespeare*. Making use of generic categories may be a helpful starting point, but it does not lead us to an immediate elucidation of the actual meaning of "comic" in Thomas Kilroy's work. Indeed, the extensive culture he shows in the vast palette of influences of other playwrights (in particular Beckett and, more generally, the theatre of the absurd) which have given substance to his work, finds its expression in the composition of a humoristic blending of styles upon which he stamps his own hallmark. While doing this, he remains faithful to a fundamental principle of his own theatrical art — a certain distancing from any reference to a model, theoretical or otherwise. This is why, short of being able to circumscribe this study to a particular subcategory, we shall broadly define a comedy here as a play which contains elements likely to bring laughter or smiles. The blurring of categorial distinctions so dear to Kilroy regarding comedy as a genre leads us into a threefold analysis of the comic appeal in *Tea and Sex and Shakespeare*. To this end, we shall observe the classic distinction between situation comedy, verbal comedy and comedy of manners, which will enable us to reach a better understanding of the way these elements fit into the play. This will naturally lead us to formulate questions as to how and to what end the comic is used, and as to its implications on the meaning of the work as a whole.

Before entering into the subject of the comic appeal included in the text spoken by the actors, it may be expedient to study the place of the spectator as a mediator of the comic. Indeed, laughter is a social and cultural phenomenon, and the way in which the contract binds the audience to the performance gives us a better insight into the way comedy functions. Do the spectators identify with the protagonists, or do they, on the contrary, hold back from what is presented before them? *A priori*, if one bases one's opinion on the whole of Kilroy's works, identification — at least as experienced in a continuous fashion — seems excluded, as the distancing from the characters and from the crucial issues addressed in the play appears to be established as a principle by the playwright. This being so, one is aware — notwithstanding the obvious influence of Brecht — of the limits of such a standpoint, for the total absence of identification throughout the performance seems unlikely, if not impossible.

The first sentence of the initial stage directions confirms the premise of a departure from reality as a mode of approach to the play. "*The scene is a surrealistic version of the top floor of Mrs. O.'s house*" (*TSS*. 13).

Further on in the text, "grotesque" as qualifying a piece of the furniture confirms the prime importance of the adjective "surrealistic." The first impression is of a departure from reality, heightened by a fake hanging ("*When the play begins Brien is discovered 'hanging' by the neck*" [*TSS*. 13]), then further emphasized by the entry of characters who seem to be walking through the walls. From here on, the phantasmagorical character of the world into which the spectator is projected is displayed in an almost provocative manner. The audience, faced with a world whose consistency escapes them — that of the writer's mind — can hardly be expected to identify with characters devoid of any tangible reality, either physical (the fake hanging) or intellectual (by appropriating a form of speech that would disqualify them as autonomous speakers). If one also takes the stage setting as an indication of the type of comedy, one understands that the surrealistic dimension, obvious right from the start, precludes the unequivocal use of epithet usually associated with the idea of the comic: high or low, bourgeois, of character, heroic, of ideas, or even of intrigue. In spite of the categorial blur surrounding the comedy being performed before his eyes and which, in itself, is not one of his major concerns, the spectator validates the comic by his laughter. Concerning the spectator's response, however, one notes that in the absence of consistent reference to reality — so alien is the world into which he is projected — he is unable to relate to the comic in such a way as to identify with the characters.

Comedy, which is akin to farce, is established right from the start thanks to the visual effects presented to the spectator. It begins as an upheaval which, like the "gigantic scissors" (*TSS*.13), serves to usher him into a world out of joint, a world for which the audience on first sight finds no explanation. From the very beginning, the comic figures exert their influence on the way the comedy works. It is worth noting in this respect that the innumerable and outlandish sources of mirth stand in the way of any kind of complicity binding the audience to the handful of ordinary characters. This mode of construction is exactly the opposite of that of *Le Bourgeois Gentilhomme* in which, by contrast, the individual extravagance of Monsieur Jourdain effectively emphasises the solid bond between his fellow protagonists and a world of reason which the audience shares. In *Tea and Sex and Shakespeare* the strategy consists, on the contrary, in setting up a comic mode by presenting a world which is totally foreign to the spectator, in which he is at first unable to find anything to identify with.

Unlike the traditional *coup de théâtre*, which habitually occurs at some point in the play as a turning-point in the action, the visual *coup de théâtre* described in the initial stage direction serves as a comic anacrusis, setting the tone for what is to follow. Interestingly, the use Kilroy makes of situation comedy is not limited to the curtain-raiser; it also serves to illustrate the way Brien experiences the agony of writing. Although this is clearly a central question in the play, the staging — oblique to say the least — of this terrible crisis once again bars the way to any serious acceptance of his speech about the anguish of the blank page.

> *He seizes typewriter and hurls it to the floor. Takes gun and fires into the typewriter with a final coup de grace. Does a John Wayne walkabout, blowing smoke from his barrel* [*TSS*. 17].

The comic aspect of the situation, as it appears in this extract, shows how Kilroy holds himself aloof from the issues he is addressing. Taken at face value, the first two sentences are not especially laughable, and their association might simply relate Brien's outrageous gestures to the expression of his suffering. The third sentence, however, deliberately throws a comic light on the question of the difficult relationship with writing and with the pain caused by creative impotence. The solemnity of the gesture — in its reference to John Wayne — magnifies the grotesqueness of the situation, and by giving Brien a borrowed role, Kilroy initiates the spectator to a double reading of his burlesque anger. On one hand, he holds aloof from Brien's difficulty in coming to terms with himself, while at the same time challenging the reality of the writer's martyrdom. On the other hand, he adds the notion of the role as a possible disguise, which means that whatever genuine, although strange, character Brien's own life might take on, it is challenged in its truth. Here Kilroy comes back to the principles of his theatrical art and uses comic distancing — in this case a pure form of situation comedy — to explore the question of the character's authenticity and, through him, that of the self. The medium of comedy enables him to share with the audience a vision in which the individual reality performed on-stage is actually an image built around an illusion shared between the protagonists and those around them, with the added complicity of the spectator which the theatrical medium allows.

Situation comedy is sometimes associated with verbal comedy, and its implications then transcend a simple challenging of the person's reality. Several times during the play, the spectator understands that Brien loses the notion of the boundary between reality — as he sees it — and what is held as an absolute reference by those surrounding him. His behavior on the telephone is a perfect illustration of this:

> BRIEN: (*On the phone*). Hello-hello? Yes. Thank you. Please put me through to Paradise. What? Yes. As in the Bible. (*He bangs down the phone, rushes into the toilet. Toilet flush. Out again. Manic dialing on the phone once more*). Hello-hello-hello! Is that Peter? Look. Could you put me through to your man? Right. OK. Hello? Is that JC? (*Pause*). Ah, I'm not too bad. Slight touch of, well constipation. Con-stip-a — Never mind. Look. When are you coming back down here? (*Pause*). You're not! Well, could you — send someone else? Something fucking terrible is going on down here [*TSS.* 20].

The idea of putting a phone call through to Paradise makes the audience smile, especially when Brien adds physiological considerations which are hardly in keeping with the horizon of their expectations. This singular conversation echoes a similar situation, in which Shakespeare lectures Brien for overstepping his quotation rights. In both cases, the procedure is equivalent. The telephone is still primarily a tool for communication, but by a stupendous technical miracle, it enables Brien to enter into contact with an immaterial world, inaccessible in its very essence, hence the laugh triggered by this discrepancy. Once he recovers from his surprise, the spectator might interpret the scene from the point of view of the boundaries between the real and the imaginary, or as a comical illustration of the hold of fantasy upon people's lives, but the real issue appears to be more complex. The spectator is invited to reflect on the idea of absence as a form of presence. The derision which arises out of the description of the divine implies a fundamental belief in the existence of God, which seems to be just as clearly established as Shakespeare's in the Elizabethan era. In the present case, doubt is banished from the construction of comedy. Indeed, the interplay between the present in its concrete reality and a virtual world which ought not to be able to intervene directly in people's lives draws gales of laughter from the audience with, as a *sine qua non* condition, the premise of the existence of God.

Both God and Shakespeare hold such an important place in the characters' daily lives that in spite of the absence of a tangible Shakespeare or God, the idea that nonexistence is the corollary of immateriality is invalidated. Their omnipresence in the speeches and in the concerns of the protagonists indicates that they are to be reckoned with, notwithstanding the material impossibility of establishing a dialogue in the usual sense of the word. Kilroy skirts round this obvious fact and, by giving a realistic appearance to what is unreal, throws the spectator off his balance. Situation comedy, associated with verbal comedy, leads to a reflection concerning the status of reality. In spite of their insubstantiality, God and Shakespeare both appear as genuinely alive at the same time as Brien. They intervene in a surprising but relevant way — if one considers their actual presence in the character's life — not only in Brien's everyday life, but also in that of the group, and this casts a doubt on the other characters' assertions about Brien's presumed madness.

Among the elements which draw laughter from the audience, we can note the verbal inventions, the repetition of which emphasizes the distance which the characters maintain between themselves and the agony of their everyday lives. The same applies to the author and his own speech on the condition of the artiste, for he raises essential questions by viewing them from the angle of futility. Paradoxically, this distancing from reality sometimes helps to create a realistic effect, because of the fact that it is acted out against a social background in which the audience is able to recognize itself. So, when Brien describes Mummy as "That collection of inflated Woolworth's balloons that you misguidedly call a mother" (*TSS.* 15), his satirical image refers to relational tensions between son-in-law and mother-in-law which have found their expression in countless comic representations in literature and elsewhere, thus drawing the audience into a familiar setting.

The transition from descriptive comedy to verbal comedy, which rests more on ambiguity than on verbal invention, sets up a new relationship between the spectator and the character. Many times in the course of the play, Brien mocks his companions without using verbal inventions, but what makes the audience laugh is that his words go beyond the understanding of their recipients.

> BRIEN: I want to dispense with real people. Just one or two imagined caricatures like yourself, Mrs. O.
> MRS. O: That's nice [*TSS*. 36].

Mrs. O. clearly understands "character" where she should have detected the stronger sense of "caricature," in its inhuman aspect, the word being almost equivalent to a denial of existence. One finds a double message here: the one Brien addresses to Mrs. O. and the one intended by the author for the spectator, a commentary which somehow enables him to justify the way in which he is constructing his play, so that over and above the portrayal of a conflictual relationship between the misunderstood artist and those around him (in particular his caretaker), the playwright is also building up complicity between Brien and the spectator.[1] When the lights go down, the last look Brien darts at the audience, inviting them to take stock of the situation, gives us a glimpse of the sort of complicity Kilroy was looking for, a phenomenon which one finds elsewhere in similar forms. One may remember, for example, that this intellectual complicity had been set up in the very first scene, through a distorted re-enactment of an extract from *Hamlet* and a humorous rewriting of Shakespeare's text, which could not but draw peals of laughter from the audience at the discrepancy between the well-known passage and its unexpected application.

Mrs. O., with her total ignorance of the lexicon and her recurrently emphasized stupidity, is one of the comic highlights of the play. However, as is often the case in Kilroy's writing, this particular type of criticism is a cover-up for the addressing of deeper questions. The humorous dimension owes its impact to the incomprehension of language, which in turn echoes the cultural schism which separates Brien and Mrs. O. At first sight, the problem might seem to concern nothing more than the sum of intellectual knowledge which, provided it is not too sorely lacking, should enable people to converse harmoniously, without any lexical deficit impairing their mutual understanding. This is clearly not the case, and the exacerbated opposition between Brien and Mrs. O. rises up as a summit which serves to reveal other, less obvious, aspects. For example Elmina, Brien's wife, who does not belong to the same category as Mrs. O., provides a fresh angle of approach to the comic. In spite of her mastery of language which together with her marital affection enables her to express herself on a variety of different modes, she still does not succeed in dissipating the mutual incomprehension from which the couple suffer.[2] At first, the audience laughs at the farcical grotesqueness of the caricature which makes a mockery of a form of expression fraught with polysemy and devoid of any unequivocal reference to reality. But behind the many repetitions, which serve to heighten the comic impact of the work, lurks the ill-concealed anguish at the loneliness which each individual endures. Beyond its comic expression, incomprehension refers to life's suffering, which invests the comic medium with a double status, as both a source of enjoyment and an expression of human pain.

> BRIEN: You are all figments of the imagination.
> MRS. O: The poor fella is off again.
> BRIEN: Mere shapes and airy nothings.
> SYLVESTER: Nonsense! (*Pleased speech*). If you prick us do we not bleed? If you tickle us do we not laugh? Aha! Shakespeare.
> MRS. O: (*Relieved aside*). 'Tis only that Shakespeare. Would you like something hot, Mr Brien? Maybe the cuppa tea? [*TSS*. 17].

The different levels of language, the opposition between absolute pragmatism and something like verbal delirium, set the audience laughing. However, incomprehension is no longer the only comic factor. The different facets of reality on which the characters are placed are also a source of mirth in their contrasting aspects. Indeed, the extravagance of their beliefs is expressed in speeches which bring out two aspects of the character with which each spectator is sure to be able to identify, at least partially. The discrepancies in the language are in fact used by Thomas Kilroy to pursue a reflection which develops ontological implications. Brien banishes Mrs. O. and the other characters to a virtual sphere in which their lives, as they imagine they are living them, are nothing but illusions. The impossibility of communication becomes further proof that the characters are deprived of what they understand existence to be — that is to say, having a tangible anchorage point in reality. Mrs. O. makes another appearance as a comic trigger-element, with less certainty than Brien for, unlike the author, the remedy she offers in any crisis contains a degree of uncertainty: "Maybe." Confronted with the statement that life — at least as she conceives it — is nothing but an illusion, Mrs. O.'s universal remedy is "the cuppa tea." "The cuppa tea," the popular *deus ex machina* of Anglo-Saxon culture, seems to her just the thing to offer as a universal answer to Brien's existential difficulties. The excessive and contrasting character of the representations staged in this extract builds up a vision of humanness which asserts itself by invalidating the forms of existence embodied by the two antithetical figures of humanity. This clearcut rejection does not lead Kilroy to advocate a syncretic vision in keeping with his rejection of the simplistic and deleterious certainties of Mrs. O. and Brien, but rather to lay emphasis on the vastness of human blindness, without promoting a middle course.

> BRIEN: Are you planning to have Mummy and Daddy for afternoon tea, Elmina? By God. If you do. I'll — I'll piss on them over the banisters!
> MRS. O: Lord save us, I'm going to try the priest. *She heads off down the stairs.*
> SYLVESTER: He dislikes your parents.
> ELMINA (*Tearfully*): He writes repulsive letters to the newspapers and signs Daddy's name. Advocating abortion and all [*TSS.* 21].

The actress's performance is sure to add an extra dimension to this scene, which will probably be better set off if some distance is observed, especially in the way "tearfully" is rendered. Now situation comedy, now verbal comedy, the play is projected against a social background which the playwright sketches indirectly. The laughable effects become more and more numerous as the play progresses, and when several people are involved in the transgression of customs, the comedy of manners comes to the fore, with the social critique it presupposes. In the present case, Brien's indecorous provocation is something which goes beyond gratuitous bawdiness. The laughable arises out of a strategy of confrontation of a somewhat colorful brand, as the social intercourse between the two protagonists is ultimately nothing more than a form of violence. This scathing type of comedy appeal brings Kilroy's comic scenes close to Shakespeare's, not without recalling Beckett's. The emphasis on the carnal dimension of individuals shows them in a caustic light, as flouting commonly held social principles. The provocative nature of Brien's words is all the more readily appreciated as the spectator is able to reconstruct in his mind the elements of a very strict moral order suggested by the list of taboos defied in the course of the play. These transgressions, further highlighted by references to guardians of law and moral order (for example the priest, second only to the tea as a performer of miracles), establish by inversion of the image they project a concave portrait of a society which becomes oppressive in the number of taboos it conveys.

Tea and Sex and Shakespeare. Hélène Montague and Stanley Townsend. Rough Magic Theatre Company, Dublin, 1988 (courtesy of Rough Magic).

It should furthermore be noted that Brien is not the only scandalmonger. Elmina, in spite of the distress she exhibits following her husband's bawdy jokes about her parents, also takes part in the scathing criticism of the system when she brazenly avows her unsatisfied sexual lust. The comedy of manners is constructed on different levels, partly hinted at in the title: the tea ritual, sex and drama both literary and factual. Kilroy's caustic vision finds an outlet in the parody of a society which seems to function in a grotesque way. Through the constant shifting of perspective and through pastiche, which gives a surrealistic air to the scenes of the extraordinary lives of the protagonists, the world as a whole is challenged in the consistency of its logic, over a disconcerting roar of laughter.

From a literary point of view, *Tea and Sex and Shakespeare* stands as a concrete and burlesque demonstration of the point of view expressed in Virginia Woolf's essay *A Room of One's Own,* in which the writer claims the right to a private (and protected) space of their own for women, so that they might gain access to writing. The nightmarish vision of Brien's suffering for literature's sake, caused by constant interruptions, adds relish to his chamber odyssey, but literature — as the title suggests — is just one of the three points targeted by the playwright. If allusions to literature find a natural place in the architecture of Kilroy's works, reference is not made to literature alone. Whether it hangs on Shakespeare, on sex or on relations with the Other, initially hinted at in the form of a cup of tea shared with the parents-in-law, the comedy owes its impact to a scathing social critique. From puns to bawdy jokes, the play gathers evidence for the trial of a world with which, in spite of its surrealistic aspects, the spectator cannot but identify. In this very special vision of the world, the comic arises out of the fact that the tragic is reduced to the fear of being forced to have tea with one's parents-in-law. As often in Kilroy's drama, comedy — of words, of situations, of manners — gradually emerges as a mode of reflection on the relation between man and the world.

Distancing is an invariable feature of Kilroy's playwriting, achieved through the use of constant incongruity, as announced in the title of the play in which the coordinating conjunctions establish preposterous links between spheres which are *a priori* completely alien to each other. As the play lacks any reliable structuring dimension, the world is presented as a place of disorder which, far from lending itself to the construction of a complex polyphony, makes the audience laugh at the absurdity of the situations staged. One cannot be oblivious to the tragic dimension in the

3. Comic Variations in Tea and Sex and Shakespeare

playwright's vision, stern and icy if it were reduced to the tragedy of meaninglessness. However, one must also bear in mind that *Tea and Sex and Shakespeare* works like a practical joke based on comic disillusion. If one takes Baudelaire's distinction between the *comique significatif*, in the sense that one laughs at something or someone, and the *comique absolu*, in which there is shared laughter, one is better able to grasp the internal impetus of this comedy. In *Tea and Sex and Shakespeare*, Kilroy offers a form of *comique significatif* which becomes *comique absolu* as the action progresses. Despite the anguish one perceives surrounding the world in which Brien and his acolytes eke out their existence, the social disorder does not end up as a loss of meaning, and the spectator eventually recognizes himself in the features of the various characters, in a kind of complicity which does not arouse in him any feeling of superiority. On the other hand though, confronted with incongruities arising out of himself, he will enjoy a moment of relief laughing at himself, a grotesque and frail figure who suddenly realizes he is staggering when he thought he was walking.

4

Space in *Talbot's Box*

Text space, acting space — the special attention given to stage production as an essential part of theatre studies prompts us to question the function and impact of textual material which has long been held as an exclusive mode of reference for the study of dramatic works. When one considers the text of a play with a view to staging it, that is to say, in the relation which must link it to a particular human and material reality, variable according to the period, one notes that the title, unlike the other aspects of the text (dialogues or stage directions), makes no further appearance once the play is produced on stage. One may well question the scope of an element which is to leave no visible trace on stage. Does it serve no other purpose than that of indexing the play, thus avoiding confusion when actors or stage managers talk about a particular piece of drama? If this primary usefulness were the only reason for putting a name to a work, one could expect that some other, non-referential form of classification, comparable to the choice of certain contemporary, non-figurative painters, might eventually replace this mode of characterization. In actual fact, the significance enjoyed by the need for a name, although by its very nature it narrows the scope of interpretation, can probably be attributed to the power that a title offers the author over the way in which his work is to be perceived.

This demonstration of the author's creative power, which lays emphasis on one character or on one particular dimension of the play, is occasionally overlooked by actors and stage managers, who fail to see in the title a major aspect of the work itself. Indeed, the fact of adding a spatial dimension to a text brings out the latent tension which opposes freedom to choose between different interpretations and the basic guidelines inherent in the content. For this reason, creative independence — regardless of the author's wishes — may naturally exert itself on the title, as on other elements in the text. In the present case, Thomas Kilroy's choice — *Talbot's Box*— offers the spectator a certain number of clues which he will naturally follow up, and also a few unknown perspectives which the unfolding of the action will clarify, thus showing to which aspects the playwright wished to draw the spectator's attention. The possessive form following the proper noun indicates that the play is to deal with a possession relationship between a person and a box, whose contents, shape and significance are shrouded in mystery until the moment when light dawns on the stage. The audience then discovers that the relationship between "the box" and the subject himself is not a metonymy, as Harpagon's casket would be, but that there really is a large box, representing a space whose possession by a human being is to be a key element in the understanding of the play.

The identity of Talbot is defined in the opening scene, insofar as the presentation of the sanctification process enables us to reach a better understanding of one of the elements of the report. The story is to be about a saint and his box, which the spectator quickly understands not to be a logical extension of sanctification, as might have been "*Talbot's Chains*," but rather as a mystery. Chains do indeed symbolize the mortification embedded in the man's flesh, and lead to the sanctification of a man whose long penitence has turned him into a saint; but what is the meaning of "the box"? The importance the title ascribes to it is manifested on stage in the initial stage directions: ("*The lights reveal a huge box occupying virtually the whole stage*" [*TB.* 9]). After the first visual encounter which underlines the all-importance of the box, the question arises as to the way this should be apprehended. If one adopts a resolutely optimistic point of view, considering that the set designer is able to achieve total compliance with the playwright's wishes, he will have to express the following aspects:

> *The effect should be that of a primitive, enclosed space, part prison, part sanctuary, part acting space* [*TB.* 9].

From a material point of view, the designing of a set representing a virgin space which conjures up the impression of enclosure is not a major difficulty. However, the second part of the sentence refers to three non-complementary, potentially antagonistic requirements, whose physical and intellectual representations are far from simple. This triple definition describes a space in the form of a tension between diverging but inseparable points of view.

The opposition between the sanctuary and the prison constitutes a dialectic through which the author seeks to demonstrate the limits of partial — hence inadequate — perception. This double orientation, consistent insofar as it bars the way to any premature and unique characterisation of the space ascribed to Talbot, is associated with a third constraint on the set design. This consists in designating as "acting space" a place which has a quasi-sacred character because of its association with a saint. This enhanced distancing effect is achieved by the introduction of a specifically theatrical orientation, which implicitly undermines the sacred status of a space perceived alternatively as punitive or redeeming. The syntactic analysis of the title put forward here has shown the importance of the possession relationship between the person and the object (as a guideline to the reading of the play); the lexicon plays a similar guiding role, insofar as it reiterates the questions which arise out of the association of the three aspects targeted by the author. The word "cell" might have seemed more adequate if we had only taken the first two perspectives into account (the prison and the sanctuary), but the word "box" refers to the distancing called for in the third part of the definition which, paradoxically, brings us back to reality by laying emphasis on the artificiality of the performance. The spectator pursues his elucidation of the title as he continues to question the object, not so much in its material form — the reality of which he will nonetheless be brought to challenge — as in its actual meaning. Whether a sanctuary or a prison, disputed by the introduction of doubt into the definitions which it suggests, the object — perceived first as a thing possessed — eventually becomes the object of a multitude of questions. These concern not only the relationship between Talbot and his box, but the saint himself, as the hint of an identity crisis has been suggested by the doubt surrounding the nature of his space.

As the hymn dies away, the front of the box is opened out from within by two men so that the audience now sees inside [*TB.* 9].

The opening of the box sets up a relationship with the audience who up to this point have been kept outside, and are now able to gaze into this closed space. Besides symbolizing the contrast between inside and outside, between those who have access to a masked form of reality and those who do not, the box, at the time of its opening, appears at once as a stage prop and as a symbol of theatrical activity, since its side symbolically refers to the fourth wall, which has become invisible in the stage-setting. According to the conventions of the realist school, it enables spectators to watch the characters living out their lives, as though they were endowed with the invisibility of omniscience.

The actions carried out just before the priest's speech, as the characters in the box take their places, form a theatrical prelude which is presented as such, since these arrangements are not hidden from the spectator. This allows the playwright and the stage manager to lay emphasis on the spectacular side of the performance,[1] thus complying with the criteria stated in the spatial definition, referring to the box as acting space. This being so, the theatrical artifice — materialized in the preliminary placing arrangements — has only a very limited impact, as preliminaries of this kind have become something of a ritual in contemporary theatre. Accordingly, space is better defined or invalidated as such through speech than by body language and stage-setting. The vestments and the statue of the Virgin installed by the priest obviously play a part in predefining the place in which he makes his speech, but only his sermon (during which he tells his congregation the story of Matt Talbot's spiritual path) imparts its religious character to the place in which he is expressing himself. The sudden interruption of his preaching by the actress supposed to be playing the Virgin Mary corroborates this analysis. Her unexpected vociferation upturns the scene with an intensity ten times that of the preliminaries presented as such, which had merely served to remind the spectator that he was at the theatre.

WOMAN (*Shout*): How long do I have to stand like this?
PRIEST FIGURE (*Aside*): Shush! you're supposed to be the statue of the Blessed Virgin Mary! [*TB.* 9]

Thomas Kilroy makes frequent use of spectacular distancing effects, which are a signal to the spectator that the vision he was about to adhere to remains invalid. The initial warning, presented in the form of stage preliminaries, was thus in no way a concession to practices currently in vogue, but rather a prelude to an intrusion by the author himself within the very structure of the play, in order to establish as a principle the existence of a multifaceted reality. In the opening scene, the staging of a near-sacrilegious double challenges in its very essence a religious ceremony (in a space perceived as a place of sanctification), and turns it into something like a show. "The Box," which spectators were about to invest with serious religious properties, suddenly turns back into just a box, a stage prop, or a prison. The halt in Talbot's sanctification process does not totally disqualify the sacred character of the box, which remains virtually present, but the upheavals brought about by the stage-setting send it back to its value as a prop, without however reducing it to a single unequivocal reality. The non-correspondence with expectations is a challenge to space itself: placed on a precarious footing by the transition from an indubitable reference value (imparted by a theatrical convention) to a concept, its status is fragile in that it depends for its reality on two different types of determination—material reality and the play of the actors. Space, through a mirror-effect which becomes obvious when certainties disappear, also serves to define the characters. This explains why the challenging of a single-faceted spacial dimension is also a challenge to the person who inhabits it. The rest of the play shows from several different angles the way the protagonists appear, depending on where they stand. In view of this, the initial complexity sets the tone for the whole in its presentation of a man whose relations with space reveal a multifaceted personality which cannot be reduced to a single perspective.[2]

While we are aware of the problems of identity linked to the absence of a stable definition of the place as a mode of characterization, we should also bear in mind that another reference to space — imperceptible because it does not appear on the stage — is also connected with questions of existence raised by the relations between the characters and space. The unpredictable events in the opening scene have served to lay emphasis on the necessity of spatial, concrete and verbal convergences, so that a given place might indisputably be accepted as such by the audience. This pinning down to concrete reality, tangibly expressed in the performance, does not exclude the fact that space may be represented differently in the protagonists' speeches, for instance in the form of verbal scenery. The special off-stage effect thus achieved broadens the scope of this reflection on space by developing an aspect which had hitherto only appeared as a reality in the stage-setting: the question of the role of space in individual lives. The words of Matt's sister — a mother figure who grieves over the solitary and cloistered life led by her brother — echo problems of identity previously mentioned, in that she evokes the past in its spatial dimension as a way of probing into life itself.

> WOMAN: All I remember we was always movin'. Here in Rutland Street. Over to Aldborough near to the barracks. Summerhill, Newcomen Court offa the North Strand, down to Monto, Byrne's Lane offa Potter's Alley, back to Summerhill again, out to Love Lane beyond Ballybough. Sticks o' furniture on top of a handcart, the small wans perishin' with the cauld. Runnin' from the Landlords. But what in the name o' God were we runnin' after? Was it anything better? [*TB.* 21].

An implicit contrast is set up between the story of their young days, when financial pressures kept them on the move, and Matt's confinement, which Susan is trying to understand. Having established this first opposition, we cannot but recognize that her final question about the meaning of the moves leads us to a similar question, based on contrasting logic, since it concerns Matt's cloistering. The prepositions "from" and "after" indicate the gap which separates two ways of apprehending the world. "From" refers to a material reality which has become overpowering for the victims of the forced removals, for it imposes a movement which escapes their understanding. "After," on the contrary, suggests a quest which breaks off from material contingencies and probes into the meaning of these removals, from which comes a reference to the divine, which seems to be the last rampart against a feeling of absurdity. The analysis of the past, in the form of a pessimistic biography, is nothing more than a list of homes forsaken for reasons of poverty, and we are given to understand that the situation has not improved. According to Matt's sister, life is one long tribulation, whose potential absurdity is all too obvious in the physical way in which people belong to the universe. Space here raises the question of the human condition, in the sense that a subject, when deprived of the decision as to the place he is to occupy, loses his freedom and sees himself as an object. The overturning of expectations concerning the subject/object status raises a question which becomes more and more relevant as the play goes on, concerning the exact value to be ascribed to the possessive case, so as to ascertain who, Talbot or "the box," possesses the other. The assessment Susan draws up naturally refers to the title of the play, whose essential element *in fine* is the link between "the box," irrefutable as a spatial element, despite the different ways it is defined by the various characters, and Talbot, whose rootedness in this place — precise in itself but viewed from diverse angles — conjures up a number of different profiles of his personality. Here again Kilroy, to whom the very idea of certainty seems to be synonymous with absurdity, is at work weaving complex backgrounds.[3] They take shape, if not as intrinsic truths, at least as sketches of identities, kaleidoscopic yet coherent, based on people's relations with space as viewed from different angles.

How are we to fathom Talbot's innermost being? In spite of the theatrical upturning of the religious ceremony which from the start challenges the meaning of the place within which the action takes place, the recognition of Talbot as a Holy Man gains ground as the play progresses. Notwithstanding the anticlerical digressions, among which one finds the role of the priest played by a woman,[4] the religious context nevertheless imposes itself as a reference, given Talbot's spiritual path. The revelations about his life as a penitent (to which are added the priest's speech and the Conservatives' observations about his possible canonization) gradually enthrone his image as a saint. In this respect, although his destiny is unique and his roots Irish — underlined in the use of idiomatic expressions — a parallel is set up between his spiritual path and those of St. Anthony and St. Catherine of Sienna. This equivalence of saintliness rests on the tangible trace of his secret, self-inflicted chastisement, whose carnal mortification only became apparent after his death. This physical proof of saintliness conditions the way some of the people around him interpret his relations with space. His mysterious confinement, together with his daily martyrdom while hidden from the eyes of the world, add up as extra elements in his path to saintliness. The portrait of Talbot as a seraph is drawn up on outside evidence which, with all due respect for the holy man, considers him as a part-time hermit, whose confinement was an extra punishment. The relevance of this vision seems to be corroborated by Talbot's last monologue which, in the final scene, describes a carpenter and his wife bidding farewell to their son, while in the background a cross is being built. Jerusalem, Dublin, or other places — geography loses its meaning; the distance fades away while a convergence becomes apparent between several different types of sanctifying commitments. Materially, the initial description of the box — mostly wood with a small amount of metal — prefigures the imminence of the cross which appears in the last scene. "The Box as a Cross" is thus one of the possible ways of reading the title of the play, laying emphasis on the idea of recurrence in the spiritual paths followed by martyrs. This interpretation presents Talbot's penitence as a historical trajectory, in which confinement in his box is likened to an updated version of the Stations of the Cross.

> TALBOT: But then I discovered something strange, Susan. (*She begins to move away.*) Having given all up, it was all given back to me, but different, y'know what I mean. All the world and the people in the world came back to me in me own room. But everything in place. Nothing twisted 'n broken as it is in the world. Everything straight as a piece of good timber, without warp [*TB.* 23].

The change of perspective makes Matt's confinement appear less like purgatory in the shape of chastisement than as a retreat in which, paradoxically, he becomes reconciled with the world by moving away from it. The withdrawal into oneself does not necessarily invalidate the idea of saintliness as held by the faithful, for it enables Matt to enter the dark inner realm mentioned at the time when he started out on the road of abstinence. Before expounding the positive dimension of his confinement, he explains to his sister that God has obliged him to give up those most dear to him.[5] In his confined space, whose darkness — negative, according to the priest — seemed to him on the contrary to indicate the presence of God, he at last finds a wholeness he had never dreamed of in the fragmented outside world. From this point of view, the elation he feels at this discovery of total harmony may be seen as an aspect of a relationship with the divine granted to a Holy Man, whose solitary confinement has been rewarded by a redeeming vision offered only to God's elect.

Confinement seen as a protection against chaos brings a slight modification to the analysis of Talbot's relations with space. They must now be seen as hanging on a complex opposition between an inner world — inhuman but paradisiacal — and the outside world which Talbot describes in Dantesan terms. This points us to a dialectic reading, for — if Matt's situation is to be taken for what it stands for in this perspective — the relation of man to the world depends upon the way he occupies space, itself viewed from two different angles, as redeeming confinement and destructive confrontation. The spectator discovers that ordinary social relations seem to afflict Matt more excruciatingly than the physical suffering produced by his chains. The encounter with the world makes him aware of his remoteness, of the distance which separates him from beings to whom he does not manage to relate. In the play, the relinquishment of the beloved is not simply a concept in the background, having no substance in staged reality, and the spectator soon understands on what grounds, on the personal level, his refusal of society does not stand as an impediment to his sanctification. In the course of an ordinary scene serving to present one of his multiple facets, Matt reveals that he is unable to establish an intimate contact with a young woman who is in love with him. The young woman sees aloofness where he sees shared experience, and their breakup is proof of his inability to love in terms of what society expects. The pain experienced by the young woman affects him indirectly and takes on dramatic proportions, although he claims to be rising to a higher level, which to him is a compensation. He then defines the outside world in terms of separation, of impossible closeness, but his acceptance of an impassable distance, which will always keep him apart from others, whoever they may be, does not conceal his deep inner suffering. The artificial paradise of his confinement in a monastic room is his response to the daily martyrdom inflicted upon him by his inability to relate with the Other in the ordinary world. At once clandestine Holy Man in secret and an ordinary workman, Matt Talbot and his twofold identity spark off differences of opinion as to the meaning of his confinement and his failure to enter into social commitments. Contrary to the faithful, the working-class community — from which he seemed to exclude himself— cast a highly critical eye on this aloofness.

> FIRST MAN: Spent his days — prayin' for the salvation of his immortal soul.
> SECOND MAN: Prayin'! Listen, comrade, there was a hundred thousand people starvin' in the Dublin tenements. What's the soul of wan man got to do with that? [*TB*. 30].

This passage rings with the echoes of Matt's aborted love relationship, but his inability to give of himself in a human relationship here applies to the whole community. Once again, the contrast between love and the religious world comes sharply into focus. The mention of anything religious has always been associated with a codified representation of space, according to which the spiritual referred to an uplifting. At the opposite extreme, the material, encompassing everything human, love included, was emptied of its value and banished to the lower regions. The traditional Christian opposition between the spiritual and the material, above and below, comes to the fore when the sufferings endured by a famished population are brushed aside as minor details. Commitment or distancing regarding social realities serve to show up the kind of relationships people establish with the world. In the present case, Talbot's inclusion in a secular space challenges his saintliness as one would never challenge that of a monk in confinement. Paradoxically, the mention of Talbot in prayer throws discredit on the very idea of saintliness, insofar as holiness is built up on a relation with the divine which transcends the grasp of ordinary society, but is oblivious of a material dimension vital to common mankind. Present in spite of himself in a world he does not understand, he is condemned by an absence whose motives, seen through the eyes of prevailing collective suffering, appear emptied of their validity and are likened to a betrayal.

In *Talbot's Box*, the relations — whether public or private — between the characters and space serve as an indication of the relations they establish with the world. In spite of this meaningful relating process, interpretation is nonetheless fraught with pitfalls. The various points of view are either invalidated or partially refuted by those of other protagonists, whose views of the same reality may be widely different. Moreover, the spectator is repeatedly cautioned against any monolithic reading of the main character, whose status gradually shifts from that of a complex subject to that of a fixed object (the staged sanctification being the first example). The Conservatives, who seek to appropriate the saint's political dimension, illustrate the dangers of such blindness by their claim to be representatives. Their biased gloss concerning Matt's withdrawal from social reality enables them to include him in a xenophobic speech. It casts doubt not only on the trustworthiness of their words but also on the possibility of ever reaching a final and comprehensive understanding of the character. At first the author's delaying tactics, notably visible in the polyphonic composition of the work, seem to explain the slow progress toward the ultimate revelation of the truth. However, as one scene succeeds another, we gradually realize that the counterpointal orchestration serves to point a highly critical finger at a meaningful but simplistic duality.

Thus, the spectator learns that after his religious metamorphosis, Matt tries to find the street musician whose instrument he stole with the help of accomplices. Talbot recounts his fruitless search for the fiddler, combing the streets of Dublin, year after year. Unlike the situations mentioned up to this point, when he had either been safe in his redeeming confinement, or else had rejected those who tried to draw close to him, his active contrition breaks away from his image as a saint in confinement, since he is the one who goes out in quest of the Other. Although this reversal is the only one of its kind, and is motivated by his yearning for expiation, it demonstrates the impossibility of defining reliable limits, upon which the spectator might construct and therefore understand the character. In spite of his repentance, he falls short of the redeeming encounter. The saint disappears, leaving the man, who is suddenly confronted with the banality of human heartbreak. His wanderings, which bring a surprising new turn to his relations with space, now add to his life the ordinariness of human loneliness. From this point of view, somewhat reminiscent of Schopenhauer, he shares in the agonies of the common mortal, and the pains of life are no less acute than those of his martyrdom.

The staging of the play, with its added spatial dimension, enables the playwright to blur the divisions between different spatial entities, and so readjust the Manichaean visions constructed around the idea of the schism separating the world of the saint and the world of ordinary beings. Thus the workman and his wife, who live under the same roof as Matt, overhear his chanting through the thin walls, while the saint hears nothing of the workman's criticisms. Drama as a mode of expression allows the playwright to defend his stand against one-sidedness by his use of theatrical overlappings, and gives him the freedom to juxtapose different spatial entities which, although separate from each other, are nevertheless brought together in various ways. These *extempore* coincidences have a double effect: they both challenge the very idea of total separation arising from the character of the saint and, over and above the humor, with the tone contrasts they bring, they serve a subversive purpose, in that they explode near-sacred stereotypes. Whether private space or public space, Matt's body is among the places upon which this subversion is concentrated. At the mortuary, the forensic scientist is obliged to interrupt his postmortem in view of the saintliness of the patient. This double status allotted to the saint's body finds an echo in the incongruous association between the mortuary and a football ground, where the forensic scientist hopes to go that evening. The telescoping of times and places in fact expresses spatial transgressions which, in the play, take on a broader meaning. In the opening scene, the use of a deodorant clearly debunks the sacred character of the saint's body, which is no longer considered as a relic, a sacred object, but as the source of an unpleasant body odor which must be got rid of. This comic distancing must not be understood as only serving to debunk the sacred.[6] The body, whose material substance is demonstrated in the fetid emanations, is not the only indication of reality. The chains imprinted in the flesh, representing reality in its most concrete form, open up a spiritual dimension, thus refuting any representation of the body limited to its physical aspects.

Between private spaces and public spaces, the recurrent problem of rejection and inclusion forms an ever-changing mosaic, whose meaning is constantly renewed to match the changes in time and space. Kilroy's approach precludes any possibility of a rigid vision of Talbot and his relations with the box, and after a judiciously constructed initiation, the spectators are able to apprehend in all its complexity the final picture of the play.

> *The great doors of the box are closed from without by the two men and the woman who stand looking in through cracks in the wall from which bright light comes which illuminates their faces* [*TB*. 63].

Logically, if one bears in mind Kilroy's particular handling of the paradox, the closing of the box is tantamount to an opening up of the meaning. The questions surrounding the interpretation of this picture, upon

Talbot's Box. Photograph by Fergus Bourke. From left to right, Stephen Brennan, John Molloy, Clive Geraghty, Ingrid Craigie, Eileen Colgan. Abbey Theatre (Peacock), Dublin, 1977 (courtesy of The Abbey Theatre Archive).

which the play comes to a close, are contained within the picture itself, a sort of visual *fermata* which suggests its highly composite nature. As we gaze at the box, how are we to decide whether Talbot is the possessor or the possessed, given that the light which beams out through the cracks — suggesting the crossing of boundaries — challenges the concept of possession? We are then reminded of the third element which, between the prison and the sanctuary, had also defined the box as acting space, thus precluding any simplistic bipolar opposition.

The representation of saintliness lends itself to a threefold reading. Although clearly respected in itself, its spiritual radiation is nevertheless rendered with a touch of humor by the lighting effect, which brings us back to the distancing in the opening scene and the use of the deodorant. Finally, its value is challenged on the grounds of its antisocial effects by the behavior of those faithful who are locked out of the sacred spot.

Together yet drawn apart: this last vision of the characters, as an image of the human condition with its unfathomable mysteries, recalls the many facets held up before our eyes in the course of the performance. The question once again arises of how reliably a person can be defined through his relation with space. There is nothing surprising in these misgivings, for the complexity of human nature makes any kind of transparency impossible. Furthermore, as the play progresses and different points of view are developed, the spectator becomes more and more wary of speeches which reconstruct individuals through the prism of their own relations with the world.

Talbot's Box ends with a visual element which refers us back to the title, without elucidating it, and for the last time addresses the question of the links between the saint and space. Unlike the act of speech and the single point of view it generally imposes during the performance, this image stands as a refutation of the one-sidedness of speech. Through this visual medium, Kilroy offers the spectator a number of different angles of approach to the truth of his character, which still remains impossible to grasp but, as he hopes, will be apprehended through the number and the variety of challenging strategies.

5

Double Cross:
The Faces of Betrayal

From union to separations, be they short-lived or permanent, wrought by human will or brought about by fate as it leaves its mark on people's lives, Thomas Kilroy in his drama takes pains to show man in the whole spectrum of his contradictions, his meanness and his grandeur. Although it is partly irrelevant to attach to a play the particular reading suggested by the precise historical situation prevalent at the time when the play was first performed, it is worth noting that *Double Cross* was first performed by the Field Day Company. This theatre company, based in Derry, produced a new play every year, before embarking on a tour of the Republic in a symbolic refusal to acknowledge the boundary between the two Irelands. Beyond the artistic commitment, then, lurked a political project, that of the refusal to accept the separation.[1] In Derry, the audience was composed of members of both communities, who probably situated the condemnation of an absurd brand of nationalism in an Irish context — a message intended for both sides.[2] In *Double Cross*, the playwright tells the story of two historical figures of Irish origin, showing some extraordinary episodes in their lives. The action is set during World War II, which gives a particular color to the choices made by each of the characters. In the first part of the diptych, Bracken appears in his role as Minister of Information in Churchill's government, while William Joyce, chief disinformant on Goebbels' radio station, gradually comes into focus in the second part of the play. The one identifies with the ideals of English democracy, while the other adheres totally to the ideology of the Third Reich. Through the sound reproduction of each other's speeches or the rebroadcasting of video extracts projected in the parts of the play dealing with the one whom the other wishes to annihilate, they construct, turn by turn, diametrically opposed political portraits. However, through their total commitment to a struggle in which each is ready to lay down his life — for no clemency for the defeated is to be expected from the enemy — they both embody, despite their antagonistic positions, a form of adherence to an exacerbated brand of nationalism. The same actor plays the parts of Bracken and of Joyce, and the physical resemblance serves to heighten the likeness in the way their minds work.[3] Kilroy reconstructs the lives of Joyce and Bracken on the basis of established historical facts, to which he adds a certain convergence, partly through the relation which each has with his lady friend. On the political level, however, their destinies diverge in that Bracken finds himself on the winning side and savors the joys of victory, while Joyce is arrested, judged and hanged for treason.

In *Double Cross*, Kilroy stages two men — together yet locked in combat — whose destinies lead them in opposite directions, in a kind of deadly war game. The author, aware of the necessity for giving some roundedness to the perfect hero, dresses Bracken up with a few foibles so as to avoid falling into hagiography, that infallible dramatic prelude to boredom. Joyce is handled differently, as he embodies loyalty to those on the losing side, who eventually fall into total disgrace. His depravity is therefore free of any sexual character, being entirely concentrated in his adhesion to an ideology generally considered unacceptable today. The wartime background and the subject matter place *Double Cross* in a somewhat specialized category of drama, and the play owes its originality to its obvious political overtones. Kilroy's usual distancing from the crucial issues at stake in the play takes on a very unusual form in this very different play. Like the original handling of theatrical distancing techniques, the almost total lack of humor is worth noting. In order to reconstruct a historical framework, the play features two narrators who play no part in the action, creating a distancing effect in the form of a putative objectivity, which excludes any possibility of derision. This objectification implemented by the two impersonal figures enables the author to lay emphasis on the factual side of Bracken's and Joyce's lives, thereby emptying them of a large part of their individual personalities. The propaganda speeches which the two characters play back also remind one of the hardships of the war years. The nationalism in the speeches is doubled with sound effects which invite the spectator on a journey to the center of wartime horror, brought back to life by the sound of bombing. The play appears to follow the course of history, as it ends with the victory of the Allied forces and Joyce's death sentence, while Bracken, face-to-face with his double yet craving for a brother, questions his own success.

In appearance, especially if the structure of the play is to taken as a reliable indication, *Double Cross* tells the story of the final events in the life of Joyce, a traitor to the British cause. From the outset, in the opening scene, Kilroy presents the confrontation between the two men in this light, with Bracken calling his enemy a "filthy little traitor" (*DC.* 22), while Joyce counterattacks with claims of treason from within, in the Minister of Information's putative depravity. Joyce's downfall — played as a parody of a happy ending in which evil is punished and good rewarded — unsettles a political standpoint hinging upon the idea of treason yet implicitly invalidated by the link between the two enemies. Furthermore, the intense nationalism of the young fascists who attend Joyce's trial and bring him their support seems also to challenge the reality of the treason, which in fact turns out to be judicially non-existent. The initial Manichaeism as a logical expression of a conflict opposing two sides gradually fades away. The obvious contrasts between the enemies lose their edge as the two characters slowly turn into puppets churning out nationalist speeches. The two shadows, empty of any real substance, have many points in common, which should lead the spectator to reflect upon the relevance of a Manichaean vision of conflict.[4]

The narrators who tell the story of the two characters' lives lay emphasis on a practice common to both, consisting in inventing for themselves a personality which is out of keeping with their origins. This personal reinvention is not surprising in itself: for Irish people, it may recall the integration process of immigrants who, once they have settled in the host country, invent themselves a new identity so as to integrate into a foreign community. The terms "invent" and "story," chosen by the two narrators to recount the history of Joyce and Bracken, enable the playwright to insist on the artifice inherent in their own creation, by underlining the subjective character of their chronicle. The playwright builds up a particular kind of hermeneutics, which gradually substantiates the idea of treason outside of war. The errors in his own official obituary — which Bracken seeks to impose — demonstrate that his anxiety to assimilate masks a desire to erase the past which far surpasses the usual quest for integration as experienced by immigrants. The idea of personal reinvention is thus given wider scope than the limited process of immigration. Writing about oneself, particularly if the chronicle is intended for someone else, as in the present case, necessarily implies a tension between private truth and protective artifice. The behavioral pastiche, in the form of

Double Cross. Stephen Rea. Field Day Theatre Company, Derry, 1991 (courtesy of Field Day).

the abjuration of an abhorred identity, suggests not only the idea of the mask, but also that of treason pervading the play. A quest such as this does not fail to set up links between the two main characters, who are brought together by their atypical approach to questions of identity. The physical resemblance between Joyce and Bracken — highlighted on the stage by the same actor playing the two roles — brings them even closer together. If their love lives are less faithfully replicated than their political careers, both nevertheless find themselves confronted with failure, which contrasts sharply with their success in politics. Indeed, both enjoy such resounding success in integrating into a system to which they had both been outsiders, that each seeks to make use of his fame to discredit his enemy:

> ACTOR (Narrator): Ladies and gentlemen, this is the story of two men who invented themselves [*DC.* 24].
> BRACKEN: The question is though: how did this chappie Joyce end up as Goebbels' right-hand man on the wireless?
> JOYCE: The question is, what does it say about democracy if such a trickster can rise to the top?
> BRACKEN: Lord Haw Haw, I ask you!
> JOYCE: Mr Brendan Bracken, Tory MP for North Paddington, of all places!
> BRACKEN: The traitor!
> JOYCE: The trickster! [*DC.* 23].

From a dramatic point of view, the use of stichomythia heightens the violence of the confrontations within the dialogue, which is perceived as an individualized echo of the war between two opposing nations. Here Kilroy demonstrates his skill in handling dramatic expression, this particular construction generally being used at a moment of intense emotion, when the verbal exchange is as deadly as a duel. This technique sometimes overflows into comedy when one of the protagonists wins the day and rails his opponent, but here the mutual neutralization of the jousters makes such a transition impossible. The use of parallel syntactic structures shows the fundamental similarities which the playwright draws between antagonistic speeches. Although opposed in matters of principle, each enemy group denounces the imposture of the other, following a single path which leads them from abuse to insult. As the tension mounts, hate becomes crystallized in words which the outside world condemns out of hand through sound effects which illustrate the wartime atrocities they generate. The terms "chappie" and "trickster" are a prelude to the oncoming insult, which seems to be the supreme outcome of partisan diatribes. This extract shows how, in the context of armed conflict, the two sides attempt to discredit their enemies, while also emphasizing, beyond this ordinary organization of conflict, the special attention paid by the author to substantiate in detail the resemblance between Joyce's and Bracken's careers. The two characters make opposite political choices, while realizing that their common Irish roots cannot account for such a commitment. The looking-glass construction and the use of the double as a way of demonstrating the similarities between the characters clearly show up the differences, in particular their modes of treason.

The title of the play announces the theme of treason, which presupposes that this transgression, committed by one or more characters, is to be offered, in one form or another, to the audience for their judgment. This is why the position of the spectators, as an essential element of the performance, must be taken into account. Indeed, the accusing speech leveled by Bracken against Joyce — a traitor to the cause of democracy in its struggle against a fascist regime, the mere mention of which conjures up the image of horror and genocide — makes it highly unlikely that the audience will remain neutral when faced with the issues at stake. The holocaust, whose tragic and unbearable reality is constantly reenacted on the stage, should lead the spectators to reject Joyce's ideas in favor of Bracken's. This partisan view, not unexpected in countries having taken part in the European conflict, is probably not so obvious for Irish spectators.[5] The variable stands of spectators, depending on their backgrounds, challenge the evidence supporting Joyce's treason. If one looks at Ireland's position during World War II, one notes that engagement on the English side was not a foregone conclusion. The oppression suffered by the Irish in the course of the centuries preceding World War II placed them in a somewhat special position. The conflict might indeed appear as a struggle between two forms of imperialism, with the shots fired against England being seen by some as fair revenge for multisecular tyranny. It would seem that this particular point of view is not rejected by the author, who remains at a certain distance from the crucial issues of the conflict, and directs his attention primarily to Bracken's and Joyce's individual nationalist commitments:

> *Upstage, flying above the scene, a hanging washing line of larger-than-life figures, cut out of cardboard representations of Churchill, King George V and Sir Oswald Mosley. When these are reversed for Part Two, they become: Dr Goebbels, Hitler and Mosley again* [*DC.* 21].

This stage-setting has the advantage of bringing together under a fairly similar banner two visions which the spectator would probably tend to visualize as radically opposed. The meeting-point in the emblematic figure of Sir O. Mosley, whose nobility ironically endows him with enhanced respectability, belongs to the same dramatic strategy followed throughout the play. The pinpointing of the differences between the main characters coincides strangely with a simultaneous erasing of oppositions, and opens the possibility of some kind of reconciliation. Kilroy's use of Mosley to bring Joyce and Bracken together in a visual way is a clear example of this. Furthermore, the provocative nature of a vision such as this is plain to see. The flagrant, undifferentiated reprobation brought to bear alike upon Churchill and Goebbels or George V and Hitler may seem surprising or even unacceptable to the spectators, for whom the tragic mistakes of the Allied forces can in no way be compared to the crimes committed against humanity by the Third Reich. The distancing from commonly held expectations concerning the appraisal of wartime behavior patterns now raises the question as to the message conveyed by the play, and its general meaning. Indeed, the refusal to set up a scale of atrocities might be interpreted as an equating of the horrors attending any instance of warfare, and consequently as an indirect rehabilitation of the exactions committed by the Germans during World War II.

The importance of the intellectual standpoints expressed in the stage-setting seemed to me of such moment that I asked Thomas Kilroy for an explanation, on the occasion of an interview. His reply[6] was that this is indeed a fundamental point in his approach to writing. Although aware

5. Double Cross 63

of the differences between the two regimes, the playwright metes out equal measures of reprobation upon all the types of abject behavior, into which any person could sink. In the present case, concerning the Irish context mentioned above, his strategy is to place the two sides back to back, condemning both Joyce's and Bracken's nationalist allegiances. The ideological convergence of the two enemies is implemented by Mosley, which marks their commitment with the seal of infamy. The values of hatred which they share with the leader of the English fascists invalidate any attempt to justify the conflict, in a display of man's primal brutality which is anything but flattering.

At this point, it is necessary to reach a clearer understanding of the nature of the treason referred to in the title. The adhesion to English or German nationalist values is condemned, as we have seen, not so much for the political commitment it entails, but probably more forcibly because of the disowning of Irish roots which this implies. When the two narrators describe Joyce and Bracken as the inventors of their own identities, can we fail to see the implications advanced by the playwright? This quasi-mythical self-creation, so highly valued on the other side of the Atlantic as a symbol of individual success, here for the two main characters takes the form of an abjuration of their own identity, a denial of their origins and of their very Irishness.[7] For Joyce and Bracken, the image of Ireland as the mother country must be blotted out before they can emancipate themselves from the initial impediments which their Irish identity puts in the way of their integration.

> BRACKEN: Vulgar little shit from Connemara, full of fight, ready to take on anyone. You know the kind of Paddy. Joined Tom Mosley's blackshirts. British Union of Fascists, that is. Tom eventually had to throw him out. Constantly beating up yids in the East End. The Irish are always being thrown out of something or other, aren't they? I'm absolutely convinced he's over there in Berlin, now, simply to be in the middle of the row. Coat off, sleeves up and bejasus we're off. Dreadful chap, actually [*DC.* 22].
>
> JOYCE: Who is this Brendan Bracken? Who is this creature who pretends to be a member of the English establishment? I can tell you, my friends. He's the son of a Tipperary stonemason who was also a dynamite terrorist [*DC.* 22].

In their descriptions of each other, Joyce and Bracken each go to great lengths to discredit the other, and the reminder of their Irish origins is a sharp arrow in the quiver of their exclusion strategies. The first speech, uttered in private company, is striking in its xenophobia, although the broadcasting of the second explains a few reserves, but every reference to genealogy contributes to marring the image of the double. The word "Paddy," an insult to Irish culture, expresses the extent of Bracken's rejection of his native country. This presentation of the enemy as an Irishman and therefore a blackguard is presented in the opening scene, when the spectator is not yet able to weigh the importance of these words. Later, when the two characters are confronted with the crucial issues of the war, their identical attitudes toward Irishness (in keeping with their personal choices) become less obvious. This convergence only reappears when the question is raised as to what treason actually means, when Kilroy breaks unfamiliar ground with his all-embracing denunciation of wartime atrocities. We then note that the focus of the play shifts from what might have appeared as an opposition between a hero and a traitor, toward a uniform vision of treason perpetrated by both characters alike in the betrayal of their origins.

The title of the play, *Double Cross*, naturally suggests treason, but the polysemy inherent in the word "cross" leads us to search for another meaning, according to which their Irish ancestry might be likened to a double cross which Joyce and Bracken refuse to carry. At first, the author's motives in condemning his characters seem paradoxical in that the self-invention he reproaches them with is likened to the very fact of existing. These motives then become clear when one considers the question of identity in its relation with origins. Obviously, each character is portrayed with his own personality, which in turn is the imperfect reflection of an unfathomable identity, but the condemnation aimed at them can be explained by their determination to disown their roots. Seen from this point of view, the disloyalty shown on stage escapes from the political arena embodied by the context of the war, and belongs rather to the area of private commitments. Although their acts commit them totally to mortal combats, in spirit Joyce and Bracken nevertheless appear as deserters. Witness Bracken's fictitious genealogy, invented to hide Irish origins too real to cope with and staged in a Wilde-like scene, with almost absurd attention to his ancestry:

BRACKEN: I am an orphan!
POPSIE: You've had those perfectly normal, nice Irish parents of yours back in the land of the shamrock. I mean, what more does one need?
BRACKEN: Orphanhood, my dear, may be as much a condition of choice as an unhappy product of the Great Reaper [*DC.* 35].

Bracken's peremptory assertion, despite the childishness which his lady friend underlines (to the audience's amusement), expresses his strong desire to break off from his roots. His determination to delete family history echoes the theme of treason, since by denying his own, Bracken leaves one world to enter into a foreign environment which is hostile toward his origins. An exclamation mark punctuates his claim to orphanhood. It expresses in the text what the actor is to render on the stage with a special vocal intensity: a surprising, almost absurd desire for self-reconstruction. The next cue, in which he attempts to give credit to a blatant lie, is a comic expression of the wild strength of his desire. In this respect, we note the convergences between the two main protagonists. Bracken's words about death find an ironical echo in the fate met by Joyce who, at the time of the German collapse, turns down an invitation to be escorted back to Ireland. He claims that a return to that country would be tantamount to a burial alive, the dramatic irony of which is underlined by the author when he informs the spectators that his body was indeed returned to that country after his execution.

The impossible escape from himself emphasizes not only the vanity of the attempt to blot out Irish roots, but also underlines the seriousness of a denial which can be assimilated to a refusal of his own essence. If one looks at the way Joyce's and Bracken's denial of their Irishness affects the course of their lives, one understands why the author lays such emphasis — at each consecutive period — on this impossible yet destructive severage, as it affects men who refuse their primary identity. On the occasion of a somewhat heated exchange with his mistress, Bracken takes offence at a remark concerning his manner of expression.

> BRACKEN: It [language] is what makes me what I am! Without it, I am nothing! [*DC.* 36].

This acknowledgment of the creative function of language, according to which speech characterizes the speaker and endows him with a social or private life, is not the first of its kind. More surprising is the dramatic intensity of this assertion and the virulence with which Bracken expresses himself. This point is worth noting, as it heightens the effect of a statement whose real interest lies in what it implies about the content of his speeches. The challenging of his mode of expression — all the more scathing as it is not meant to be hostile — affects him deeply, as he considers his mode of expression as a representation of his true self. Although it is obvious that the character in all his complexity is not to be apprehended in a monolithic perspective, it is also true that in the eyes of society Bracken is defined by his wartime harangues, behind which the many facets of his personality disappear. Such a deletion owes nothing to chance; it stems from a desire to put on the mask of a nationalist, behind which he may take refuge. In the same way, Joyce dissolves his identity in a warmongering creed which provides him with an artificial sense of being. The fake identity he builds up in his speeches on the radio, in which he puts across an ideology with which everybody identifies him, effectively hushes up the liaison with his lady friend. This almost insignificant ellipsis gives us a side view into a deletion strategy common to the two enemies, principally centred on their Irish origins.

To return to Bracken's convictions, one notes that in his opinion a man's mode of expression reflects what the man actually is. Given that Joyce also associates the verbal expression of his ideas with his personality, it stands to reason that their standpoints are to be seen as the cornerstones of their very existence. Consequently, albeit paradoxically, the implicit rejection contained in the verbal attacks against the Irish and their roots is an essential factor in the definition of their inner selves. By adhering rigidly to a brand of nationalism which fundamentally challenges them — if not as men, at least as Irishmen — Joyce and Bracken illustrate how their total adhesion to an ideology actually amounts to inner treason. This spurious access to a new life, which makes a clean sweep of the abhorred geographical ties, brings with it a destructive betrayal which leads them to annihilation. Their acceptance of this forged identity turns them into puppets dancing in the hands of irresistible forces and yet, in spite of themselves, wondering who they are. In the course of the play, Thomas Kilroy uses various strategies to bring Joyce and Bracken together. Without merging them totally in similar mental constructions, he nevertheless insists on the convergence of their behavior. He refuses to condemn Joyce for the nature of his commitments and establishes a portrait of Bracken which is far from heroic, in such a way that the spectator gradually comes to change his expectations concerning the handling of treason in the play. As the two enemies fall into equal disgrace, owing to their adherence to nationalist ideology, the playwright deserts the political sphere to direct our attention to the individual level. In this way, he demonstrates how the denial of one's origins as a mode of asserting one's identity finally leads to an annihilation of the self. In view of this, the quest for identity assumes greater importance than political combats whose legitimacy is unclear. Consequently, the deletion of their Irish ancestry constitutes the supreme treason. Kilroy postulates that people who disown the identity of their ties and deny their inner individuality fall prey to their basest instincts.

Although this relinquishment can in no way explain their attitude during World War II, a small token of fidelity toward their origins might have prevented Bracken and Joyce from identifying with the dehumanized type of speech denounced by the author. Indeed, the original treason of cutting themselves off from their own identity — as appears in the systematic association of abusive terms with the Irish world — seems to be the origin of the total refusal to recognize the Other as a person.

> ACTOR: Our transposed Irishman, born in Brooklyn, New York City, but raised in the West of Ireland —
> ACTRESS: After a short period as an ultra-Englishman in England he ended up a naturalized German citizen of the Third Reich.
> ACTOR: To summarize: He was American but also Irish. He wanted to be English but had to settle on being German [*DC.* 60].

Kilroy's refusal of "mental immigration," which he defines in terms of alienation, here develops its full meaning. This quotation highlights the unreliable character of national ties, making Joyce's and Bracken's positions even more vulnerable as they take refuge — almost by chance — behind a brand of ideology which at the same time stifles them. This course of action obviously tends to appear grotesque although it is not portrayed in comic scenes, probably because of the tragic nature of the setting. Faced with the medley of nations entering into the summary of Joyce's life, the spectator may raise two questions.

The first question, upon which the playwright himself urges us to reflect, challenges the intrinsic value of the nationalist standpoints embodied by Joyce and Bracken, given the unforeseen opportunities which have led to their commitment. The second, no less fundamental but not suggested by the author, challenges the importance given to the question of treason compared to the real importance to be ascribed to the person's origins. According to Kilroy, the disowning of one's origins is tantamount to a denial of one's very existence, and this refusal of the past and of the ancestors is assimilated to a life-draining betrayal. However, the absurdity of nationalist opinions founded on geographical ties, underlined in the play, is contradicted in a certain way by its own implications regarding the roots of individual people. Given the unforeseeable nature of each of their careers, one may well question the true importance of Joyce and Bracken's Irishness. In the present case, their destructive attitude as a powerful echo of the forces of evil within them may be more important than geographical definitions. The question remains open, partly owing to choices made by the author concerning the staging. The refusal of an intimist stage-setting, for example, together with Joyce and Bracken's lack of roundedness, reduces the scope which one might ascribe to the internal drama of the treason. The absence of real emotion, upon which the spectator might feed his understanding of the dramatic issues, weakens the handling of the "Irish" betrayal. Indeed, no spectacular artifice comes up in the course of the performance to highlight the betrayal as a wrench from deep-set roots, against which the characters might be seen to struggle. Instead, it seems more like a minor detail.

The sometimes unenthusiastic response of the public (Tom Kilroy speaks in the preface of "hostility, especially in the treatment of sexuality in the lives of the two men"), and a possible future rejection of the way Kilroy handles the idea of treason underline the gap between the playwright and the audience. Indeed, he places on a par two men whom most spectators would classify in separate categories (because of their allegiance to Churchill or Hitler, even if the playwright made it clear that such a reading would be inappropriate in the first interview reproduced in this book). When published and performed on stage, the text achieves a kind of autonomy, and partially — or totally — escapes the author's possession. Because of this extreme dispossession, and in all likelihood ironically, *Double Cross* illustrates a discrepancy in perspective which, probably for some time to come, cuts off the author from his non-Irish audience. Until the passing of time allows the spectator to concentrate less on the conflict and on the downfall of the traitor, *Double Cross* runs the risk of generating a few betrayals.

6

Lighting Up the Masks: *The Secret Fall of Constance Wilde*

A stage performance inevitably bears the stamp of its time and of multifarious and changing cultural trends, and therefore sets up an ever-renewed relationship between dramatic works and the audiences to whom these are revealed. Some timeless features are passed down unchanged, some ephemeral mutations sink into oblivion, while other characteristics surface recurrently, conveying meanings which vary with the changing times. Among these constant, intrinsic elements of theatricality itself stands the mask — sometimes almost invisible — used in a variety of ways according to places and times. As a play, *The Secret Fall of Constance Wilde* must by definition have some bearing upon the question of the mask, and Thomas Kilroy, anxious to stage some of the subterfuges of theatrical expression, lays special emphasis on the artificiality of performance. In this dramatic work, he explores the question of the masking and unmasking of the inner self as an invisible oppression. Characters, puppets and language are among the devices the playwright uses to fuel his reflection, and in *The Secret Fall of Constance Wilde* he attempts to probe into the very essence of a person's being. To do this, Kilroy rewrites the personal history of Constance Wilde, a woman engaged in battles both private and social, who finds herself face to face with her own masked non-existence.

With respect to its content, the play links up with the trend in theatrical history represented by Oscar Wilde, the character, and by a filiation with Yeats which finds its expression in a variety of ways; firstly by comparison with Yeats' theory of the mask and more noticeably in its connections with Asian theatre. The Androgyne figure/character, for instance, suggests a convergence with oriental theatre on the symbolic level, and the correspondences with the *Kabuki* clearly emerge for example when we compare this image with the *onnagata*, a mixture of virile force and feminine delicacy.[1] Furthermore, the use of puppets as non-realistic masks representing hidden truths epitomizes the connection with a theatrical world totally at odds with the dramatic constructions of the western world and the immediacy of their realism. Although the effect is not of a total merging of very different cultures, the use of puppets nevertheless stands quite apart from the usual ways of portraying a person. Full use is made of the stage as a place of disguise and artifice, a place to reflect upon masks — visible masks or invisible ones, masks perceptible as institutions or masks hidden behind normality.

In its form, *The Secret Fall of Constance Wilde* breaks away from present-day conventions while linking up — in the spirit — with literary heritage. Although Kilroy makes use of extraneous dramatic forms which are likely to contrast sharply with commonly recognized cultural models, he nevertheless takes us into a familiar world, that in which Oscar Wilde lived. The partly outdated set of social conventions enables him to focus on the type of behavior expected in society at the time, which in turn mirrors the question of masks and what they mean in society today. How do two time-spheres which are *a priori* quite foreign to each other connect? This question is raised each time a discrepancy occurs between an event and its staging at a later date. *The Secret Fall of Constance Wilde* takes us into the past, and the theme expressed in the adjectival part of the title might seem somewhat old-fashioned, particularly in view of today's transparency cult. However, the once slow-moving metamorphosis of Irish society — slightly out of step with developments in other countries — made it seem more contemporary, given that other social changes, brought about by the newborn reign of the "politically correct," might even give Kilroy's reflection on the mask an air of avant-garde.

Then two other attendant figures lead Oscar and Constance into the spot, onto the disk, rather like hospital attendants with frail patients [*SFCW.* 11].

The opening ceremony reminds one of a certain number of Kilroy's works in which the very first speeches bring out the spectacular and artificial nature of the theatrical arts. The obvious physical frailty of the two protagonists serves to situate Constance and Oscar at a certain point in their lifespan, but it also endues them with a certain originality and makes characters of them, rather than just people played by actors. Paradoxically, given the distancing effect produced by this mode of introduction, their arrival on stage immediately gives substance to their decline.

6. Lighting Up the Masks 71

As their bodies cannot hide their degeneration, this very special moment is to be seen as a lowering of the masks. Worse still, this baring of the two old people's physiological dilapidation is not the only aspect of their loss of physical autonomy. More importantly, the presence of an attendant regulating their movements raises the question of their freedom as human beings, thus conditioning the way the audience interprets the events to come—which actually occur prior to the opening scene—and inviting spectators to pursue this reflection throughout the play. This initial question about people's status (subjects or objects?) is reiterated by another indication in the stage directions which confirms the vision of inhibited freedom, taking the form of a staged rendering of the reflection concerning the mask.

> *Constance crosses the stage at the back, walking with difficulty, holding the child puppets, in sailor suits, by the hands. Suddenly the puppeteers whisk the puppets away in a wild, childish run and then they are gone* [*SFCW*. 62].

The mother and her children move on two different planes, since the part of Constance is played by an actress, while Cyril and Vivyan are metaphorically represented as puppets. In spite of this obvious estrangement, Constance holds her children by the hands, which endows them with a symbolic flesh-and-blood existence.[2] Conversely, the link established between the puppets and the actress has a certain impact on the actors' status, and detracts part of their authority from Oscar, Constance and Douglas, as it is an indirect challenge to their reality. When the children run away from Constance, they appear as playthings in the hands of higher powers which carry them away against their wills—a situation which brings us back to the opening stage direction in which Constance and Oscar seemed to have lost control over their movements. The children's flight is a reference to the duality between artifice and the authentic (expressed here in the way the children are pulled off the stage). The puppet materializes the shattering of an illusion and the negation of the identifying process which links the spectator and the actors, all the while contributing in its own way to the illustration of the status granted to individuals. If one looks at it from the point of view of Claudel's theatre, in which the puppet is a word in action, one realizes that it implements a distancing effect which enables a masked truth to be unmasked. In the present case, the characters lose some of their reality, but gain in credibility. Indeed, the puppet as a frail shadow of their real identity is in fact a figure of their inhibited freedom. It unmasks the iron grip of society upon individuals and likens the power of social conventions to an individualized dictatorship. The characters thus appear not only as subjects, elements making up the performance, but also as objects, and potential victims of dominating powers.[3]

> CONSTANCE: What you have to understand is that we women are trained from birth to conceal. Otherwise, you see, men would be unable to behave as they do. This is what is known as society [*SFCW.* 30].

Among the ideas addressed in the play, womanhood is the first area viewed through the parallel drawn between the puppets and the characters. Constance's scathing vision, almost Ibsen-like, brings her very close

Jane Brennan in *The Secret Fall of Constance Wilde.* Photograph by Amelia Stein. Abbey Theatre, Dublin, 1977 (courtesy of The Abbey Theatre Archive).

to the inanimate beings which haunt the stage. The generic portrait of the woman as an object, fettered with the shackles of social codes, effectively brings out the obligation brought to weigh upon her of wearing a mask. The reproaches directed against this forced concealment — an excrescence of the male community's demands, keenly decried for their injustice — make up the first round of a social critique which becomes more penetrating and more vituperative as personal dramas come to the surface. The convicting evidence brought against the male clan becomes even more incriminating when Constance talks about her married life. She reveals that the necessity of concealing oneself does not only apply to social codes in the broad context of the community. It also concerns the couple's private relations, where the possibility of expression remains inconceivable in certain areas. Having been deprived of his sexual attentions by her husband, for reasons she discovers later, Constance exposes her misery and doubt, exacerbated by the unqualified view whereby the woman is naturally responsible for every failure in this area.

Sex — that prohibited question — is one of the community's banned subjects. However, in spite of the taboos which hush it up and the masks it puts on faces, some, under the cover of false compassion, make allusions to it and try to pry into the private lives of those whom society marginalizes. The scandal, that delectable occasion when respectable citizens revel at the sight of masks wrenched off, gives the full measure of the importance of social codes. Constance thus finds herself faced with malicious gossip, slander and perfidious questions about her husband. She explains to Oscar how she has succeeded in fending off the attacks by stepping into the role of the model wife, but also by making use of the protective barriers set up by other taboos. For Constance, then, the mask acquires a redeeming power as, unable to defend herself, she relies on religion to avoid being stigmatized as a woman whose husband has fallen from society's favor. Religion, itself marred by the idea of impossible transparency — as is shown by the performance of the Catholic ritual in the play — is used by Constance as a shield against an ill-inspired inquisition.

> CONSTANCE : (*Self again*). Actually — I said to them in my best nonchalant, wife-of-a-celebrity voice — Christ came to him in his cell. That stopped them in their tracks, I can tell you [*SFCW.* 30].

The tone she uses, the "wife-of-a-celebrity voice," elsewhere described as "wifely," shows that Constance measures all the power of social expectations. Faced with her opponents' attempts to pull down the masks and savor the joys of a humiliating strip-off, she shows by her counterattack that she is quite aware of the way everybody deftly avoids committing a *faux pas* which would focus the group's reproof upon themselves. Indeed, the appraisal of the Other appears as a crucial factor in the regulation of society, and the consequences within the community of a transgression of the rules are proof of the all-powerful virtue of self-restraint. Oscar's prison term shows that public disapproval is not the ultimate form of chastisement, and the most horrendous punishments await the perpetrators of extra ordinary practices (homosexuality for example). The game society plays with masks indicates that this general regulation extends beyond the limited scope of sexist oppression and applies to the community as a whole. In this respect, it is worth noting that Oscar, like Constance, is perfectly aware of the rules of the game concerning appearances and compulsory concealment, even if he overestimates his ability to resist. Oscar appears at once on the side of the victims and on that of the slanderers. This duality becomes clear in the course of the play, and precludes any Manichaean reading which might turn him into a martyr.

Social codes set up as absolutes make it necessary to put on a mask, but the play challenges the validity of uncrossable boundaries.

> DOUGLAS: That there are no absolutes except in the desperate imagination of men and women. No black. No white. No good. No evil. No male. No female. Everything runs together and runs in and out of everything else. But human beings cannot abide such glorious confusion. So they invent what is called morality to keep everyone and everything in place. I am quoting, I believe, from the testament of the beloved apostle, St Oscar [*SFCW*. 56].

Here, Douglas reiterates the vision held by Wilde, upturning the foundations of socially defined categories and implicitly confronting them with contradictions to be found in the real world, in the area of sex for example. The manifold points of view expressed in the play might give one to understand that Kilroy himself refuses to take sides. One notes, for instance, concerning the cast, that the roles of Douglas and of the androgyny may be played by the same actor or the same actress, in a deliberate confusion between the two genders knowingly orchestrated by the playwright to combat the idea of uncrossable barriers between the sexes. In a much less controversial way than Douglas, Kilroy also distances himself from beliefs held as certainties by the community. Homosexuality features among the problems he raises in *The Secret Fall of Constance Wilde* to illustrate his critical reflection on the problematic interface between norms and reality. In this particular area, his refusal of predefined limits which oblige people to conceal themselves whenever they stray from the narrow path of customary requirements gives the play political overtones.

Kilroy's analysis of society has implications which go further than a simple black-and-white criticism of a community's regulations. Through his handling of the many dead ends which occur in the lives of Douglas, Oscar or Constance, he explores the long-term consequences of an individual defense mechanism consisting of putting on masks. Faithful to his favorite between-the-two technique, which one might define as an approach to reality in which he maps out a field of exploration yet refuses to commit himself to it, Kilroy observes a constant distance from the issues addressed. Confronted with the total, almost absurd, rigidity of the moral rules he denounces, he sketches the beginnings of a counterargument by pointing at the suspicion which surrounds Douglas's attitude toward Oscar's children. The arbitrariness of the moral standpoint is disputed because it claims to be absolute; notwithstanding this, its social necessity does not seem to be denied as such. It is thus upon the consequences of this moral dictatorship, which obliges everybody to clothe themselves with respectability, that the playwright heaps his disapproval.

> CONSTANCE: Stop it, Oscar! Stop it!
> OSCAR: What? What?
> CONSTANCE: Playacting!
> OSCAR:— not playacting!
> CONSTANCE: You never face the situation as it really is. Never! Nothing exists for you unless it can be turned into a phrase [*SFCW*. 11].

Here at the end of their lives, Constance upbraids Oscar for continuing to play roles, as his behavior prevents any real exchange between them. She reformulates what she had once said in reply to questions about her married life before the trial:

> CONSTANCE: People keep asking me: What was it like, Constance, really like, to be married to him? Of course, they're thinking of you-know-what. It's as if they were undressing me with their eyes. Why, I answer in my best wifely voice. It was theatre, m'dears, theatre! Theatre all the way! You know what Oscar is like! Every day a different performance. With frequent costume changes, of course [*SFCW*. 15].

According to Constance's indications, the repeated changes of "costume" in fact reflect Oscar's very heart. A champion in the art of dodging, Oscar sidetracks language and draws part of his strength from this verbal discrepancy which puzzles those around him. Instead of the superficiality one might expect to find in keeping with his lifestyle, his portrayal in the play reveals strong human feelings, showing that he is in fact the first victim of the games he thought he mastered. In spite of this, one may question the genuineness of his need for concealment. Indeed, given the fallacious representation of himself that society requires, it would seem more likely that his character parts are a series of strategic answers rather than a mirror revealing his personality.

As is often the case in Kilroy's theatre, contradictory elements prevent the spectator from fixing his choice on any specific reading. Behind the forced masquerade, Oscar's behavior is ultimately a defense mechanism, not only against society but also against himself. His playacting might also be accounted for by his awareness that he is unable to define a truth about himself which Constance, on the contrary, believes to be non-equivocal and readily apprehended. Another hypothesis not be excluded is the fundamental philosophical belief that the mask has an ethical value as an ideal mode of representing a certain form of truth. The fact remains that in the general frame of the play, his behavior has other motives. By sporting a multifarious façade, Oscar resists the social oppression which — as Constance herself recognizes — strains to encage him within a single immutable role. In a certain sense, the futility of his behavior is a cover-up for an act of resistance as he seeks, by showing himself under a great number of facets, to safeguard his freedom to be what he would be. Here again, these praiseworthy attempts to conceal his inner conflict might deserve some public recognition; instead, they arouse the most scathing comments. The mask has thus become a necessary mode of liberation from community oppression, although in the very first cues of the play it comes under violent criticism for its deleterious tendency to reify its wearer. Constance admonishes Oscar for his chronic use of the mask — a subject which particularly affects her as she suffers an oppression of which her husband no longer seems to be aware. This conditioned reflex with which he steps with ease into different roles according to circumstances in fact reveals that he is quite unable to show himself the way he really is.

The theme of the mask, as one sees it in *The Secret Fall of Constance Wilde*, is developed within the context of a social critique concerning a bygone period. However, as the performance necessarily occurs in a contemporary context, the question must be raised as to its interactions with the social realities of today.[4] The attacks aimed at the dictatorship of appearances come into better focus when the challenging of prevailing standards of correct social behavior reaches beyond a mere criticism of institutionalized hypocrisy. From these particular instances it gradually extends its hold as a moral dictatorship, inhibiting the freedom of the individual within the community. So, the initial discrepancy with contemporary society becomes irrelevant as evidence is gathered for the trial of a world which the spectator understands to be not only that of Constance and Oscar, but also one which gradually expands to a universal dimension.

This broadening outlook then takes us from the intimate circle of the Wilde family to the wider context of certain aspects of Irish reality which are never very far from the center of Kilroy's preoccupations. The interest he shows for the mask may at this point be linked with the more general theme running through his other works, of Irishness and the relations between man and the world in an Irish context. The escape from material reality also broadens the play's outlook and adds weight to the critical analysis of a long-colonized society where concealment, once a primary necessity, eventually becomes part of everyday life. The would-be resistance fighter must don a mask, and individuals mechanically make up character parts behind which they run the risk of disappearing, which accounts for the concern expressed in the play as to what it means to exist.

Before exploring the final aspect of the question concerning the relation between Constance in her surprising role as the main character and the theme of concealment, we shall focus on the special relationship between Kilroy the playwright and his illustrious predecessor. Thomas Kilroy in his endeavor, if not to clarify, at least to underline, a few mysteries, seems to have gathered from his university education a taste for prefaces as a means of guiding his readers through the meanders of a complex literary production. Had he wished, he might have included in the foreword to the play some indication as to the setting of *The Secret Fall of Constance Wilde* and some guidelines concerning the reflection on the mask. However, quite inhabitually, he refrained from doing so. The absence of a preface, that privileged place where the author is able to express himself in his own name, free of the constraints of theatrical language, adds to the subtleness of the work. By staging another playwright — Oscar Wilde — he directs the attention of the spectator to language as a form of concealment, thus driving a wedge between himself and his theatrical production. He thus invents a new way of playing with masks by creating a new literary genre, the virtual autobiography, defined by Oscar Wilde in the play:

> OSCAR. Everything I write is autobiographical. With the facts changed, of course [*SFCW.* 25].

In this respect, given the liberties which Kilroy takes with history, his affiliation with Wilde is obvious. On the strength of his position regarding the mask, Kilroy enjoys complete freedom to reinvent Constance's drama, all the more so as, had it really taken place, the customs of the time would have obliged him to conceal it. The author, through his invisible presence in the world represented on the stage, weaves an extra thread of complexity into the play. Ordinary reality thus takes on a new, fictitious dimension and turns into what the playwright makes of it — a world riddled with artifice and concealment in which, through a paradoxical play of mirrors, theatricality becomes a means of probing into the truth, the essence and the freedom of the individual.

In *The Secret Fall of Constance Wilde,* Kilroy offers a reinterpretation of the past, while at the same time constructing a link with the present-day situation, as silence — women's silence — is the starting point of his analysis of the relation between man and the world. The question of childhood, briefly alighted upon, features as a secondary concern but is not developed to any extent in the play although it belongs to a similar theme. Indeed, the playwright draws the substance of his reflection from the contrast between two tragic realities embodied by Oscar and Constance, so as to show primarily how programmed non-existence was once a part of womanhood. The study of masks enables him to focus on a form of oppression of which people, at the time, were hardly aware.

> CONSTANCE: You said to me, you're different, Constance. Remember? That long ago afternoon in Merrion Square? You're uncontaminated by life, Constance. That's what you said. What utter rot! You needed to invent me because you couldn't face life as it really is [*SFCW.* 66].

Beyond its dramatic irony, Constance's statement owes its impact to the fact that it brings to light a social code accepted by everybody, including Oscar. The forced tone and the conceited banality of his suitor's speech are based on the assumption that he detects in the woman he courts a difference which he spontaneously understands and which leads him straight to her innermost essence, and contrast sharply with his usual originality. This devastating fragment, so intellectually mortifying, shows us the full extent of his submission to social expectations, for his estrangement is revealed by the very fact that he is unaware of his own narrow-mindedness. Love, whether met as a painful misfortune, discovered as a fresh start in life, or experienced as the first step toward shared fulfilments, portends some new form of enclosure. This strange perception of love which reinvents the Other, thereby failing to recognize her as a real person, symbolically kills her.

Kilroy's exploration of the essence of womanhood takes him further than merely portraying the oppression women endure. Accordingly, their sexual experiences, insofar as these may be reprehensible, are not brought to public exposure, unlike what happens for men. The incestuous rape which Constance suffers — and conceals, as is expected by society — unconsciously brings her nearer to Oscar, in whom she confusedly senses a similar experience of decline. Later, when his downfall and his homosexual activities come into public view, Constance's "secret fall" is opposed to Oscar's "public fall," and Oscar finds himself banned from society. His condemnation affects him profoundly yet also sets him free, for it takes him into the innermost recesses of his being, to his true self. Constance, on the contrary, was not able to express her suffering. As she could not or would not say who she was following the aggression committed against her, she holds herself partly responsible for her failure and paints a bleak picture of a life wasted behind masks which she had accepted as such.

Deeply pained by the inhuman violence of the scandal, Oscar is probably not aware of the relief which Constance feels after the final speech she delivers, which verges on a kind of exorcism. She overturns the cultural and social determinism which has made of her an inert mask, emptied of any life, and bestowed upon her the role of a puppet in a masquerade whose rituals celebrate the funeral of her true self. The confession which she wrings from herself is an implicit reference to the sacrament of penance, after which she at last feels free to live her own life. Talking about the rape she has endured helps her to transcend the moral suffering and at last start a new life. She dashes down the masks and asserts herself in her moral nudity, withered and worn out — like her body, which no longer conceals its decline — but free at last to show her true inner self.

The last image of Constance, busily engaged in writing a letter to her children to express in her last wishes the desire that they should keep a positive image of their father, once again stages her in a role, that of a mother who up to the last moments of her life takes the moral well-being of her children to heart. This picture might lead us to believe that once this moment of speaking out the truth is over, everything will spin around and Constance will once more find herself a prisoner of stifling masks. This is not the case. Her mother-image with its mask-like appearance is freely chosen, for she is not forced by any social obligation to wear it. Furthermore, the sorority which Oscar requests and Constance eventually concedes is proof that the old boundaries are now abolished, with both showing themselves to be just what they are in their innermost selves, united by their shared suffering as human beings. Masked and further obscured with partially consented blindness, the paths followed by the protagonists paint a grim picture of life, but, as a redeeming contrapuntal voice, the assertion of their ipseity opens the gateway to a real form of existence. In this respect, the final conversation between Oscar and Constance (with an obvious reference to Beckett) features as a positive endgame. The mirror held up to the audience now becomes more imperious as the two characters become simply man and woman. The freedom they have won by dropping the masks and accepting the multifaceted human decline, from which they nonetheless launch out into a new life, is the first stage of their rebirth.

7

Skywork for a Symphonic Theatre: Scenic Images in *Blake*

The first sentence of an article Thomas Kilroy wrote about playwright Brian Friel reads as follows: "We write plays, I feel, in order to populate a stage."[1] This statement, which his latest assertions have confirmed, stressed the continuity in the playwright's mind between text and stage. It also implied that the visual aspect of staging played an important part in the conception of his dramatic projects. In a different way, this quotation also characterized Kilroy as a playwright. It exemplified his continued reflection on drama, which he still discloses not only in his introductions to his plays, but also in articles in which he provides articulate outlooks on theatre.[2] Many years have elapsed since he asserted his views on the Irish theatre of the 1960s, in a famous article entitled "Groundwork for an Irish Theatre."[3] To summarize his evolution, one might note — together with a distancing from social concerns and a move toward more intimate questionings — the growing intellectual complexity of his theatre projects, in which practical aspects of the staging lead to reflections about theatricality.

Blake falls in line with this evolution. Not unlike William Blake's artistic achievements, when he printed his "illuminated books" and combined poetry with illustrations, Kilroy's dramatic composition seems to have moved toward a more global art form. In keeping with his past works, in which he used different techniques to illustrate specific points, in *Blake*—probably because of their relevance to the subject—Kilroy resorts heavily to scenic images. In doing this, the playwright links up with theatre customs which go beyond the limits of Irish traditions. Before defining his specific approach to scenic images in *Blake*, an overview of the way in which he had handled them up to this point may be a useful way to measure the changes which have occurred.[4] Beyond a comparison between *Blake* and Kilroy's earlier plays, one may also wonder whether increased use made of scenic images amounts to a redefinition of Kilroy's dramatic views.

Thomas Kilroy's vast dramatic culture enables him to include scenic images in his play in ways which go beyond the use of a mere theatrical device. He is well aware that etymologically, the theatre is linked with vision and, for instance, the *tableau vivant* which appears in scenic image 57 may be connected to an 18th-century tradition. Faced with this powerful type of staging technique, one thinks of Bertinazzi, but also of Diderot, and later, Gogol. In a contemporary environment, it recalls the work of stage directors like Peter Brook.[5] As for Irish dramatic traditions, Yeats's influence can be traced through the importance of potentially unrealistic visual images. Regarding the relationship between image and reality, especially with respect to distancing, Brecht comes to mind, but in *Blake* his influence seems to have been far less important than in Kilroy's former plays. In the circumstances, Eastern modes of representation, with a substantial part granted to rituals in Bunraku or Noh theatre for example, may have had a greater impact.

In all his plays, Thomas Kilroy takes into account the staging of the text, which simply cannot be disconnected from its spatial enactment. While he hardly ever uses stage directions as a means of guiding actors in their personal performance, he sometimes provides indirect staging information through scenic images. Naturally, when the play is performed, no matter what the playwright recommends, his suggestions are bound to vary in their factual realization, since stage directors, actors and decorators alike will leave their own mark on the performance. Despite all idiosyncratic addenda to the author's initial perspective, the audience is nevertheless likely to discover scenic images corresponding to the playwright's own expectations.

Apart from *The Death and Resurrection of Mr. Roche*, no play by Thomas Kilroy is realistic. However, a number of the scenic images he conceives bring a realistic touch to some situations. In *Tea and Sex and Shakespeare*, for instance, he underlines a gesture common to all the characters:

> *In the pause, everyone turns directly to Elmina, awaiting her response. When it comes, it comes in a low, exhausted monotone* [*TSS*. 66].

The stage direction brings to mind an almost realistic vision of the scene, even if the common, almost mechanical, gesture of the protagonists might lend a fake — hence comic — touch to the characters' behavior.[6] Kilroy creates a scenic image which is a mixture of proximity and distance, in that the audience will realize how close this image is to their everyday lives, while probably taking the hint of the caricature he stages. The stage direction reveals that the scenic image falls in line with the general situation in that it does not seem totally incongruous. Still, its ephemeral occurrence — as it tends to blend into the course of the play — deprives it of any specific importance, so that it cannot become a major semantic item which the audience would retain in their minds as a deeply significant visual episode, as would be the case for a *tableau vivant*, for instance.

As opposed to the minor part granted to some scenic images, another stage direction in the same scene demonstrates that a scenic image (the gesture) may prevail over language. In the circumstances, the playwright precedes mime with a mixture of ordinary and surrealistic conversation. He insists on the inanity of what the characters say, as a prologue to the principal — visualized — event that is about to take place: the tea ceremony. "*A mime of tea-drinking, sugar-passing, bun-eating*" (*TSS*. 68).

The mime is made up of a series of scenic images to which the audience relates. The distancing effect produced by the mime reinforces the accuracy of the ritual. At the same time, the playwright deprives the rite of meaning or, more precisely, insists on the deep social emptiness that this type of ceremony conveys. In both cases, the coherence between situation and scenic images is blatant, to the point of turning the characters into puppets, whose machinelike gestures illustrate the mechanical content of their social behavior. While some scenic images prolong the content of the text — a more or less distanced illustration of the action — others bring echoes of classical images, and change the perspective put forth.

With a sudden, startling energy, he rises on the trolley and flings both arms out in the shape of crucifixion. As he does so, blinding beams of light shoot through the walls of the box, pooling about him and leaving the rest of the stage in darkness [*TB*. 17].

Through the visualization of the scene, Kilroy establishes a link with a cultural background that most spectators will share. This scenic image — mainly created thanks to light — brings to mind a number of paintings in which sanctity is represented not only by the crucifixion of Christ, but also by light, which symbolizes His holiness. In the circumstances, one might see this scenic image as a prelude to another one — used in *Blake* — which corresponds to plate number 76, "Albion before Crucified Jesus," of Blake's *Jerusalem*. This scenic image helps Kilroy convey a message, but it also refers to other works of art, or at least to expected modes of representation, which enclose the dramatic work within an artistic frame highlighted by the playwright.

In his readiness to use and play with cultural references in his dramatic works, Thomas Kilroy initiates a tension between his acceptance and his rejection of social codes. This enables him to resort to scenic images as tools to implement his distancing effects. In *Talbot's Box*, for instance, the opening scene stages a mass, an established ritual which the playwright very rapidly subverts. First the audience is faced with a priest (who is a woman), then with subversive distancing from expected forms of presentation, which materializes in the attitudes of the priest and the Virgin Mary.

> PRIEST FIGURE: Body — hold on a moment — in the church! Retain your pious pose! (*Produces large aerosol can, jumps down from pulpit spraying all about intoning prayers in Latin.*) There you are! (*Looks about in satisfaction.*)
> WOMAN: It's only getting worse!
> PRIEST FIGURE: Remain on your pedestal at all costs! (*Further spraying about.*)
> WOMAN: I will not! (*Jumps down from pedestal, goes upstage in disgust, removing costume.*) I'm near choked with the stuff out of that can [*TB*. 10].

As is shown by this short excerpt, this technique very effectively challenges expected modes of representation. Whether they merely prolong the content of the dialogues, bring more information — which may include references to other art forms — or function as distancing techniques, scenic images remain one of the tools the playwright uses to assert his dramatic vision. When he addresses serious religious or political issues, Thomas Kilroy sometimes skillfully resorts to scenic images as subversive tools. In such cases, the tension resulting from the contrast between speech and image enables him to make his point — more often than not merely calling into question socially fixed representations — while avoiding the trap of didacticism.

Like most of Kilroy's plays,[7] *Blake* leads the audience into a meditation about human nature which, as usual, the author combines with a reflection on theatre. Shaping his dramatic approach in accordance with the central issues of his works, the playwright adapts his techniques to his subjects, and in *Blake* he resorts heavily to scenic images. In order to gain a better understanding of their dramatic importance, all ninety-eight scenic images will be listed in order of appearance. The figure ninety-eight is significant in terms of dramatic technique, and a comparison with Kilroy's earlier plays shows that scenic images have gradually become a major theatrical device of the playwright. Apart from images eighty-nine to ninety-eight and image fifty-seven — which correspond to Blake's paintings[8] — all the others result from specific gestures or attitudes of actors, on stage.

1. Upstage: A ramp or significantly raised space above a wall. This raised area will become, at different times, the gallery of Finchley Grange Asylum, the Blakes' lodgings in South Moulton Street, London, and other locations. The wall below opens at various times, making up cells and entrance gates to the asylum.
    Downstage: lower level, main acting area, at different times becoming the "white room," the garden and the yard of the asylum etc.[9]
2. Catherine Blake, with a chamber pot in the first-floor window of the Blake rooms in South Moulton Street, London. Dr. Hibbel comes on with two of his asylum keepers on the street below.
2. Catherine throws the contents of the chamber pot into the street, some of it catching Dr. Hibbel.
4. Dr. Hibbel: *(Sniffing himself)*
5. (Blake) Suddenly appearing beside Catherine at the window.
6. Blake is seized and put into a straitjacket.
7. Appearing in the open doorway.
8. Dr. Hibbel and the keepers drag Blake off, leaving Catherine alone.
9. She runs off after the others.
10. Dr. Hibbel is in the gallery with his guests, Sir James and Lady Fetchcroft and a lady attendant. Below them, in the white room stands a solitary keeper.
11. The keeper leads in a beautiful young woman.
12. The silent woman remains behind, standing to one side, busy with her work before her on her tray.
13. Blake is conducted on, still in the straitjacket. He is by now in a pitiable condition, frantic and moaning.
14. Suddenly, Blake and the silent woman become aware of one another and everything changes. He begins to circle her in a kind of awe, while she watches him intently.
15. As the keeper releases Blake.
16. He touches her cheek.
17. She becomes terrified, tries to break away from him, making inarticulate cries of fear but he pursues her, almost bullyingly.

18. A device falls from the tray and she runs and cowers away from him. He lifts the object up, gingerly, to the light and explodes in a rage.
19. Throws the object... She runs off.
20. The two keepers do so and Blake stands trial.
21. As the keepers seize him.
22. He stalks off, with dignity.
23. A disheveled Catherine staggers in with the keeper. She can hardly stand with the fatigue and her blistered feet.
24. A pool of light, Catherine in a chair, Dr. Hibbel by her shoulder. Other figures dimly seen in the background.
25. Reaching out a hand to lead her away.
26. Crying out as he leads her off into the darkness.
27. Blake is listening intently to the singing, far off, standing silently in the asylum exercise yard with three other male lunatics. All four are in white asylum shifts.

    One, standing motionless to the rear, is a black man, a Catatonic, frozen. The second is a Frenetic figure whose body and lips move ceaselessly. The third is the Murderer who never takes his eyes off Blake.

    Blake clearly dislikes him and would try to shake off the man's attention but cannot.

    The yard is an enclosed space, backed by a high, brick wall with, near the top, a kind of barred window. This grill is a peephole or window, one of several such devices in the asylum, to observe the lunatics within.

    Keepers on guard to one side.
28. The keeper ignores him.
29. Ridiculous pose.
30. Observing him. Long pause.
31. The Keepers hesitate. Then one nods to another, one of them leaves.
32. Blake glares at him. Then he rushes back to the Catatonic, looks at him. Reaches out and takes a hand as in greeting. Lets the hand go. Much to his shock it remains pointing out to him. Blake retreats, watching the Catatonic's outstretched hand.
33. Blake is about to strike him but changing his mind rushes back again to the Catatonic and lowers the outstretched hand gently.
34. Bursts into tears.

35. Blake is moved. In spite of his dislike he tries to comfort the Murderer, putting an arm about his shoulders.
36. Sudden shift, a manic cackle, finger pointing.
37. A keeper comes in with paper and pencils for Blake. Blake grabs them eagerly turns his back on the Murderer and begins to sketch the Catatonic. The Murderer becomes extremely agitated at all this.
38. The Murderer produces a shard of broken glass from beneath his shift and lunges at Blake with a roar. He is grabbed by the keepers who disarm him and drag him off, his hand streaming blood. Blake hardly pays any attention to this but returns to his sketching of the Catatonic. He also remains indifferent as a loud bell-ringing takes place off. The spying grill on the wall swings open to reveal Dr. Hibbel and Lady Fetchcroft. A high metal barred fence is drawn across the stage and female lunatics are shown in, with their keepers, on the other side of the fence, opposite to where Blake and the two male lunatics are contained.
39. Among them is the Silent Woman who is without her work tray and is now taking some interest in what is around her. She looks across at Blake. When the women enter the Frenetic immediately gets a large erection and hurls himself against the fence. He is pulled off by the keepers and for the first time Blake looks up from his sketching. The Frenetic, still sexually aroused, is dragged away by the keepers.
40. Catherine, dressed like the other lunatics in the white shift, is brought into the women's side of the fence. She stands, confused.
41. Blake points at the Silent Woman.
42. Catherine is dragged away with the other women lunatics.
43. The grill before Dr. Hibbel and Lady Fetchcroft closes and Blake is left alone with the two other male lunatics and keepers.
44. A pool of light on a darkened stage. Blake and Catherine sit close together on a simple bench in this light.... At some height, as if suspended in the air, the lit head and shoulders of Dr. Hibbel, recording details in his notebook.
45. BLAKE: (*Hands to ears*).
46. Threatening to hit her.
47. Dr. Hibbel, above, claps his hands and disappears from view.
48. Catherine jumps in surprise but Blake pays no attention. Female keepers come forward and take Catherine off into the darkness.
49. Blake puts his hands to his head and sinks into a seat once again.

50. The male and female lunatics emerge out of the darkness, chanting, each one taking different names, first the males, then the females. They gather about Blake and the effect is of a wild chorus around his head.
51. Blake sinks as under a great weight and the lights come down.
52. A night scene. An empty, brightly lit cell in a pool of darkness. The door of the cell facing audience is a floor to ceiling iron grill. Blake steps out from one side and looks into the cell through the iron grill door, an "audience" to what follows: a kind of staged, animal-like, coupling.
53. Two keepers bring on a table into the cell. A veiled Lady Fetchcroft is conducted on by her woman attendant and a female keeper. They bend Lady Fetchcroft across the table, facing audience and uncover her body from the waist down. The keepers bring on the Frenetic who is already sexually aroused. He quickly mounts Lady Fetchcroft from the rear and the action is swift and brutal before the Frenetic is hauled away again. The women rearrange Lady Fetchcroft's clothing.
54. Lady Fetchcroft lifts her veil and looks at Blake through the grill. She stretches out her hand towards him.
55. Blake throws himself against the iron grill, shaking the bars in his fury. It is as if he is now a caged animal trying to break out. Lady Fetchcroft and woman attendant cower away from him on the other side of the bars.
56. Lady Fetchcroft turns away and her woman attendant helps her. The two women rush away.
57. The naked figure of the Murderer is chained to a wall, metal collar around his neck, manacles on each wrist. The effect is like a one-man *tableau vivant* of Blake's Plate No. 26 from *Jerusalem:* the naked cruciform figure of Hand/Satan splayed in rising flames. This effect is very brief, a flash of projected light, a glance from Blake's eye, as it were.
58. We are left again with the naked Murderer with two keepers hosing him down with water. Dr. Hibbel is in attendance to one side.
59. The keepers hose him again.
60. Dr. Hibbel signals the keepers and they beat the Murderer with rods until he sinks to his knees, whimpering and bellowing with pain.

61. The keepers hose him down again and pour water in his mouth.
62. The keeper runs after Blake and Dr. Hibbel stands, helplessly, with the other keeper and the chained Murderer.
63. Dr. Hibbel's office in Finchley Grange Asylum. A desk and chairs. Catherine Blake, still in asylum shift, is conducted in by a female keeper and made to stand in front of the desk.
64. Dr. Hibbel bustles on and takes his place behind his desk. He is waving about a sheaf of papers.
65. Takes the pages, looks at them and stops.
66. DR. HIBBEL: (*Following him*)
67. CATHERINE: (*Following both of them*)
68. Catherine, dressed in her own clothes, comes bustling on leading a reluctant Silent Woman by the hand. The Silent Woman is carrying a cloth bag.
69. Blake turns to the Silent Woman who shrinks back from him. He kneels in front of her.
70. The woman becomes even more agitated at this and tries to break away but he holds her by the knees.
71. Catherine now grabs the cloth bag from the Silent Woman and holds it up.
72. Between them, Catherine and the Silent Woman have produced four large keys from the cloth bag.
73. The Silent Woman hurries away.
74. They go off together.
75. Three cells in the asylum open towards us, their doors facing us are closed, floor to ceiling iron grills. The cells contain the Murderer, the Catatonic and the Frenetic.
76. Catherine, with a lantern, leads Blake, still in the asylum shift, across the front of the cells as they make their escape. To her annoyance, Blake dallies before the cells.
77. To the other lunatics, as Catherine drags him away
78. Dr. Hibbel rushes on with two keepers.
79. A keeper searches the cells. To the other keeper... Look in the garden! The keeper rushes away.
80. Hibbel and the keepers rush away. Catherine and Blake appear above.
81. They hug.
82. He breaks away excitedly.
83. Below, the front gates of the asylum are thrown open and a

dishevelled, wild-eyed Dr. Hibbel appears in the opening. Within, the lunatics crowd about, peering over his shoulders.
84. The lunatics, in their white asylum shifts, wander out past him, dazed, both frightened figures and menacing figures. He turns back and the doors close behind him.
85. They continue forward in a line, a mixture of menace and fear, until they stand, facing the audience, a brief moment of indecision. Then they turn as one, backs to the audience, straightening up with a new alertness.
86. At once, the lunatics drop their white shifts; they are now wearing gold coloured robes beneath.
87. Blake and Catherine appear in their small work room above, their faces and hands dirtied with inks, wearing leather aprons, both working furiously, she printing, he etching. The effect is of two people familiar with a tiny work-space, knowing what to do and how not to get in the way of the other. Their dog Thomas sits quietly to one side, watching them.
88. The lunatics raise their arms towards the Blakes. A large white sheet is lowered at an angle above the heads of the Blakes, a single, blank page.
89. Blown up copies of ten plates from *Jerusalem* (as follows) drift upwards on the white sheet during the singing of the single male voice and the choral singing of the lunatics. Plate 1: Los the London Watchman
90. Plate 2: Frontispiece of Jerusalem
91. Plate 6: Los in his Forge
92. Plate 25: The Torture of Albion
93. Plate 26: The Crucifixion of Hand
94. Plate 28: The Lovers on the Lily Pad
95. Plate 76: Albion before Crucified Jesus
96. Plate 78: The Birdman
97. Plate 99: Jehovah Embraces the Androgyne
98. Plate 100: The Final Plate

The striking point in this succession of visual scenes — apart from their number — lies in their importance as elements conveying significant messages. Indeed, the list above consists of a series of images — some more striking or momentous than others — which, whatever their status, create a visual summary of Kilroy's dramatic work. Despite their kaleidoscopic nature and divergent types, grouped together they provide a global reading of the whole play.

In his introduction to *Blake*, Thomas Kilroy stresses the fact that it is a "fiction,"[10] and not an attempt at retracing the "real" life of the poet. Notwithstanding the assertion of his right as an artist to invent the lives of his characters, the author depicts generally credible life scenes in an asylum of that era. In fact, he uses the majority of the scenic images he conceives to give credence to Blake's reinvented life-story. As opposed to *The O'Neill* or *Talbot's Box*, in which he resorted to challenging scenic images to call into question expected social or historical representations, in *Blake*, scenic images often serve the opposite purpose. They tend to build a coherent and believable illustration of the misfortune of Catherine and William Blake.[11] Because of this unexpectedly realistic approach, almost half of the scenic images could be characterized as ordinary[12] since they reproduce the common movements of characters.

Beyond Kilroy's peculiar use of realistic scenic images — which does not correspond to his usual style but brings a credible aspect to the play — one notes that seemingly plain movements do not merely correspond to physical representations. For instance, while image two matches banal gestures which are immediately meaningful, others turn out to be more complex. Some significant attitudes may, for example, reveal the state of mind of a character. This is the case for image nine, in which Catherine's running off after Blake indicates the extent of her worry and disarray.[13] In the same way, images thirty-three and thirty-five epitomize states of mind and relationships between characters. They precede the obvious break in the two men's relationship, in image thirty-eight, when the murderer tries to kill Blake. One then realizes that what matters is not so much a succession of factual images, but the global information conveyed to the audience through visual means. It illustrates that drama, according to Kilroy's conception, is not restricted to a text turned into speech, but encompasses a prominent visual dimension. Consequently, the series of scenic images adds a different layer of meaning, which does not quite correspond to the characters' speeches, but brings another level of significance to the play.

Beyond their realistic utility, some ordinary scenic images may have a more extensive value. Indeed, there are discrepancies between scenic images, and one discovers during performance that their status varies. The staging of the play — as interpreted by the stage director — will obviously define the way in which scenic images are used and performed. Even plain depictions, like image ten, which inform readers about the spatial situation of the protagonists, can — depending on performing choices — become more deeply meaningful. Bearing in mind Kilroy's use of scenic images in his other works, one feels that through light or reduced speed of movements, the gestures of the characters could become ritualized. Obviously, such a reading of the stage direction amounts to an interpretation, but in this way, the characters would gain an almost godly force — used to manipulate individuals — as their location on the gallery seems to indicate.[14] Kilroy's insistence on space in the description, combined with the implicit role of the attendant as the introducer of a show gives more depth to the action. Through precise spatial requirements, the playwright organizes the staging of characters in ways that create an impression of the play within the play, and remind spectators of their own position as an audience.

Scenic images can also work together, even if they do not appear one after the other. For instance, images ten, twenty-three, forty, forty-two and forty-four gradually build an inverted picture of the opening scene (image two), when Catherine had thrown part of the contents of her chamber pot over Dr. Hibbel. Visually, the reversal of power is mainly expressed by gestures ("Catherine is dragged away with the other women lunatics"[15]), alterations in the characters' costumes and also changes in space. While not equivalent to the Brechtian distancing techniques used by Kilroy in other works, scenic images nonetheless put forth revised perspectives. In the circumstances, Dr. Hibbel's loss of power — a situation that appears suddenly through image eighty-three, an echo of scenic image two — illustrates the instability of intellectual perspectives, a reminder of Blake's own words on sanity and lunacy.[16]

> CATHERINE: *(Considerable effort)*. You must say that your visions are a madness! *(Pause)*. Then we may go home. The little medical fellow said so [*BL*. 32].[17]

During performance, Catherine's comic speeches challenge the relevance of the social condemnation which Blake endures. The audience might be willing to side with her, especially if one takes into account the almost universal contemporary admiration of Blake's artworks. On the other hand, wary of one-sided interpretations, Kilroy carefully hinders any identification process on the part of sympathetic audiences, and Blake does not quite correspond to the perfect heroic figure of a sane but misunderstood genius. Consequently, spectators can never really side with him against society, or vice versa. Unable to find a position between apparent rationality and professed madness, the audience is then invited to look elsewhere for more open modes of understanding that may not be expressed through words but — possibly — through visual experience.

In *Blake*, vision appears as a defining feature of individuals, and not merely as a representation of the world. Plain ocular perception leads to an interrogation of the levels of reality, which diverse forms of recognition turn into visions. The question of sight concerns the artist, Dr. Hibbel and other characters, who try to probe into the unknown, in order to express or explain obscure perceptions. William Blake's misfortune testifies to the importance of viewpoints. His socially unacceptable misinterpretations of what he sees results in a harsh sentence passed by his brother and sister, who define him as lunatic.

Focusing on the peculiar intellectual history of William Blake, Kilroy stages a character whom he deems representative of mankind,[18] an ordinary alien who reveals the blindness of people, his own included. The playwright refrains from turning him into a hero,[19] but shows that with the passing of time his challenging views become acceptable, not to say banal, to a contemporary audience. Through Blake's unfortunate experience, spectators are able to measure up the peculiar rationality that prevails in the characterization of the unknown, and also appreciate something of the unfathomable realization of what it is to be normal or mad. If to see is to be, then — from a religious point of view — a denial of access to vision may be understood as a condemnation to non-existence:

> BLAKE: "I see the New Jerusalem descending—" Not true. I see nothing! Nothing anymore! I am condemned [*BL*. 46].[20]

William Blake realizes that his loss of vision amounts to a divine condemnation. His sightlessness, a form of punishment, results from his misbehavior as an eyewitness, which revealed how unworthy of any divine perception he was:

> BLAKE: I watched with Satan from the tree while the couple writhed on the grass.
> CATHERINE: What is this?
> BLAKE: Transgression through the eye is greater than transgression through the body's hole because the eye is portal to the mind and the Divine Imagination and we are its keepers. So. I have failed [*BL*. 56].

Blake explains the nature of his curse. To express this, Kilroy links his speech about vision with a biblical image, which echoes his moral misconduct when he observed the sexual encounter between Lady Fetchcroft and the Frenetic. No matter what reaction spectators may have when they watch this scene, it is very unlikely that — during performance — any of them will perceive themselves as sharing Satan's attitude. Condemning his response, and implicitly that of any viewer, Blake raises the issue of perspectives which lead to the passing of judgments. In the same way, when he had been confronted with scenic image fifty-seven, he had acknowledged his mistake regarding his interpretation of a vision which each spectator had also briefly visualized.[21] From the tension between what he sees as an individual and his reproduction of it as an artist, he makes the audience wonder about the accuracy of their own perception of reality. In this, his speeches about vision play a part equivalent to the distancing scenic images used in other works, where they underlined the irrelevance of what characters said, or went against the expectations of the audience. Here, following an inverted process, speech calls into question the perception and understanding of images, and arouses a lurking, albeit unconscious, query in the spectators' minds during performance, if Kilroy's repeated interrogations are perceived in this way.

Because of their polysemous nature, the reading of scenic images proves difficult, especially so as one might overemphasize the importance of "echoing" pictures in Kilroy's works. Still, thinking of the obsessive invasion of Shakespearean quotations in *Tea and Sex and Shakespeare*, one feels that in *Blake*, Kilroy follows a similar path with scenic images. With scenic image eleven, for instance, the youth, beauty and purity of the young woman give her an Ophelia-like aspect,[22] and her strange madness raises the question of its visual importance for spectators. This latent evocation of Shakespeare's heroine calls to mind the many paintings which depict Ophelia's tragic plight, and widens the scope of this scene.[23] If this mental course corresponds to Kilroy's expectations, it would mean that the audience would undergo a process similar to that experienced by Blake, whose mental images do not quite correspond to the reality he is supposed to perceive. These visual alternatives providing mental echoes of different shapes would then effectively bring out the fragmentary aspect of the play's reception, a point in keeping with *Blake* as a challenge to the relevance or even the possibility of unique or unified perceptions.

While some scenic images lead to multiple interpretations, others serve a different purpose. Faithful to his conception of the theatre as an alembic of deep emotions, in *Blake* Kilroy resorts to crude scenic images and draws close to Artaud. In the circumstances, the prominence of scenic images, together with their challenging nature, brings strong echoes of Artaud's theory of drama, which was hostile to the predominance of the text. With regard to the violence of some scenic images, the asylum as an almost realistic mirror reflecting society — added to some hardly acceptable representations of what it is to be human — is likely to be overpowering for some spectators. In terms of public reception, Lady Fetchcroft's sexual acts will certainly prove challenging, and will possibly lead to censorship, depending on the country of performance.

> *They bend Lady Fetchcroft across the table, facing audience and uncover her body from the waist down. The keepers bring on the Frenetic who is already sexually aroused. He quickly mounts Lady Fetchcroft from the rear and the action is swift and brutal before the Frenetic is hauled away again. The women rearrange Lady Fetchcroft's clothing* [BL. 41].

The crudity of the scene, which reminds one of the ritual which attends the mating of a stallion with a mare, underlines the animal-like behavior of Lady Fetchcroft. She expresses physical needs which society hides or codifies so that the bestial nature of individuals is masked. Thus, the fakery of society's expectations regarding people's saintly nature is exposed. At first Blake condemns Lady Fetchcroft, but he later understands that he had no right to judge and condemn her. Kilroy joins Blake by exhibiting unconventional attitudes and refrains from condemning her. Nakedness and bodies — those of the Frenetic, the Catatonic and the chained Murderer — echo Blake's paintings. Indeed, some of the artist's works represent half-human, half-animal beings. Here Kilroy turns them into almost ordinary visions of human nature. It follows that the refusal of one's basic animal needs seems absurd, even if it corresponds to society-imposed restrictions, which the audience is likely to approve. Therefore, scenic images contribute to a building up of tensions between what society — hence the audience — deems acceptable, and a presentation of humanity that moves one step ahead of Blake's graphic presentations of people, Kilroy showing up mental *écorchés* in the play.

> *They continue forward in a line, a mixture of menace and fear, until they stand, facing the audience, a brief moment of indecision. Then they turn as one, backs to the audience, straightening up with a new alertness.*
> *A single male voice begins to sing, at first in the distance, then coming closer and closer.*
> *At once, the lunatics drop their white shifts; they are now wearing gold coloured robes beneath* [BL. 65].

In the last scene, the audience faces a major shift in perspective. As often, Kilroy uses a scenic image so that spectators can measure the extent of their delusion. Despite the apparently conclusive contrast between what people used to be and what they become at the end of the play, clear-cut oppositions do not work. Characters are now defined by their dress, but their former identity as lunatics has not disappeared. As human beings, they belong to both sides, and thus retain seemingly contradictory features. This point proves essential if one keeps in mind the impossibility of imposing limits, which prevents any one-sided conclusion to the play. Indeed, although the final images provide an ending, a basic uncertainty prevails. The transformation of the asylum into a New Jerusalem is not temporally defined, and the ultimate metamorphosis remains open to interpretation, thanks in particular to the ephemeral visual presentation of Blake's plates.

In terms of structure and conception, the ending of the play is obviously part of the whole work. Although, apparently, Kilroy makes his bow and ushers Blake's vision onto the stage in the forms of his paintings, the shift in perspective fits into the playwright's own global dramatic design. In the same way as gold-colored robes did not eradicate white uniforms, blown up copies of Blake's plates do not replace what had been prominent before: text, scenic images, music and more generally, performance. They bring a final touch to Kilroy's theatrical approach, in which the extreme importance granted to vision outlines what may be characterized as "symphonic theatre." By this expression, we understand a form of total theatre in which the various elements of performance — text, scenic images, music and acting techniques — will be used extensively, not as the result of a stage director's choice but because, initially, they are at the core of the playwright's dramatic vision.

One of the striking elements in *Blake* lies in the convergence which appears between the playwright's continued research into dramatic modes of expression and Blake's technically innovative project of the illuminated books. Blake tried to combine text and pictures in order to enable his readers to gain access to the nature of his mystic poetic endeavors. In *Blake*, Kilroy once again breaks away from a dominant Irish tradition, and refuses conventional storytelling in favor of a more complex approach. His refusal of realism, together with the openness of the play, hinders the assertion of any conclusive one-sided interpretation. Kilroy's renewed and ambitious dramatic perspectives echo Blake's daring scheme, but also bring to mind other audacious predecessors in the field of drama. In this respect, one thinks in particular of the challenging views expressed in *Le Théâtre et son double*. Contrary to Artaud's perspective, however, in *Blake*, the text retains a relatively significant role as *one* of the features of performance defined by the playwright. Here, the ritualized aspect of the staging, in which music and scenic images play a major part, contributes to the creation of a different rapport with the audience. Thanks to a convergence of emotions produced by a combination of senses and imagination, spectators may fully relish Kilroy's dramatic visions, and thus share his insight into life. Kilroy's "symphonic theatre" does not overstress fragmentation, despite its multiple levels of interaction. Thanks to these, it reaches a higher level of significance because, through a new approach to the stage and to performance, it reintroduces the audience to the mysterious essence of drama.

8

The Shape of Metal: Portrait of a Successful Artist

The Shape of Metal was first performed at the Abbey Theatre, Dublin, in 2003. Faithful to his writing approach, which consists of varying his dramatic techniques, Thomas Kilroy altered his artistic perspectives for his new play. In performance, the most visible changes were the choice of a realistic setting, as well as the fact that the three characters were women, who introduced the audience to an exclusively feminine universe. Nell, an eighty-two-year-old sculptor at the apex of her glory, is forced by Judith, her younger daughter, to explain her past behavior with her elder daughter. Their conversations mainly concern their former family life, but their encounter leads to numerous reflections on art and the status of the artist both at a social and personal level. Nell looks back on her life, but *The Shape of Metal* is not a memory play, since a questioning of the future parallels Nell's inquiry into her past. This staged portrait of a successful artist provides the audience with familiar Kilroyan themes. Through an external and an inner depiction of Nell as an artist, the playwright wonders about the creative process, questions the relevance of success, and challenges contemporary myths about art. The social value of art is at stake, as are gender issues, but beyond this, the looming problem of failure paves the way for ontological questionings.

Thomas Kilroy has staged artists in several plays, sometimes granting them a central role. If one thinks of the depiction of a playwright, *Tea and Sex and Shakespeare* or *The Secret Fall of Constance Wilde* immediately come to mind. *Blake, The Madame MacAdam Travelling Theatre*, or even his adaptation of Chekhov's *The Seagull* also bring to light the importance of artists. His most recent work partakes of his staged reflections on art.

The Shape of Metal was published thirty-four years after *The Death and Resurrection of Mr. Roche*, his first play, and this probably corresponded to a time when Thomas Kilroy looked back questioningly on his theatrical experience, as the content of the play seems to suggest. Indeed, the point in common between the author and Nell is that both approach their works in ways which differ from those of the young writer in *Tea and Sex and Shakespeare*. In *The Shape of Metal*, Kilroy does not need to engage in a telephone conversation with Shakespeare to seek advice about the ways of shaping a play. His doubts no longer concern the capacity to create, but relate to the value of creations. The nature of queries has changed in time, but the intensity of the questioning seems to have grown, gaining in scope and depth.[1]

Despite the force of the quest, Thomas Kilroy keeps a distance between his personal experience and what he stages. His fascination for the achievements of artists and the mystery of creation appears in the title of the play. It lays stress on shaping as a crucial feature of artistic work, and his choice of a sculptor enables him to focus on the creative process. If one had doubts about the converging perspectives between sculpture and playwriting, Nell's definition of her creating process would make a convincing case:

> NELL: What one does, actually, with one's pieces, I mean, is add one more, yes, presence. That's what we do in sculpture, we — populate [*SM*. 42].

Nell's views on sculpture echo some remarks on playwriting made by the author when he offered a critical view of the dramatic production of his friend Brian Friel.[2] The close connection established between theatre and sculpture is meaningful in that it reveals the personal involvement of the playwright through his depiction of a sculptor who looks back on her artistic practice. On the other hand, one should not restrict the significance of Kilroy's choice of sculpture to an indirect autobiography. As was the case in *Blake*—where painting enabled the playwright to bring forth his meditation on art—a dramatic expression through a different art form helps him widen the scope of this reflection.

In *The Shape of Metal*, Kilroy focuses more on artistic production and on the artist as an individual than on the nature of the relationship between an artist and society. In this specific context, he provides the audience with a vision of family relationships when one of its members is a creator. The social figure of the artist hardly appears as such, except through the positive communal response given to Nell's sculptures, and the material consequences of fame, which she emphasizes: "Going to put them into that museum in Kilmainham. A Nell Jeffrey Room, no less! What a lark!" (*SM*. 15). Despite this restricted social outlook, one notes that when Nell speaks to her daughter, she sometimes stages herself as an artist.

In the opening scene, the audience discovers Nell both as Judith's mother and as a sculptor. Certain social expectations about artists arise in an initial clash of perspectives between the two women with regard to what may be defined as acceptable language. Judith reminds her mother of basic principles concerning the respect for individuals, but Nell claims an inalienable artistic right to express herself in the way she wants, even if it does not correspond to accepted standards. In doing so, she tacitly reminds her daughter that being an artist implies that society expects her to be and to act like a truth-seeker, hence her insistence on her right to speak her mind freely. Consequently, Nell's antics are part of her artistic status, a point which Judith challenges as a daughter:

NELL: Good! Now we're getting somewhere!
JUDITH: Oh, no, we're not: Not playing that game! [*SM*. 14].

Judith understands that her mother's resorting to well-rehearsed speech modes will prevent them from reaching a common ground of discussion. Faced with what she sees as a mask, she refuses to grant Nell the privilege of performing the reassuring but empty role of the artist. Both women know their parts, and while the staging of such a dialogue might provide some solace for their inner worries, Judith is aware that accepting such a mode of conversation will lead them nowhere. Thanks to this challenging dialogue in the opening scene, Thomas Kilroy resumes a long-standing reflection on masks, on social hindrances to the expression of the self, even through what should help one express one's "true" self. The compulsory staging of artists leads to a paradox. Artists are supposedly truth-seekers, but their socially expected performance weakens or even invalidates the strength of their statements.

Thanks to Nell's initial portrait, Thomas Kilroy calls into question a number of stereotypical perceptions. To do so, he starts with a successful sculptor, thus inverting the banal image of the poor and misunderstood artist. He puts forth the danger of compulsory performance, but his taste for paradox prevents him from equating the shallowness of socially expected artistic discourses with an emptiness of reflection. On the contrary, Nell's later assertion according to which her daily introspection seems to be part of her nature comforts the relevance of a perception of artists as compulsory truth seekers. However, at that level too, Kilroy cautiously avoids the trap of myth-making. His humorous depiction of Nell's meeting with Beckett and Giacometti — whose conversation almost exclusively related to footwear — expresses his rejection of romantic portrayals of artists.

The initial focus on the artist as a social element enables Kilroy to bring the question of art into perspective. However, in *The Shape of Metal*— contrary to *The Secret Fall of Constance Wilde*—social issues are less prominent, and he resumes his inquiry into the process of creation in a different way. Nell's initial remarks — prolonged in the rest of the play — lead to a reflection on the recognition of artistic production.

> NELL: Do you know the young are right. Put your urine in a row of bottles and exhibit them. Arrange some rubbish in a corner according to some design that is only known to the rubbish artist. Art! So be it! There is some extraordinary revelation in the times we live in. Do you know why? Because this is a time of relentless, artistic mediocrity [*SM*. 53].

Nell had already alluded to Giacometti's theory of *visione*, according to which distance proved essential to make out what one could not decipher at first sight. In doing so, she had initiated a questioning on the public reception of art. Using Nell's comments, Kilroy moves beyond socially determined demands concerning the role of artists, and shifts to artistic production. The words "rubbish" and "artists" link creators to commonness, and assert the existence of a category to which some contemporary artists obviously belong. The association of "art" and "rubbish" brings echoes of different periods in the history of art, when artists have created works deemed unworthy by the public. In the circumstances, an opposite perspective prevails. Condemning pseudo-challenging artworks judged valuable by the public because of their deliberate difference, Nell starts from an inverted image of the romantic artist. At the beginning of the twenty-first century, disconnection has apparently lost its flattering romantic aspect, especially since success has little to do with any form of creative achievement. Indeed, according to the new approach to art which Nell exposes, "rubbish artists" no longer face deep personal demands which would grant some value to their works. Consequently the unquestioned social acceptance of their voluntary difference challenges the relevance of their artistic production. Paradoxically the words "rubbish artist" exclude a philistine approach to art. Nell's sharp critical attitude asserts the vital importance of art as a challenge, which is inherently alien to mediocrity.

In performance, her statements question the audience on the role of the public and its capacity to adhere to complex artistic projects. Thanks to Nell's repeated assertions, Kilroy builds the play on a dual level: the plot and a meditation on art. The audience might relate more easily to the disclosure of the reasons for Grace's departure than to Nell's reflections on art. Still, Kilroy intertwines the two perspectives, especially through Nell's complex thought process, which involves a gradual discovery of the major issues which being a mother and an artist involve for her. The two levels meet through the notion of failure, which concerns Nell both as a mother and a creator, but also through the links between creation and destruction.

Resorting to traditional images, Judith equates the creative process with giving birth. Interestingly, the play brings forth a more complex view of creation, which includes destruction, for instance when Nell smashes her last sculpture. Yet, her gesture — spectacular in performance — is no attempt at escape. Her deed calls into question the validity of what has been created, knowing that the failure embodied by the sculpture will forever remain in her mind. Looking back on Nell's past — not exclusively on her artistic experience but rather on the two intertwined levels — it seems that creating means destroying people, or giving birth to broken individuals.

As for the creative process, Nell links it to self-delusion.

> NELL: I have spent a lifetime trying to create perfect form. The finished, rounded, perfect form. Mistake. No, take that back. Colossal fucking blunder. And B, I knew it. All along, I knew this. Knew what I was doing. Knew it was an illusion. And still persisted [*SM.* 53].

In performance, the audience is likely to perceive her speech as an echo of Tom Kilroy's reflections on his dramatic experience. Nell gives a wide scope to her meditation. She does not view the creative process in terms of success or failure for specific works, but more as a deep-rooted but flawed necessity. She also insists on the demanding nature of her artistic attempt: "Trying to create perfect form," which led to what she sees as a failure. She understands that her creative urge amounts to a vain but paradoxically essential endeavour, which echoes her former condemnation of artistic mediocrity.

Thanks to this and to other dialogues, Thomas Kilroy puts his reflection on art at the core of the play. Nell's conversations with Judith — together with her monologues — enable the audience to discover the tension between a need to create and an urge to destroy, in a process which the artist fails to master. Between dedication, survival and self-destruction, the creative process seems to result from the assertion of the ego as a compulsory mode of truth-telling artistic expression. In this respect, social hostility to creation makes sense. The lack of discrimination in the field of art enables society to protect itself against the unpleasant truth which the works of artists are likely to expose.

Starting from the status of the artist and a questioning of contemporary creation, Kilroy continues with his quest. He probes the creative process in an unaccustomed way for him, since the artist whom he stages is a woman.

In the opening scene, Grace bonds motherhood and creation:

> GRACE: Busy fingers pressing and shaping, lump of stuff, stone or metal to be transformed into Grace finally at peace, head still and quiet, no terrible dread anymore, no mad panics to run out into the fields screaming, no dreadful terrors for Gracie anymore, Mummy kneading the head, ... [*SM*. 11].

Art, motherhood and peace — in her ghostly initial conversation with Nell, Grace expects that thanks to her artistic skills, her mother will bring her peace. Unfortunately, contrary to Grace's idyllic expectations, the play recounts Judith's discovery of Nell's destructive attitude toward her elder daughter. Thanks to its balanced human complexity, Nell's rather unflattering portrait is nevertheless captivating, and *The Shape of Metal* is no Manichaean rewriting of *Medea*, which would only stress lethal maternal powers. Starting from Grace's naïve Botticelli-like vision of a Virgin mother with her child (which recalls paintings illustrating the supreme healing power of mothers), Tom Kilroy redefines mother-daughter relationships. To do so, he calls into question the myth of motherhood, the essence of which might be selfless, healing motherly love.

This dramatic strategy strikes a familiar chord; as often in his other plays, the playwright exposes the stifling and dangerous aspects of compulsory social masks which prevent individuals from showing their real nature. Both Nell and Grace suffer from Nell's incapacity to play her maternal role in ways which would correspond to common expectations.

In spite of the political stance which Tom Kilroy takes when he exposes fake but socially-expected feminine attitudes — together with his choice of a female creator — he does not opt for a feminist perspective. Without a doubt, child-bearing provides a unique experience to the woman artist, but the playwright stops short of elaborating on gender issues.

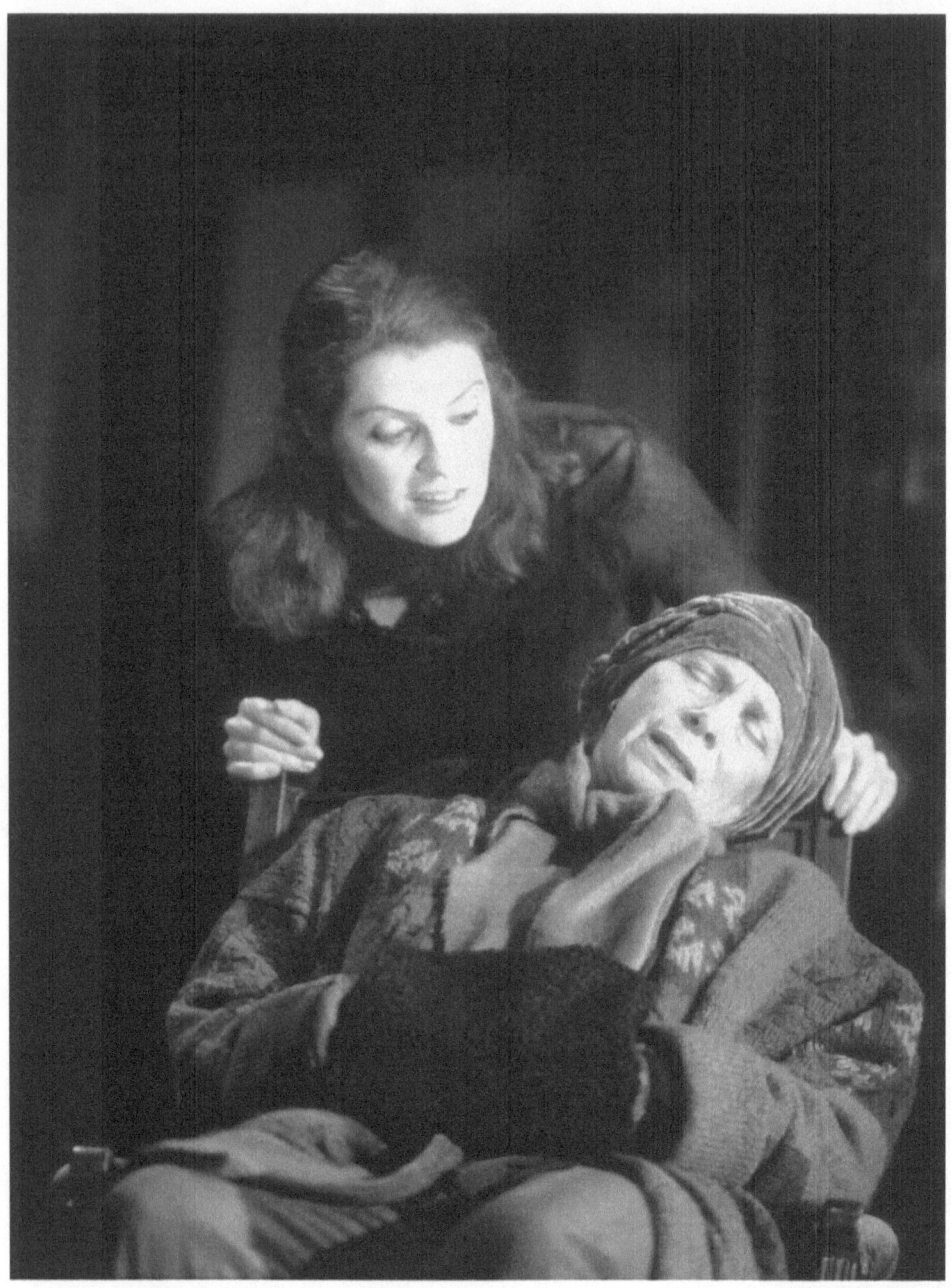

The Shape of Metal. Photograph by Tom Lawlor. From left to right, Justine Mitchell, Sara Kestelman. Abbey Theatre, Dublin, 2003 (courtesy of The Abbey Theatre Archive).

8. The Shape of Metal

Paradoxically, despite acknowledged differences, selecting a woman as the artist becomes significant precisely in that he wishes to go beyond gender issues. Choosing a woman artist enables him to challenge global stereotypical views of creation in a different way, and to expose — beyond sexual questions — the falsely reassuring images that society conveys of artists.

> JUDITH: Kowtowing to male greatness! You've never done this! All your life you've struck a note of independence from men–
> NELL: Down to the banal. Down, down further, down to the common animal–
> JUDITH: You are a great artist! You don't need a male example, never have, which is why women look up to you! I know something of the battles you fought, Mother, remember–
> NELL: Snuffling and scratching and guzzling and breaking wind, that's the base! On which everything is constructed! [*SM*. 56].

Contrary to Judith's expectations, Nell refuses to acknowledge the relevance of the gender limits which her daughter traces. While Judith analyses her mother's creations in social terms — a possible response to male artistic supremacy — Nell strikes a different chord. She insists on the depth of her quest, explaining that contrary to what her daughter thinks, she is not in search of a male model. In fact, her vision of art takes her beyond gender issues. To her, creating implies an initial, earnest introspection. It later leads to forms of artistic expression to which socially-constructed gender images may relate. However, rather than oppose men and women, Nell insists on the common bond between artists, but not necessarily from a conciliatory viewpoint. The meeting points she finds between male and female artists do not belong to the most flattering kind, as her allusion to the common animal shows.

Such a statement could seem contradictory to her initial acknowledgment of failure because she had striven to create perfect form. In fact, the tension between the animal and the immensely demanding attitude of creators might illustrate the nature of the challenges which artists have to face. Nell defines creators as people who are caught between unflattering physiological realities and their need to invent genuine art forms. The task is enormous. It is so perilous for an individual that gender issues seem almost irrelevant compared to the artistic and metaphysical questionings inherent to a pursuit which, according to Nell, is bound to fail in some way.

> NELL: Failure. It really is just a question of how great are one's failures. That's all. And how one lives with them.
> JUDITH: (*exasperated*) Mother!
> NELL: (*Lost*) "The piece of sculpture must embody its own particular failure."

"*Son propre échec.*" That's what Giacometti said that day on the Rue Hyppolyte-Maindron, in 1938, or at least some time before the Hitler War. "Indubitably" Beckett answered from a corner of the room [*SM.* 44].

Nell's reference to famous artists of the past enables her to give a more universal scope to her statement. In doing so, she also connects artistic production to time, which paves the way for her later assertion, by which the artistic creations of former artists have become less relevant for her contemporaries. Nell relates her encounter with Beckett and Giacometti to explain what creation means. To her, artistic production does not correspond to Judith's understanding, which reflects common but false social images. In fact, the fundamental truth which she asserts goes against expected visions. It links artistic production with failure, making it part of its essence. Nell knows from experience that artists can achieve something, but they should not delude themselves into believing that they will create perfect form.

Nell's views mean that artists cannot but fail. Any other attitude would be complacent, hence the oxymoronic nature of the "successful artist" which society deems her to be. Starting from this principle, public recognition cannot be a convincing form of success, and external approval might even hinder the artists' awareness of the limited scope of their achievement.

As for the work of art embodying its own failure, Giacometti's sentence makes one wonder about the failings of *The Shape of Metal*. Ironically, the flashback might illustrate the point, showing the need for the artist to ignore the public expectations of his time. One could view the staging of this event as an unconscious consequence of Kilroy's disappointing experience with *Tea and Sex and Shakespeare*. The unsatisfactory response of puzzled audiences faced with the complexity of *Tea and Sex and Shakespeare* might have hindered the audacity of the playwright for his new play. It is true that the 2003 Dublin production of *The Shape of Metal* led to a positive audience response, especially thanks to Sara Kestleman's commanding interpretation of a powerful Kilroyan text. Yet one may regret that the audience did not have to fill the gaps in Nell's story for themselves, without being told about Grace's love affair, because their mental discovery of missing elements might have made *The Shape of Metal* an even more powerful play. On the other hand, one should be cautious before blaming the clumsiness of a mature playwright. Indeed, this critical vision might illustrate differently a point which Kilroy makes, failure resulting this time from an inadequate critical response to a work of art.

Failure is part of the artist's quest and life, but the audience may feel that Nell's lingering questions gradually extend beyond the scope of art. By the time mother and daughter leave the studio, the successful artist has come to embody humanity, made of individuals at the core of a perpetual war between what society would call their basest and highest instincts. The outcome of past battles has shown that neither camp could prevail. Being human means that both sides have to remain together, as is shown by the work of the artist — a series of more or less elevating failures — which may well consist in giving a shape to this vital tension.

It is difficult to conclude on the portrait of a *successful* artist, without adding a coda to Kilroy's own coda. It seems necessary to devote some attention to the way in which Kilroy widens the scope of his dramatic work to the very last instants of the play. The change from immobility to slow movement proves a meaningful feature of the final scene. Judith and Nell walk together into the garden, but Nell's former speeches preclude any optimistic interpretation of their last exit. The two women stand for a world which has come to an end, but *fin de siècle* does not mean nostalgia. In fact, one may even add that Kilroy's main interest lies in the future. Nell's concern with "the new woman, Femina Nova," whom she sees as the bearer of future undertakings gives us a clue on that point. Because of this double temporal dimension — a world coming to an end, and a world about to be born — *The Shape of Metal* is both a concluding and an opening work for future generations. In the last moments of the play, after Nell and Judith have left, the playwright visually calls for a new beginning. The final image — an empty stage — might be Tom Kilroy's most significant dramatic message. Not a wink to the public this time, as was the case at the end of *Tea and Sex and Shakespeare*. He concludes *The Shape of Metal* with an empty stage, which bears the full force of the challenges that await future creators. Thanks to this last image, the playwright closes *The Shape of Metal* with an invitation for the generation of "the new woman" to "populate" the stage in ways which are still to be imagined.

9

Irish Disconnections with the Former British Empire: Thomas Kilroy's Adaptation of *The Seagull*

In the course of the twentieth century, the relationship between Ireland and England was significantly altered, with climactic crises such as the Easter Rising of 1916, the War of Independence, and also the repetitive tragic events that have characterized life in Northern Ireland since the late 1960s.[1] In Ulster, the place where tensions are still acute, many Catholics regard themselves as the victims of a persistent and lurking form of colonialism, while some Protestants pride themselves on their attachment to the former Empire. Repeated, intense political crises have left their mark on people, but also on art and artists, among whom there is Tom Kilroy, whose plays and adaptations of dramatic works such as Chekhov's *The Seagull* echo past and present conflicts resulting from Ireland's colonial history.

As was seen in the previous chapters, some of Kilroy's personal writings supply valuable information regarding his vision of relationships between England and Ireland. However, because his adaptation of *The Seagull* initially constitutes a rewriting of colonial history, a study of Kilroy's standpoint as an adaptor of Chekhov may prove even more rewarding than a reflection on his original works. To understand some of his perspectives on Ireland's colonial and post-colonial history, the reasons which persuaded Kilroy to make the literary choice of adapting *The Seagull* will be analyzed. The mere fact that Kilroy referred himself to a famous play instead of writing a new one provides a number of clues, not only as to his own status as a playwright who adapts plays, but also with regard to the new trends informing the relationship between Irish drama and world drama. The next question that comes to mind is how Kilroy's adaptation of *The Seagull* to an Irish colonial context sheds light on his uncommon perception of past connections with the former British Empire. Finally, beyond the playwright's personal or literary motives, the political significance of his work on *The Seagull* needs to be examined in a context of connections with or disconnection from the former British Empire.

In 1981, Max Stafford-Clark, an English artistic director at the Royal Court Theatre in London, asked Kilroy to write an adaptation of *The Seagull*. This initial request, which some might be tempted unjustifiably to view as an extended form of colonialism, went exactly in the opposite direction, as will be shown further on. The reasons why an author translates the literary production of a foreign writer differ from artist to artist. Still, they can be roughly explained by a wish to give one's fellow citizens access to the specific works of an author, whom the translator deems important on a number of grounds. As far as the decision to adapt a foreign masterpiece is concerned, the motives for such a commitment can less easily be explained since the works of the foreign author in question are already available to the public. No single answer may prevail, but undoubtedly, through his particular dialogue with Chekhov, Kilroy found the means of redefining past and present Anglo-Irish relationships.

To start with, one should note that a dramatist's willingness to adapt plays is one of his distinguishing traits. Indeed, it forms an integral part of the process of self-definition as a writer in general and as an *Irish* writer in particular. Through his renewed approach to this foreign play, Thomas Kilroy found himself in a position to play a role similar to the almost creative one of translators, since his adaptation — as opposed to previous translations — gave an Irish touch to otherwise English-sounding texts. In the Irish playwright's own words:

> Max felt, and I agreed with him, that some English language productions of Chekhov tended towards a very English gentility where the socially specific Chekhov tended to be lost in polite vagueness. He believed that an Anglo-Irish setting would provide specificity, at once removed from, and at the same time comprehensible to an English audience. He also felt that an Irish setting would more easily allow the rawness of passion of the original to emerge, the kind of semi-farcical hysteria, which Chekhov uses in the scenes between Arkadina, Treplyov and Trigorin in Act Three.[2]

Furthermore, what Kilroy wrote in his preface to the play about Max Stafford-Clark's offer indirectly relates to Ireland's colonial history:

> I was well aware that the history of drama is a history of adaptations. The good adaptation is always a substantial tribute to its original and it should send us back to that original with an enhanced view of it, as I hope this version will do.[3]

The perspective put forward, being part of a general culture — a stage in the history of drama — sheds some light on the nature of Kilroy's complex undertaking. This quotation becomes even more significant if one thinks of *Tea and Sex and Shakespeare*—a comedy in which he had humorously depicted a young playwright's unsuccessful attempt at eradicating compulsory English cultural references when he tried to assert himself as a writer by lessening Shakespeare's influence on his works. Kilroy's serious approach to Chekhov partakes of the same idea as that described in *Tea and Sex and Shakespeare*. Indeed, at a social level, adapting plays that do not belong to a specific English heritage opens new doors to an extended literary fund that, so far, had only been available to Irish people through the frame of English culture. On that matter, it is worth noticing that other major Irish playwrights such as Brian Friel and Frank McGuinness have taken the same path and adapted famous works by foreign writers.[4] Each playwright thereby connects himself with his illustrious predecessors, but socially, individual accomplishments take on a wider significance. They also indicate that new cultural perspectives are emerging in Ireland in relation to world drama, through a literary disconnection from the former British Empire.

Regarding Kilroy's involvement, one should remember that adapting plays can be a risky venture in terms of ensuing publications. This is unfortunately proven by the fact that contrary to his adaptation of Ibsen's *Ghosts*, his adaptation of Pirandello's *Six Characters in Search of an Author* has not been published. His work on *The Seagull*, though, was published even if, at the time, about ten translations were available to the public. Regarding his choice of authors and plays, one notes that family relationships and crises, together with people's connections with society at large bring indirect echoes of a paradoxically close Irish world. On a wider cultural level, the professor's presence is felt behind that of the playwright. Indeed, plays such as *Six Characters in Search of an Author* added to the culture of theatregoers, who may have been unfamiliar with daring works that challenged conventional opinions of what theatre should be.[5] Consciously or not, Kilroy's creation of cultural landmarks that are initially alien to British culture reinforces his disconnection with the former British Empire.

Besides experimenting with the theatrical genre and offering a reflection on art, Chekhov's *Seagull* and Kilroy's adaptation also present

Six Characters in Search of an Author. Photograph by Amelia Stein. From left to right, Katie Monelli, Barbara Brennan, Rory Keenan. Abbey Theatre, Dublin, 1996 (courtesy of The Abbey Theatre).

parallels on the social and political levels. The painful economic situation of the Anglo-Irish in the West of Ireland in the late 1870s strongly echoes that of Chekhov's gentry. For instance, the Big House[6] becomes a focal point where people from all walks of life meet, in an atmosphere that forebodes feared changes and characterizes a dying world. The signs of impotence reflecting common impoverishment are also reinforced by some characters' awareness of the distance that separates them from the capital and a power they are supposed to represent. In Kilroy's adaptation, the

Anglo-Irish stand for *foreign* power, which introduces the dimension of colonialism, one that is absent from Chekhov's work. Moreover, various short addenda made to the Russian original also generate specifically Irish political themes and gradually build up a colonial background in the play, as illustrated in the following extract:

> SORIN: And after dinner I accidentally fell asleep again and now every joint in my body aches. I feel as if I'm going through a nightmare, when all's said and done.[7]
>
> PETER: And there I was, after dinner, snoozing again in the chair. It's no wonder half the neighbourhood lives in England. This country is asleep [*SEA*. 18].

Kilroy revisits a specific period of Ireland's colonial history. Like its Russian equivalent in Chekhov, the Anglo-Irish land-owning gentry has now disappeared. On this basis, Kilroy transforms Russia into Ireland. The first significant alteration concerns space, when geographical references turn a Russian landscape into an Irish one. For example, "The whole district" becomes "this side of the river Shannon"; in a similar vein, "the other side of the lake" evolves into "beyond the lake near Kilmore." These transformations illustrate the passage from a Russian to an Irish background, but after Brian Friel's play, *Translations*,[8] it would be difficult to view the adaptation of names as a purely innocent phenomenon. These changes help Kilroy ground his play on Irish soil, so that the situation of the Anglo-Irish will bring to his audience echoes of not quite forgotten days. Verbal scenery creates a fake reality to which Irish — or even English-theatregoers are likely to relate, since their cultural background will make them fully realize that through his depiction of helpless characters faced with a predicament they cannot master, Kilroy, an Irish playwright, provides a personal outlook on Ireland's colonial history.[9] If one compares Chekhov's text with Kilroy's, one can easily measure how the two plays differ when characters talk about the political and financial situation, as is shown by the contrast below:

> POLINA ANDREEVNA: He sent the carriage horses for work in the fields, you know. And misunderstandings like this go on every day. If you only knew how it worries and upsets me! It's making me ill. See, I'm trembling ... I can't stand his rudeness, I can't.[10]
>
> PAULINE: It's not as if he runs the estate properly. He doesn't. It's bankrupt like every other estate in the West of Ireland. You know they've stopped paying rents again this past month. The land leaguers will have nothing to take of what's left, [*SEA*, 44].

In both cases, the depicted economic situation derives from the owner's vain attempt at running the farm in a profitable way. However, in pre-Revolutionary Russia, the characters' impotence is individualized as the direct result of personal behaviour or habits, while the Irish perspective differs. The desperate financial state of the farm does not represent an isolated case highlighting a specific situation. On the contrary, it reflects on a wider scale a common poverty shared by landowners who — in the West of Ireland — find themselves in financial straits.

Although Kilroy mentions the tension between various social classes, colonial oppression does not however stand out as the major cause of it. First, similar social tension has occurred at various stages in the rural history of European communities; moreover, the lurking conflict spurs an almost metaphysical questioning that goes beyond ready-made answers about the harmful rule of England as a colonial power. Landowners undoubtedly thwart communal well being, but their human incapacity to turn Nature into a satisfactory provider seems to prevail over their origins when it comes to the source of conflict.[11] It follows that the Land Leaguers merely add to the list of elements that prevent landowners from hoping to make some profit out of their farming activities. Kilroy refrains from taking sides, an approach that corresponds to that found in his other works on similar issues since, apparently, both parties endure a fate that precludes any attempt at improving the general situation.

By depicting the mental background of a dying world — a recurring stage in any communal history — Kilroy connects the specific past of Ireland to a world history of rural desolation. In this respect, his adaptation can be perceived as a way of building new links, of asserting a common ground between Irish people and the rest of the world. To return to the earlier mentioned links that exist between Kilroy's adaptation and its original, Russian people, in different circumstances, have also endured the harsh consequences of incompetent landowners, symbolizing a general human disconnection with Nature. Consequently, Kilroy's adaptation becomes a way of underlining this connection between two peoples because it underplays the foreign element inserted in the Irish version of *The Seagull*. This strategy adds to the distancing effect from colonial issues, and reinforces the impression of a gradual intellectual disconnection from the British Empire.

While, at first sight, this literary tactic does not seem to give prominence to colonial issues, Kilroy — who thrives on ambiguity and paradoxes — also uses this unorthodox approach to Ireland's past to reconnect Irish people to their history. Subjectively, he reacquaints them with episodes of their past, and invites them to reconsider their relationship —

if not with the former British Empire, at least with the present legacy of their colonial experience. Kilroy challenges expected divisions in several ways. First, he acknowledges — but does not overemphasize — national antagonisms.

> ASTON: And you people. I know nothing about you. Indeed, I rather find the whole experience in this household strange, if you will forgive me, yes, foreign. I have great difficulty in understanding what precisely, is being said by you Irish at any particular time. And yet we appear to share the language [*SEA*. 49].

Aston's insistence on the impossibility of understanding the Irish was added by Kilroy in his adaptation, in order to stress the disconnection that existed between a representative of England and an ordinary Irish woman. The word "foreign" sums up the extent of their estrangement, but while this colonial opposition is marked, one should note that this state of alienation does not merely concern English citizens. Peter, a former civil servant in Dublin Castle, where British Imperial power resided, is now forced to live in the country, in the West of Ireland, but feels he does not belong there. For the younger generation, the issue of belonging is even more complex. The Anglo-Irish, as their name indicates, are torn between their loyalty to England and their attachment to the country where they were born and raised. As the son of a Galway pedlar[12] and a famous London actress, Constantine suffers from this feeling of alienation. Identity confusion obviously affects the Anglo-Irish, but Catholics like James and Dr. Hickey are not spared either. Blind to the needs of his future wife, James fails to understand the challenges that his marriage to Mary, a Protestant, entails in terms of self-definition.[13] His complete approval of the values of a dying world, together with his acceptance of a ready-made social identity for himself can only lead to a fake harmony. In fact, beyond the religious divide, the major threat to the contemplated union seems to lie in personal interrelationships. Mary, a Bovary-like character, will eventually agree to marry Peter, but their defective marriage will serve to underline their intimate disconnection. Here, as in many of Kilroy's plays, the capacity of individuals to relate to someone else is questioned and exposed as a major existential challenge, a view that diminishes the importance of the colonial legacy, whose importance as an obstacle appears reduced compared to the feeble human capacity for mutual understanding.[14]

Adapting Chekhov proved a challenge for Kilroy who attempts to keep a critical distance from the political problems which he raises. He rejects realistic theatre[15] but tries to remain authentic, avoiding the trap of the folklore–like Irish identity which George Bernard Shaw had derided as ludicrous in *John Bull's Other Island*. Like geography, language plays an important part in the transformation of Russia into Ireland[16] but other devices underscore familiar situations to which the audience is likely to relate:

> MARY: Oh, I'm stiff with the cramp — (*She goes*).
> DR. HICKEY: She will go in there and have several stiff drinks before her lunch.
> PETER: She's desperately unhappy, poor thing.
> DR. HICKEY: She will convince herself for a few, brief hours that she is — ecstatic.
> PETER: Who can blame her? Dreadful situation. What difference does it make, if the poor thing finds it easier —
> DR. HICKEY: You will forgive me sir, but you are talking dangerous nonsense — [*SEA*. 40].[17]

The characters' remarks about Mary's drinking habit echo the familiar speeches of capitulation found in Chekhov, speeches which reveal a fatalistic acceptance of an unfortunate destiny. Kilroy is however wary of overemphasis. He knows the danger of turning his adaptation of Chekhov into a pseudo-realistic portrait of yesterday's Ireland, and adds very few elements that give an Irish touch to the play. Though restricted in number, typically Irish details — some of them unpleasant, like alcoholism and the type of delirious ranting that results from it — are nonetheless sufficiently present to enable the audience to connect past and contemporary political situations.

While economic circumstances have evolved, the perception of Dr. Hickey and James as Catholic outsiders, together with the Anglo-Irish schizophrenia, contains strong echoes of the present state of affairs. In this respect, the geographical transposition and literary assessment of a specific era that Kilroy makes in his adaptation of Chekhov prove politically significant. Indeed, they represent the first steps in an attempt to question and redefine a non-colonial Irish identity. For this purpose, Kilroy resorts to the play within the play, proceeding from the principles that if theatre is a place of artifice, it can also bring some truth when it exposes itself as a mere show. Constantine's play, rejected by his mother as "One of those Celtic things" [*SEA*. 13], proves interesting in that an outsider — an Anglo-Irish playwright — deals with the issue of Irish identity. He seeks a cultural foundation beyond present divides, and traces the way to discover new roots through an approach that disregards colonialism.

LILY: Once in every thousand years I speak out and my voice is a voice in the emptiness. And I shall speak again until the spirit of Darkness is defeated and the spirit of Light shines over the land of Banbha [*SEA*. 28].[18]

From what is staged in the play, one understands that the spirit of Darkness rules. In his search for renewal — one not limited to the theatrical arena — Constantine aspires to a spiritual rebirth.[19] The fact that an Anglo-Irish character initiates the quest for identity should be noted because the distant references in time — "once in every thousand years" — invalidate Catholic claims of a unique and authentic Irish identity. In his first steps toward a redefinition of Irish identity, Constantine partly seeks answers in legends, which deny the relevance of present religious divisions. Once pre-Christian times become the accepted framework of reference, British colonialism is reduced to an episode, a period of darkness during which people wait for the spirit of Light to reveal to them who they really are as Irish individuals, and not as the bearers of predefined and stifling social masks.

Chekhov's play *The Seagull* parallels the tragic fate of a bird with that of a fallen woman. One may wonder to what extent, in Kilroy's adaptation, the destiny of the seagull or of Lily does not also become that of Ireland in relation to England and the British Empire. As a country chosen then left alone in its struggle for survival, the consequences for Ireland are close to those experienced by Lily. Proximity means destruction because of the loved one's lack of response. Therefore, links need to be severed so that life may start again, different, plain, perhaps offering few perspectives of success, but at least providing Lily, and maybe Ireland, with the opportunity to be themselves. This point concurs with Kilroy's work as an adaptor and the new bonds that it establishes with world literature. Being unable to shed the burden of a colonial past is similar to the fate of Constantine, who finds himself in a deadlock. He cannot summon up the strength to start a new life, a desperate echo, possibly, of the quandary that afflicts contemporary Northern Ireland. On the other hand, Lily shows him the way, by accepting an unflattering self-definition which nevertheless has the merit of affording her partial disconnection from her past and from the historical past that casts its shadow on Ireland. Obviously, Kilroy is too subtle and cautious to turn *The Seagull* into a political tract. However, one feels that he might favour self-assertion for Ireland and Irish people, and that his adaptation of Chekhov's *Seagull* represents a personal example of such a belief. Consequently, Lily's advice regarding her mental acceptance of what she is may also be understood in terms of a hoped-

The Seagull. Photograph by Suellen Fitzsimmons. From left to right, Mary Rawson, Alex Coleman, Jarrod Fry (Constantine), Catherine Moore, Martin Giles, Jessica Bates (with wings spread), Ben Lawrence, Darren Eliker, Helena Ruoti, Michael Ramsay, Hal O'Leary, Mairtin O'Carrigan. Pittsburgh Irish and Classical Theatre, Pittsburgh, PA, 2001 (courtesy of Suellen Fitzsimmons).

for, beneficial and final disconnection of Ireland from the former British Empire. She thus sums it up: "what matters is being able to go on with some small dignity within oneself. That's all, really I feel that, now. I'm not afraid of being alive anymore" (85).

10

Conclusion

Rather than finish on a single perspective, which would be contradictory to the principle of this book, in which other people express their views on the theatre of Tom Kilroy, I should like to conclude in a rather open way. First, I highlight some significant features of his works, inviting readers once again to further their acquaintance with the playwright, before giving a more personal view of the plays.

To cast a final look on the plays, it might be useful to remember the pre-playwriting stage of his career, when Kilroy published the famous and seminal essay "Groundwork for an Irish Theatre," in order to trace a few close or distant echoes of this article in his dramatic production. As a starting point, in "Groundwork for an Irish Theatre," he stressed the need to push aside a literary heritage which hindered the emergence of new dramatic forms.

> Too often the view from our modern Irish windows is cluttered-up with distracting monuments to the dead and glorious past of politics and art.[1]

He expressed his discontent at the worrisome state of Irish theatre, and later indirectly conveyed this message in his dramatic works. Both the content of his plays and his cravings for a renewal of the aesthetics of Irish theatre went against standard expectations on the Irish stage at the time. However, his rejection of the past turned out to be less radical than one might have expected, judging from the intensity of his condemnation of conventionality. He successfully overcame the danger which an automatic rejection of tradition might have caused, leading to uninspired provocative plays built upon a mechanical inversion of conventional models. Like those of other aspiring dramatists, Kilroy's "modern Irish windows" were cluttered up with the works of his predecessors. Still, his scope of reference extended beyond the confines of Ireland. Consequently, his wide knowledge of theatre may have helped him in his compulsory distancing from Irish traditions. Former Irish dramatic models may also have proved less troublesome to eradicate than he imagined when he wrote his challenging article, because of the intensity of his aesthetic and thematic quests.

Another significant feature in his initial critical outlook on the state of Irish theatre was the idea of theatre resting upon collaborative work.

> It is useful to look upon the theatre as a community. The writer is just as much part of this community as the actor, director and designer.[2]

Initially, he insisted on this point because he hoped that the particular dynamics of a community would enable future playwrights to find renewed but adequate modes of expression through collaborative activities. Up to now, for the first productions of his plays, Thomas Kilroy has remained faithful to his original desire for an encounter with the stage. Being involved — included in the staging process — remains a necessity for him, not merely because it turns the author into a living stage director who can shed light on unclear aspects of the text, but also because, on an intellectual level, rehearsal proves vital for the pursuit of his continued aesthetic explorations.

His original insistence on "theatre as a community" was sincere, and attending a rehearsal never meant challenging the role of the director. The author's role is that of an active guest, who simply contributes to the communal work of the staging process. Judging from his experience of production, the playwright enjoyed working with directors who provided creative interpretations of his plays, which implied that the author's part remained limited.

The stage is a place where the text sometimes comes to life in unexpected ways. Starting from it, directors and actors build their own version of the play in ways which might not correspond to the author's original vision. Moreover, while the text is more than a blueprint, rehearsals may lead to alterations. The author's note for *The Madame MacAdam Travelling Theatre* illustrates the point: The text of the play as printed may differ from that of performance [*MMTT.* viii].

One should be careful not to equate this statement with an expression of authorial impotence. Thomas Kilroy's writing strategy merely takes into account performance as the place where the final touch is given to the play, hence the potential changes which he mentions. His acknowledgment of the provisional status of the text implies that he accepts the possibility of a post-writing collaborative work — a direct echo of his initial vision of "theatre as a community." While not a draft, the text of the play is finished but comparable to a musical score in that it is open to interpretations, a point which helps define the nature of the Kilroyan dramatic approach.

In "Groundwork for an Irish Theatre," Tom Kilroy condemned Irish theatre for not being "rooted in the society which supports it."[3] If one judges his work by his own standards, one notes that most of his plays relate to Irish society. However, even when the playwright chooses public figures as his main characters (Matt Talbot, Oscar Wilde, Hugh O'Neill...), the audience might not consider that his works are "rooted in the society which supports them," because Kilroy refrains from creating pseudo-authentic images of reality. His plays extend far beyond a parochial range, but the apparent rootlessness does not result from this enlarged perspective. It proceeds from his refusal of any superficial, expected approach of the issues at stake. For the author, a "theatre rooted in the society which supports it" implies probing into the depths of obscure realities. In other words, he never provides reassuring mirror images of reality. He challenges the notion of unified reality because, according to him, a playwright has to delve into the core of a complex, multilayered universe. He meets his own criteria, drawing nourishment from society, and bearing dramatic fruits thanks to which the community can thrive, but paradoxically the authenticity of his dramatic search forces his audiences to call into question traditional social visions.

The next point is a follow-up to the previous one:

> Our dramatists today are inclined to shirk the painful, sometimes tragic problems of a modern Ireland which is undergoing considerable social and ideological stress. The serious dramatist should fulfill the role of commentator on current values, practising espionage for everyman [195].

Thomas Kilroy never tried to be a successful but shallow entertainer, and he corresponds to what he defined as a "serious dramatist." Acknowledging this point, which no one could seriously challenge, leads to a question about the sort of commentator he turned out to be. Expressions such as "social and ideological stress" and "current values" create a number of expectations about what a playwright should be. In "Groundwork for an Irish Theatre," the importance of politics means that the playwright should be politically involved, which only partly corresponds to the content of the plays. Indeed, for Thomas Kilroy, being a serious dramatist implies refusing ready-made visions — whatever their political side might be — in order to stage the very complexity which one-sided political perspectives reject. As a "commentator on current values," he favors multiple outlooks, and the central element which characterizes his social commitment is that he privileges a dramaturgy of questioning to one of assertion. The tension between farce and serious philosophical reflection helps define the role he assigns to theatre in contemporary society. In doing so — and the importance of questioning proves vital for most of the plays — Thomas Kilroy addresses deep social, religious and existential issues.

In his representations of history, for instance, he challenges usual viewpoints, and introduces doubts to question the relevance of narrow historical outlooks. He also highlights the masks of his characters in order to underline their alienation, resorting at the same time to varied dramatic modes to expose the omnipresence of hidden realities. Seen from tragic to comic angles, his protagonists often appear under different guises, illustrating conflicting images of the self. In many works, the author invites spectators to meditate upon life as a system of representations, and stresses the inanity of unquestioned beliefs. His queries about identity, sanctity, the image of others, or of life as a mask, force the audience to follow an intellectual path set with various traps revealing multiple forms of delusion.

As for the continuity of the playwright's social commitment, one notes that political topics seem less central in his latest works. Not that he disregards them, and his characters still question accepted ideas, but in the more recent plays more intimate interrogations prevail. His meditations on life have more to do with unanswered philosophical questions than with formerly compelling political issues. On the other hand — central to his work — his continued reflection on theatricality and on the essence of theatre has remained unchanged.

A major critique in "Groundwork for an Irish Theatre" was that people deluded themselves with the pseudo "dramatic wealth" of the Dublin stage. Consequently, the lack of "creative theatre" explained the need for a renewal of dramatic styles. In this respect, one may consider that Thomas Kilroy has fulfilled the expectations raised by his article. Rejecting conventional models, he has brought to the Irish stage a different way of approaching theatre, both through the content of his works, and through unconventional techniques.

Like other dramatists of his generation, his adaptations of Pirandello, Ibsen, and Chekhov have widened the scope of what the public could see on Irish stages. On an individual level, he has brought original perspectives to life since his writing ventures have often been attempts at creating new dramatic forms. Faithful to his belief in collaborative work, his innovation has come from a thoughtful exchange with designers, lighting designers, movement directors, stage directors, actors, and musicians. A list of the plays would show how, at different times of his career, he has had a close interaction with members of the theatre community, which showed in the text of the plays.

To a certain extent, one could characterize Kilroy's theatre as a theatre of the unexpected. This is not merely due to his use of distancing techniques, to which he resorts less systematically than Brecht. In the circumstances, distancing not only means questioning in performance, but for the playwright it also includes a continued examination of what it means to write a play, involving an endless reflection on the aesthetics of theatre.

The strength of Thomas Kilroy's plays extends beyond the intensity of his dramatic quest and his skilful use of dramatic techniques. It results from a capacity to meet the deepest interest of spectators. Even in the darkest plays, the author's message always remains positive, because of his firm belief in the meaningfulness of an almost absurd existence. Attempting to reveal some hidden truth, Kilroy sheds rather unflattering lights on the human condition, but shows some empathy for the frailties of his characters. He thus responds to the challenge raised in the essay "Groundwork for an Irish Theatre," which consisted in not shirking "the painful, sometimes tragic problems of a modern Ireland which [was] undergoing considerable social and ideological stress."[4] To do this, the playwright sometimes resorts to comedy so that the audience may face the moral nudity of his characters. Provided they do not restrict their views to the latent darkness of the author's writings and his unswerving depiction of the harsh vicissitudes of life, spectators may receive Thomas Kilroy's meditations on existence and human beings as a breath of fresh air.

Part II
Interviews

11

An Interview with Thomas Kilroy, 2001

by Paul Brennan and Thierry Dubost

First published in Etudes Irlandaises, *September 2001.*

PAUL BRENNAN: In one of your plays, Tom Kilroy, *Double Cross*, one character declares: "There are Irish and there are Irish and then there are other Irish." What kind of an Irishman is Tom Kilroy the playwright?

THOMAS KILROY: Well, I take it you mean as a writer, as an Irish writer rather than as a person?

BRENNAN: Yes.

KILROY: I would see my playwriting as not being very typical of the contemporary Irish theatre scene in the sense that the kind of prevailing style, or prevailing image of Irish playwriting is strongly realistic. It's social, sociological, a theatre of contemporary realism, what we say in English, "in your face realism." My work is, on the contrary, highly stylized, a kind of theatre of artifice, one which may use realistic elements, but which in effect, asks its audience to suspend its sense of realism. So, I would say I would not be very typical in that regard. Now, I'm not alone, working in this kind of non-realistic theatre. There are people like Tom MacIntyre and Frank McGuinness who would share something of the same kind of use of the stage.

THIERRY DUBOST: Playwrights often declare that attending the performance of their works can be an ordeal, possibly because of the discrepancy between what they wished to convey and what they see performed on the stage. Have you suffered in this respect?

KILROY: Actually this has to do with the relationship between the playwright and the director. If that relationship is a collaborative one, where the director is more than just simply an interpreter, where the director becomes, as it were, a kind of helping presence, or helping genius in the creation of the work, then the experience of rehearsal, the experience of production is always exciting and good. And I have been very fortunate in my relationships with directors, both Irish and English on first productions of my plays, so that I enjoy that particular relationship. And for that reason, my work for the theatre is always in a preliminary state when I come to rehearsal. Now this is in sharp contrast to someone like my friend Brian Friel, who produces an absolutely finished text, and whose relationships with directors have not been entirely happy over the years. I mean he's had wonderful productions, but he himself would have an ambivalent attitude to the function of director. He and I differ greatly on this. I see the director as someone who will help you to imagine the final text.

DUBOST: The next question is a follow up on the previous one. What positive lessons as a playwright, have you drawn from seeing your works performed? You mentioned stage directors, but what about actors, what about the staging of the play itself?

KILROY: Well, there is this thing that actors will say to you that they are incapable of saying a line, or sometimes, they will say "he or she would never say this." Now, again, some playwrights find this very intrusive, and very impertinent. I actually trust actors. Actors very often cannot articulate why they feel this, you know. But they become so possessive of the character that they will, as it were, challenge you. Is this authentic to this character? I find that by and large, when that kind of question comes up in rehearsal, it's a very very good question, and that in some way, you have allowed a distortion into the writing, which you then try to repair. Now that's a small example of the kind of things, which I get of value out of rehearsals. I don't attend all rehearsals, because I believe that there should be a period in rehearsal where they can bitch about you. You know, where they can kind of attack you and say all kinds of things and in fact, where they can have a period of play. So that's usually around about the third week. And I go away (*chuckle, laughter*) on that occasion, and come back then for the final technicals, and the final polishing.

BRENNAN: Can this dialogue with the actors bring about a change of text, a rewriting of the text? To what extent?

KILROY: I don't think it would... I would not want to give the notion that I arrive at rehearsal with a completely unformed text. I think that the text is formed, and I think that the conception of character is formed. What it does do is that it, for example, it helps you — and me in this instance — in cases of overwriting, or in cases of an elaboration which might take the character in a wrong direction. So that, by and large, it's a very good dialogue. Now, I also have to say that there are performances in my plays which I don't approve of. You know, which I would feel are actually not the performance that I would want for a particular part. But that's what theatre is about. Theatre is a communal thing and I don't think that the playwright is an authoritarian figure in that community. There is a fate attached to every play, and the fate is its production.

DUBOST: In the case of Eugene O'Neill — we mentioned him before the interview — there would be huge cutting of the text during the production. You seem to mention changes, but very slight changes of the text itself, what about their length? Just a few sentences rewritten or...

KILROY: Yes, it would not be very much more than that. I mean the cutting is very important because for a play to work across a period of time, it has to have an energy which cannot be lost, and there are moments in writing where you may actually lose it. You know, even very skilful playwrights will lose this rhythm, this energy, and rehearsal will rediscover it. So that a good director, or indeed a good actor will find ways of making jumps, or making adjustments, or even moving script around to restore that energy. It's an instinctive kind of thing. The thing about playwrights, directors and actors, is that they all carry audiences inside their heads. And so they are testing stuff against audience reception all the time, particularly actors who are alive to this. So that you listen very carefully to what they have to say about keeping this energy going.

DUBOST: In the stage directions of *Double Cross*, one reads that the portraits of the King, Churchill, and Oswald Mosley become those of Goebbels, Hitler, and Mosley. I can't help thinking that such a change (two sides of the same coin) is not merely due to the needs of stage-directing. I see it as a wish to keep a distance, to refuse to condemn individuals on either side. Can that be interpreted as the wish of a playwright to avoid the trap of writing one-sided plays? If such is the case, how, as an individual this time, can you explain your point of view, about the interchangeability of roles? As a Frenchman, I find this lack of difference rather disturbing, namely can the holocaust be put on the same level as the bombing of Dresden, for instance?

KILROY: I think that that strikes to the heart of what I'm trying to write about in a lot of plays. The first thing I would say is that of course, there is a scale. There is a gradation of evil, and one is constantly aware of that. But I would add to that the fact that every human being is capable of profound evil. It just depends on what kind of mechanism civilization has created to keep that under control. You know I believe the human race is actually at a very primitive level of evolution. Given the kind of vision and insight that we have about human possibilities, we are a long way from anything like fulfilment. Now the distancing thing, it seems to me, is also crucial, because when I think of my own work, I mean the Irish writing that I admire most is the writing out of the Anglo-Irish culture. I admire the Anglo-Irish writers precisely because of their distancing from their material. The creative distancing, in the way for instance in which Synge looks at peasant Ireland. It is not realistic, never was, never intended to be. It's an elaborate, highly artificial treatment of peasant life. But highly artistic, with a very fine aesthetic sense. That is the kind of work I like, and it is the kind of thing which I get into my plays, I hope. When it's related to morality, it seems to suggest a kind of relativism. It seems to suggest a lack of fixed point, but I believe I am a very moral writer. And all I'm simply saying is that the kind of black and white, stereotypical morality is totally inadequate to account for human behaviour. And morality is a process of constant vigilance, and of constant discovery.

DUBOST: So, you're very optimistic for the very long term.

KILROY: Yes, very optimistic.

BRENNAN: But in the very long term?

KILROY: Well, I think we were talking about this today. I am fascinated by contemporary biotechnology. I have no doubt whatsoever that if we don't blow ourselves apart, or if Saddam Hussein doesn't get all his germs out into the air, that biotechnology will in fact accelerate evolution.

DUBOST: I was concerned about this lack of distance between the two sides, because I was afraid of a rather quick reading of your plays that would entail a vision which would become nightmarish in the long term.

KILROY: Sure.

DUBOST: That's why I wanted to ask this question.

KILROY: Well, you know, that particular play, *Double Cross*, was written out of a kind of rage. A rage against the whole nature of fascism. A rage against the kind of power residing in role playing, in costuming, in uniforms, a rage against militarism, and I was writing about two characters, two figures, that really came out of anger in me. Now, you can't actually produce something worthwhile on that level. So, what actually happened to me was that I had to find within myself a lot of empathy for these two individuals, or at least understanding, or whatever. But the distancing, I think, has to do with, again, kind of forcing the audience to cut loose from easy solutions.

DUBOST: Have French writers influenced you?

KILROY: Well, the first thing about that is that my knowledge of French would be so limited that I would be relying upon translations anyway. But, as a young man, I read a great deal of people like Claudel, and Mauriac. In the theatre, well, Beckett. You know, we look upon Beckett as somebody who actually, in some curious way, bridges our two cultures. There was one particular production, I go to theatre when I come to Paris, which is as often as I can, and there was one particular production which had a profound effect upon me, and in fact still stays with me, and even stays behind my latest play. This was a production at the Odéon, before the students tore it apart, a production by Maurice Béjart, with Jean-Louis Barrault. It was a stage adaptation of Flaubert's *La Tentation*. It was an extraordinary production, a kind of total theatre in its day. The big influences upon me in that period were the Royal Court theatre in London and seeing shows like that. I also saw a Polish company in Paris, around about the same time, a kind of a mime company. Coming from Dublin theatre and seeing this kind of work in the sixties was just mind-blowing. So, those are the things really that stand out for me.

DUBOST: Why Claudel? Does it come from your shared interest in Eastern civilization?

KILROY: Yes, there was that. There was also obviously at that period of my life the fact that I came straight out of Catholic culture, and Irish Catholicism. And to have, in the case of Claudel a kind of intellectual mind working in and through the Catholic thing was fascinating for me. We were talking about Mauriac earlier today in relation to John MacGahern, Mauriac was immensely exciting because one recognized so much in the novels. Now, I don't have the same kind of rapport at the moment with contemporary French writing, for whatever reason, but they would kind of be there in the genesis somewhere.

BRENNAN: The bridges to French culture, there would be several bridges, wouldn't there? There would be the Beckett bridge, which is not a Catholic bridge, and then there would be Mauriac and there would be this other bridge, wouldn't there, linking the two cultures?

KILROY: Yes, that's right. You know, as an academic, as a scholar, I would have read a certain amount of French literary theory, and I would have (*laughter*) lots of angry views on some of the theories involved, but you know I would have had some contact. Now I am not aware of contemporary French theatre, I would like to know more about that, but I would be aware of other matters.

DUBOST: What about the influence of Japanese theatre on your works? Do you see yourself as a successor of Yeats in this respect?

KILROY: Well, I am one of these people who actually admire Yeats's plays a great deal. I think it is very difficult to find a theatre, a contemporary theatre, which can house these plays properly. The interest in Japanese theatre really came about in the last six or seven years perhaps. I went to Japan as part of the Irish Studies escapade. I went out on a conference. It was just a week-end conference, and they organized this little lecture tour to go with the week-end conference, and at the end of it, I said to my host, I'd love to come back, and I thought no more about it. He suddenly came up a few years later with this extraordinary foundation thing in Kyoto University and I went there for about three months. While I was there, I saw a great deal of classical Japanese theatre. I found contemporary theatre very difficult to understand, to clue into, but I had very little difficulty responding to Bunraku and Kabuki and at a lesser extent, the Noh plays. So that, for example, the conception of puppetry in my most recent play, started out as a kind of use of Bunraku puppeteers. We lost those as the thing went on, and they became something else, but the notion of figures, mute figures on a stage manipulating things appeal to me greatly in relation to the Oscar Wilde material for a variety of reasons. I also was trying to play around with some techniques of Kabuki, of transformation of character in that play as well. But this is a fairly recent thing. You know I am not a poet, so I would not see myself in a Yeatsian line of succession in that way. But I do admire his work. I do admire the plays, and I think that they're dismissed unfairly.

BRENNAN: Talking about Yeats, that brings us back to the first Renaissance, but there's a lot of talk nowadays about a second literary renaissance in Irish writing. Would you agree, would you go along with this idea that there is today a second literary renaissance, and if you do agree with it, how can it be explained?

KILROY: Well, I think there's a great *quantity* of writing — an extraordinary quantity of writing. For thirteen years or so, we ran in University College Galway a national writers' workshop and I sometimes blame that for a lot that has happened since (*laughter*). The workshop was run by a different established writer each year, John MacGahern did it one year and whatever. It covered fiction, theatre, poetry, and so on. Many of the younger writers that took part in that workshop are now established writers. But the quantity of writing, and the sheer output is just overwhelming at the moment. Now I think that the quality is very uneven. For me, the most interesting material is in fact coming from young women writers, and many of them, just kind of beginning. I would also say something else, and that is that the whole postmodernist thing, which we could talk about at great length, is in a way hostile to the product of the great writer. In many ways, postmodernist culture is antipathetic to the highly individualistic figure like the great modernists. And I don't think we do have a figure of that dimension, like a Joyce, or a Yeats, or a Beckett. I think it would be extremely difficult to see the circumstances contributing to that. One of the things about the modernist period is that the whole culture as it were, the whole edifice of culture, supported this product of a major, individualistic figure. We have wonderful writers, of course, but that notion of a writer as it were, totally comprehending a world, totally enclosing a world, totally as it were, fabricating a universe, I think that the whole postmodernist temper would be impatient with that. Instead, you have a different kind of momentum. A momentum of spreading the thing as wide as possible, the notion of the individualistic artist is not as important as the notion of art making as the property of all. And that momentum is huge and powerful at every level. It's at the level of publishing, it's at the level of university teaching, and it has percolated around, so that you have a great output of writing and it's wonderful to see people expressing themselves, but one wonders how much of it in fact will last. So, I would not call it a renaissance. I'd think of something else; it would be a kind of equivalent of film making in France. There's a lot of vitality, and many people are expressing themselves in every way but you don't see the major works too often, if that makes sense.

BRENNAN: So you wouldn't accept the idea of renaissance, you talk about vitality. Now, what about the other part of the question? That is, I spoke of an "Irish" renaissance, would you accept the idea of "Irish" vitality?

KILROY: Oh, yes. And that's one of the things which makes me question it, a literary renaissance, an art renaissance, who can explain why these things happen? But very often they happen at a point of revolution, or a point when there is a total disturbance, an impending disturbance in the culture. I think for example of the English renaissance under Shakespeare. A period where English culture was suffering profound anxieties as to what was going to happen after Elizabeth. You know, you had this kind of sense of things disintegrating and falling apart. In Ireland today, you have very little anxiety about the place. On the contrary, you have an immense outpouring of self-confidence, and achievement, and money-making (*laughter*). I don't think that is the kind of atmosphere in which you have a ... because great art is always disturbing, always something which is always profoundly questioning the nature of things. You don't have that really, I don't think you have it.

DUBOST: To come back to French culture, supposing that you had to teach a course on drama to our students and were asked to recommend three plays written by three different playwrights, what works would you choose? And why?

KILROY: We'd be talking about Irish playwrights, wouldn't we?

DUBOST: Not necessarily.

KILROY: I'll interpret it as Irish playwrights. I would do something like *The Herne's Egg* of Yeats, I would do *The Playboy of the Western World*, and I would do something of Beckett, *Endgame*, possibly. The reason why I would pick those three is that it would allow me to look at a particular kind of visionary quality in those three playwrights, Yeats, Synge and Beckett. I would also see those plays, as plays from which I have personally drawn a great deal of inspiration. For me, they are, all three of them, even though they are very different, all three would be life-enhancing, which is a curious thing to say perhaps about *Endgame*, but they would have this quality of theatrical vitality. Outside that, I suppose I would have a great difficulty as it were, going into the English language theatre outside Ireland, and picking just three plays, for this reason that I would be immediately faced with two very competing areas. One is classical English drama, which I would like to have a go at teaching, starting with Shakespeare and going through the Jacobeans, and coming up to the eighteenth century. That's one area, the other area is twentieth century American playwriting. You certainly couldn't as it were, mix those with any degree of coherence, I don't think. But like you, I would like to teach O'Neill, Tennessee Williams, and Albee, all those playwrights, Miller. I would have a ball teaching American plays.

DUBOST: To come back to Yeats, you chose *The Herne's Egg*, why not *Purgatory* which was Beckett's favorite play?

KILROY: *The Herne's Egg* for me is an extraordinary demonstration of ritual, which fascinates me, and it's ritual as violation. I mean the central thing in it is a rape, a multiple rape, but it's violation, which Yeats is portraying as something which is almost sacramental. So that there is that element in it; it's also a play which looks at the Irish saga material, all that world of Irish mythology in a most unusual way, in a very anarchic way. One of the key features of the three plays actually is that in each play is a disturbing look at life, and if you read *Endgame* as the work of an Anglo-Irish playwright rather than as a metropolitan playwright, then you can see it as a very disturbing look at the kind of prized connection of family in Irish social life.

DUBOST: I was very surprised that you should choose *The Playboy of the Western World* and *Endgame* because one play is very life enhancing, while the other one seems to be very bleak and pessimistic. It gives us a very dark vision of the world, I think. So I'm very puzzled by this choice.

KILROY: I don't see Beckett as bleak at all. I see Beckett as unswerving in the way he looks at things. And for me, that is a huge consolation. Now he looks at the phenomena of family, of paternity, and maternity in that play. I mean, Hamm, in addition to being the actor Hamm, or whatever, is also a kind of father figure, he is the authoritative figure, which Beckett would know from his own class. You know I'd love to see that play done some time with a real Anglo-Irish twist to it. But he looks at those things with such a degree of bravery.

DUBOST: Yes, but he is looking at the destruction of Man. I mean this is a total destruction of a father and a mother, and even the future is more than bleak. So I guess there is a sort of contradiction between a French vision possibly and an Irish vision.

KILROY: No, I think you're right. The play is very much a play of the early period of the Bomb. You know people were constantly living under the threat of total annihilation. It comes out of that as well. And that threat of total annihilation is always there in the twentieth century.

BRENNAN: So, to come back to your own writing, your play on Constance Wilde is coming to a very successful end in Dublin at the moment. Now in *Double Cross*, you mention Oscar Wilde's idea according to which one ought to turn one's life into a work of art. Do you share this view?

KILROY: No, I don't at all. I think it's one of the many things in Wilde, which come out of the Dandy, the dandified performer. That aspect of Wilde — it's intended to shock. But it's also part of the cult of art itself which Wilde shared. But he shared it as a kind of defence, a kind of way of keeping certain realities at a distance, and I wouldn't share it at all. I have a passionate belief in the value of art, but I see it as just simply just one limb of the human endeavour.

DUBOST: Well, coming back to the first questions. This is taken from your last play. "Everything runs together and runs in and out of everything else. But human beings cannot abide such glorious confusion. So, they invent what is called morality to keep everyone and everything in place." As a playwright, you seem to be very critical of morality but some people might say that promoting the abandon of moral values might lead us into meaninglessness. What do you think — bearing in mind what I said about Beckett?

KILROY: This is something we've talked about a bit already, isn't it, when we were discussing this question of distancing and so forth. The thing to remember about this statement is that it's the statement of Douglas in the play. It's a statement which he attributes to Wilde — Wilde being his kind of mentor or father figure. It is contradicted by Constance. Really what I was trying to do in the play without being too schematic about it, was to set up two different world views, one of which is represented by Constance and the other represented by the Wildian gay frivolity and that whole world of Douglas and Wilde. The Constance point of view would be one which would demand a visible morality, a coherent system of morality. The Wilde view would be that in fact, one can't rely on that; one has to explore life in all its dimensions, and out of that achieve some degree of meaning. Both of them are ways of trying to find meaning, it seems to me. And I would say this: neither is offered in that play as a model. All that is offered as a model is the model of the conflict between the two sides. And as far as I am concerned, I think that when morality becomes systematized, it becomes calcified and rigid, and — maybe this is somebody talking out of the Irish Catholic background — when it becomes systematized, when it becomes ideological, then in fact, it ceases to be of all that much use in life, unless you want to retreat into a fixed system and stay within that. Many people need that, and I wouldn't for one moment attack anyone for that reason. But it's not my way of doing things, and I simply feel that morality is something that one discovers. I also think that Beckett is a profound moral writer. But what he is simply saying is "this is my vision, this is what I see." It's a vision that actually takes in a totality. It's horrendous, but we live with it, and we laugh with it. For he's a great comic writer. So that, as I said before, is not simply a consolation, it's actually moral.

DUBOST: Maybe this was a French vision because we are missing a sense of morality at times, and we are about to fall down the cliff, and this kind of statement, the great notion of meaninglessness which is looming in the background of the everyday lives of people, is a sort of danger for us as contemporary human beings.

KILROY: Sure. I absolutely agree with you. I think that human beings are constantly living on the edge of the abyss. And the abyss is meaninglessness. The search for meaning, the discovery of meaning takes many, many different forms. But it is undoubtedly the one kind of heroic thing that keeps us in place. But I think that search is ongoing, it is never finished. I don't approve of teachings which would suggest that it's finished. I don't think it is, and I think you are at it until you drop.

BRENNAN: So, continuing on your play, *The Secret Fall of Constance Wilde*, you stated recently that this play was not a history play. Does that mean that Irish playwrights in general are abandoning history for new themes?

KILROY: I don't think that was what I was trying to get at. What I was trying to get at was the thing we talked about over lunch. That is if a history play is to be a play, is to be a work of imagination rather than a work of history, then you have to have some kind of personal possession of that. You have to find some kind of personal way into it. Otherwise, it will remain as a wordy reproduction of historical fact. You have to — in some way — engage it at a very personalized level. There is that. The second thing I think I was getting at was that more than any kind of historical play that I've written, this one tries to subvert the known history of the Wilde story. Partly by taking the play from the point of view of Constance, but also the fact that Constance is very deliberately an invention. That is to say, she is not the historical Constance. I don't think the Wilde is, either, in the play, but he's closer perhaps to the Wilde that we would be familiar with. But she is quite distinctly an invention on my part. Therefore, the historical value of this play is pretty limited. I think that young Irish writers and young Irish students and intellectuals are very dismissive of history. Not only are they dismissive of it, history does not simply register with them to the extent that it did with preceding generations. So that when you talk to Irish students now, you have a sense of youngsters who are engaged in the immediate moment, and it reminds me very much of American students. Maybe it is part of the Americanization that is going on. But it's the immediate sensation of the here and now; and the colour and the taste and the smell and the sound of that. That's what is important to them. And I think that the writing reflects this, like that Alex Johnson play we talked about, the new cinema which they are producing. When it's not pastiche of the American film noir, it's an attempt to try to catch something that's passing right across in front of them at the moment. So yes, I think that history is in danger.

BRENNAN: So the immediate moment would be the sort of vitality that we spoke about earlier on.

KILROY: That's right. It's the new money. It's the new confidence...

BRENNAN: It's the seven per cent of the Celtic Tiger.

KILROY: Yeah, it's all of that (*laughter*).

DUBOST: In the same work, one reads, "what you have to understand is that we women are trained from birth to conceal." Writing a play with Oscar Wilde as a character was a challenge but what interested me most was the question of identity. Changing the word "women" into "Irish," would I be right to state that one meets here with an essential issue, which I would call the curse of the Irish, namely the impossibility of being oneself?

KILROY: Well, you know, I was talking recently to an Irish feminist. She was talking about the struggle of feminism in Ireland as being one of a struggle with what we call in English, low self-esteem, in women. We talked about this for a while, and she was saying that the Irishmen did not have this because of their patriarchal role in traditional Irish society and that this has not changed, and so forth. But I was arguing with her that in fact the low self-esteem — as you have rightly suggested — was actually a character of the Irish world, men and women, wherever it came out of. It led to all kinds of things, including a fascination with role-playing. So that they say in Ireland: "he is a great character." What it means in fact is that he performs; he may even adopt several different roles in performance; he is a storyteller. And these are all activities which are brilliantly colourful, but they are in fact connected to the other thing that you're talking about, which is the kind of impatience with relying upon yourself, the inability to rely upon yourself. Now, like everything else, I think that this is changing. I think that this is going to be less a feature in the future. But certainly it is there. I mean, the postcolonial scholars will give you all kinds of explanations of this, as indeed will the feminists in relation to Irish women. But there is a new self-confidence, and this new self-confidence actually is itself impatient with the role-playing. So that the kind of "broth of a boy" Irishman who dominates the pub is now an out of date figure. I think that the kind of pious Irish woman who subjects herself to a kind of a nunnish life, even if she is not a nun, I think that young Irish women will find that stereotype a gross irrelevance.

DUBOST: I was actually connecting your works with those of Eugene O'Neill, and thinking of Irishness in terms of being in the United States, and being Irish in the United States being a challenge. If the characters fail to take it up, they are destroyed. Only if they accept to be Irish can they be themselves and then stop this degrading process which leads to the destruction of characters. I was wondering whether there was not a link — a sort of danger, once again cropping up in Ireland today — in that there was a loss of identity because you said that American identity could be found everywhere.

KILROY: Well, you know the American quality of self-invention and self-development, and self achievement, that kind of thing which we associate with America at its best. I think that that quality is related in turn to the nature of capitalism. It leads to horrendous things for that reason as well, but that kind of model of behaviour, and model of aspiration and of ambition is certainly coming into Ireland, and it is also creating the kind of social problems which we associate with American capitalism. We have a very rapidly changing pattern of income in Ireland and for the first time ever, we have very wealthy twenty years olds, thirty-year-olds, and we have the gaps widening. Irish poverty was always a thing which virtually every Irish family would have had some association with. Now this is changing beyond belief. In the case of O'Neill, my sense of O'Neill was someone who carried with him — in his bones — a lot of the kind of tribalism of his Irish background. I think he was haunted by several of these burdens, you know. To that extent, in some respect — a strange thing to say — he does not come across as a typical American writer.

DUBOST: Yes, and he once declared: "the most important thing about myself is that I'm Irish."

BRENNAN: We were talking about low self-esteem. Maybe our interview is very postmodernist because we haven't yet mentioned the word "English," so would you agree that this low self-esteem is a sort of a pure product of colonialism? Of English colonialism?

KILROY: That has to be part of it. For example, in relation to writing. Irish writing is pervaded with the presence of English literature. In all kinds of different ways. It's also dominated by the English market place and the outlet of English publishing and English agents and all of that. So, you have that element there. It has led to distortions in Irish writing. It has led to a kind of distorted writing towards that kind of market. There is also the fact, in another kind of way, that the English readership and English audiences get certain notions of what Irish writing should be. And they have great problems with something which actually breaks away from it. A very good example is John Banville, who is not a typical Irish writer in many respects, and they have great problems with John Banville in Britain, including his last book, which was actually a superb pastiche of the English themselves. So, that kind of Irish writing, and I think the same might even be true of some aspects of Oscar Wilde, when they break the mold... But the English are very happy with Irish peasant plays, or with realistic Dublin street drama, or novels...

BRENNAN: Roddy Doyle, for example.

KILROY: That's Irish.

BRENNAN: That's Irish? Roddy Doyle is Irish?

KILROY: Yes, Roddy Doyle is Irish, whereas Banville would be looked upon as something bizarre.

DUBOST: De Gaulle, during his press conferences, when he was President would sometimes pretend he was asked a question on a subject he wished to treat. He would then go ahead and answer his own question. It is your privilege today to do likewise and choose the last question for this interview.

KILROY: I haven't a clue. The only thing I could think of is perhaps what I'm working on now. I'm just finishing a novel. This will be just my second novel. I'm about to start on the second draft of a screenplay of one of my plays for Channel 4. I'm moving gradually towards a new play, a new stage play. I was reminded of it, talking about John Banville's novel. It's a new stage play, which will have to be written for a London company, because it's a play about William Blake, the eighteenth century English poet. So there, I'm selling out (*laughter*).

DUBOST: Thank you very much indeed.

KILROY: Thank you.

12

An Interview with Thomas Kilroy, March 8, 2004

Writing Process

THIERRY DUBOST: Tom, I'd like to start the questions with the writing process. In 1971, you published *The Big Chapel* but after this initial success, you've limited yourself to playwriting. Why?

THOMAS KILROY: Well, I think that playwriting represents the best outlet for my particular kind of talent. That's a general answer. Actually, *The Big Chapel* may be coming back into print. The curious thing about it is that very recently I was asked by RTE, the Irish radio, to do a radio play based upon *The Big Chapel*. I went back and read it, and found that the thing was very alive for me, to the extent that I found myself rewriting and I wrote a whole lot of new scenes for it, so that in any new version of it I would have new material. It's important for me because in fact I've gone back to writing fiction again. I've gone back to a piece of fiction which I started around about the time of *The Big Chapel*. I'm encouraged now to go back and see if I can make a novel out of it. I'm fascinated by the novel. I've taught the novel. I think that my reading of prose fiction has actually contributed in some ways to the different layers of my plays. So that I don't see them as two different citadels. I see them as related in my work, and I think that my novel has a lot of theatrical kinds of qualities to it.

DUBOST: How do you proceed when you write a play? Do you draw a sketch that physically represents the stage?

KILROY: Well, I think that the understanding, the sense of the world of the play is as important to me as the language. That is to say that each play invites or assumes a particular stage world, a particular kind of stage. A place where it happens, and this has to be there for me before I can actually start to write. Now, I sometimes make sketches, very rough sketches, but by and large, it's more imagining the stage where it's going to happen. Not the kind of setting in history or the setting in social reality, but the stage, and I think if you have this sense of a stage, then in fact you're part of the way towards being a playwright. You actually have to think of an artificial space, and how that space is dressed, how it's lit, and how you can actually move actors around on it. So that, yes, you have to have a very strong sense of space, I think. At least, I do, for my own work.

DUBOST: So, still in this writing process, could you give us examples? How do you remember your writing process concerning *The Secret Fall of Constance Wilde* or *Talbot's Box*, for instance, which are obviously major productions in terms of thinking about space during the writing process?

KILROY: It's a cumulative thing, I think, because you begin with an initial image, and it's a physical image. Then, as you develop the play, you are also developing the imagery, side by side with that. One is feeding the other. Then, the process actually does not complete itself until rehearsal, and until you actually see a ground plan, and you see scenic designers' design for the play. Then in fact you get, at least, I get additional inspiration. With *The Secret Fall of Constance Wilde*, the whole use of puppets, and as it were, a kind of circle on stage, a white circle on stage, this was there from the very beginning. So that I had this conception of the play that came to some extent out of my interest in classical Japanese theatre. Bunraku, particularly, where I was fascinated by the kind of conjunction of so-called real images and puppet images. It also came out of Wilde, and Wilde's fascination with puppetry, and with his whole idea of the actor as being a kind of marionette. It also had to do with the thematic concerns of that play, the fact that I was dealing with three people who were to some extent puppets of fate. You know that they were manipulated by forces that were actually bigger than anyone of them. So, it's an organic thing, rather than reaching for effects.

DUBOST. Has your writing technique changed between 1969 and today?

KILROY: That, I don't know. This is one that I would have difficulty answering with any kind of clarity. I think, possibly, less technique than preoccupations, in the sense that a play like *The O'Neill*, which is the very first play that I wrote had a lot of the stylistic interests that I still have today, such as making the stage a very prominent thing in the play itself. I love the staginess of plays, the fact that plays have this kind of artifice. I love drawing attention to the fact that what's happening is something happening on the stage, that is not competing with the world outside. So that, I think that's been there from the beginning, and that is very much part of the style.

DUBOST: In *Double Cross, Talbot's Box, The Secret Fall of Constance Wilde, Blake, The O'Neill* you chose famous people for the plays. Why did you choose them as models?

KILROY: I'm fascinated by history. I think that when you're fascinated by history, you are fascinated by the possibilities of changes in history, and of tampering with history. Playwrights who write historical plays love to find gaps in the record. I'm stimulated imaginatively by unanswered questions in history, or maybe taking a historical thing and twisting it, and seeing what would happen in the process. So, it's less a matter of famous people than of trying to, as it were, provide an imaginative record and competition with the actual record.

DUBOST: So you wouldn't start with an exhaustive biographical study of the characters, you would just tend to focus on a general outline...

KILROY: I read a great deal, but I read a great deal that in fact never appears in the plays, so.... It's just when the imagination is sparked off by something in the reading. When that happens, yes, I do read a great deal then, but I'm always trying to find the questions in the record, what the historian cannot answer. That, for me, is a kind of goal of the imagination, and it's the old thing, you know, that you do research for the creation of fiction in order to forget the research, and it's only when you can start to forget it that you take off.

DUBOST: In *Talbot's Box*, you used the idiom of the Dublin Streets. I should like to know whether it was a starting point that shaped the play, or if it came as an added feature when you were writing?

KILROY: Well, the first thing about that play is that this figure of Matt Talbot in Irish iconography, or Irish history, whatever you want to call it, is a very controversial figure. For me, he was a figure that you could have very little respect for. And I first started to write that play as an attempt to attack this icon, and to write a work of satire, of mockery. As sometimes happens, when the character was created, the character would not allow me to completely satirize him. In other words, he took on a dimension that I had to respect. I had to find some kind of respect for him. So, it's very strange. I mean, this is a play about a religious figure, I am an agnostic, and I was an agnostic when I wrote that, but I was fascinated by the hold that he had on the Irish people. I was trying to — as it were — undermine or attack the nature of that role which, for me, is sadomasochistic, and is the worst aspect of that type of religion, but what emerged was something entirely different. Now, that is moving somewhere towards your question, because to write a play about this figure, you had to write, you had to find the idiom of the Dublin streets, and when I came to do that, which is a question of ear, and of your ear telling you what it is, I came up against the huge figure of O'Casey. O'Casey's presence was so strong here. Now O'Casey is actually a playwright that I don't have a great deal of personal feeling for. I can admire his work and so on, but I also would be highly critical of a lot of O'Casey. So that I found myself parodying O'Casey in my play. There is a good deal of parody in it, almost mock O'Casey, which fitted in, I think, into the seriocomic tone of the work itself.

DUBOST: Do you read your plays aloud as you write them?

KILROY: I don't necessarily read them as I go, but again it is a question of ear, and it's almost a musical thing. The way I describe it is that the distinction between a playwright and a writer of a novel is that the playwright hears voices. Literally hears voices, so that you are like a nutcase, with these voices going on. It's not just a question of hearing the voice of a character. You create characters and then you very often create characters through hearing them first, not seeing them, not thinking of their characterization, their behavior or whatever, or their social history, but actually hearing the voice. When you do hear the voice, then in fact, you could go on indefinitely. The problem then is to stop the voice. But you have to hear something else as a playwright, and this is what's interesting. You have to hear the voice of character, but you also have to hear the actor speaking that voice, and that's the really difficult thing. If you don't have that second skill, you'll write dialogue, but they'll never be plays. They'll never work in a theatre. You actually have to hear an actor speaking. Now there are some playwrights who write specific parts for specific actors. I've done that myself in the past, and I didn't get the actor, but that didn't matter. I was able to hear the actor actually delivering the speeches. When you do hear that, then you know that you have what you might describe as an actable play. A play which can be acted. But you have to have that double thing, the voice of character and the voice of the actor.

DUBOST: A last question about the writing process. One finds a portrait of the writer in *Tea and Sex and Shakespeare* and in *The Secret Fall of Constance Wilde*. One feels there is a message about an almost unbearable loneliness of individuals. Were writers just an example, or did you specifically want to insist on the importance of the loneliness of the writer?

KILROY: I think it's really what you know. I think I do know a great deal about writers, and writer's habits and the like. But of course, the condition that you're talking about is only of interest if it's common to all people, and of course it is common to all people. I have a close friend of mine who is another playwright, an Irish playwright, who admired *Tea and Sex and Shakespeare*, but he said, why didn't you make it a plumber? He had a point, but on the other hand, if the character in that play were a plumber, you wouldn't have the particular kind of structure that the play has. I find writers — not all of them — but I find the whole burden of writing a fascinating topic, and it is a topic which actually allows me to explore what you've just said, which is in fact the loneliness of the human condition.

DUBOST: I'd like to move on to radio plays and television scenarios. I have two questions, the first one is: Why did you decide to write for the radio and television?

KILROY: There are occasions when you're actually asked to write something. For example, I'm writing a radio play at the moment for Irish radio, simply because I'm a friend of the producer and she said, would you please write a play for me. So, I'm writing a play about the making of the movie *The Quiet Man*, which was shot just a few miles up the road from where I live, and I know this countryside very well. I'm writing a play essentially about John Ford, and about the relationship between John Ford and John Wayne, and I'm having a lot of fun with it. It's going to be called *The Cowboy and the Colleen*. I don't know which of the two is the colleen, but I'm having fun with it anyway, but that's an example of where a radio play comes out of. The very first thing I ever wrote that was given a public hearing was in fact a radio play. I wrote that for a radio play competition, BBC competition. It won first prize and it was performed on BBC radio. The same is true of television. I was approached, really, by people, to know if I'd write for television. They are totally different media to theatre.

What I love about radio is the fact that there are limitless possibilities in the writing of a radio play. You can move anywhere, and into any time, you have this great freedom of movement in radio. Television is very different. As you know, it's a medium which is actually dominated by the camera. In a sense, like film, generally, it's not a writers' medium at all. It's a medium where the writer produces something which is then just simply worked on and worked up.

DUBOST: Were there changes in your writing technique?

KILROY: Yeah, I think the whole aim of writing for the camera is to write less, and to provide ideas, visual ideas. Providing visual ideas in a narrative or in story-telling is as important as language, more important than language. So, you have to kind of suppress your interest in words, and find another way of telling the story. It's very different.

DUBOST: I'd like to move on to intertextuality. You worked as a professor in many universities. Did this help your work as a playwright?

KILROY: Um, that's a difficult one, because there's a way in which the whole business of teaching and scholarly research, and the whole business of the academy cuts across imaginative work, and interferes with imaginative work. I remember having this conversation with Frank McGuinness, the Irish playwright, about this and the fact that you have to almost compartmentalize yourself, where you switch off, in order to enter into the world of the pure imagination. Having said that, I think my experience in the academy was very fruitful in this regard that it forced me into a very thorough knowledge of classical drama. So that my particular field was early seventeenth-century English theatre, but I taught drama right across the centuries over the years, so that I read a great deal of plays, a great number of plays, and this was bound to affect me, in the sense that it forced me to drop any kind of restrictions that I might have in relation to what was possible on the stage. For me, everything is possible on the stage, because we see this in the tradition of theatre itself, and that was a great — it was an education in every sense of the word, including an education as a playwright.

DUBOST: Yes, but conversely I was thinking of *Tea and Sex and Shakespeare*, and of the writer being overwhelmed in a way by Shakespeare telling him how to finish the play. I was wondering whether being a university professor teaching drama could be a hindrance to your work as a playwright.

KILROY: One reason why this particular play is a comedy is that one of the ways of tackling that huge presence of great theatrical work behind you is to make fun of it. If you take it too seriously, it could become a terrible drag, a terrible burden, so that in that particular play, I have fun with the large presence of Shakespeare who is, of course, just huge. But I think that you need to, you certainly need to fight the seriousness of scholarship, when you come to work at a practical level in theatre. You can't bring that with you.

DUBOST: Do you limit the level of intertextuality in the plays which are full of allusions, quotations, and variations on other texts, and which spectators may miss in performance?

KILROY: Yes, I think there is a serious danger of that, actually. Generally speaking, my plays are reduced versions of what I start out with. So that I am constantly trimming work, and losing as much as I can of the allusiveness which would actually just bother an audience, and be confusing. So, I would say that if you have a play which is too allusive, then in fact, it won't work entirely in theatre itself. It would block an audience. Audiences shouldn't be puzzled; you don't puzzle audiences. I mean the allusions are there for anybody who can get them, but hopefully the play will survive without them.

DUBOST: You have adapted Pirandello's *Six Characters in Search of an Author*, Ibsen's *Ghosts* and Chekhov's *The Seagull*. Why did you choose to adapt these three plays? The next question is a follow up to this one, how do they relate or not to Irish culture?

KILROY: Well, it's a bit like the cinema and radio thing, television and radio, in that each of these adaptations came about because I was actually asked to do them. *The Seagull*, I was asked by my friend Max Stafford-Clark, who at the time was artistic director of the Royal Court Theatre in London. He actually had the notion of transposing *The Seagull* into a west of Ireland Big House situation. It was his idea. It came out of his experience as a student in Ireland. He had just read *The Big Chapel*, and he felt that I might be able to do this kind of thing. *The Six Characters*, again came out of a request. Patrick Mason, who was artistic director of the Abbey Theatre, and the young director John Crowley, both approached me and said, would you do a version of *Six Characters?* Similarly, with *Ghosts*, Siobhan McKenna, who is now dead, the actress, and a woman called Phyllis Ryan, who is a very good independent producer in Dublin, both had the idea of doing *Ghosts*, updating *Ghosts* into an Irish setting. It was very much Siobhan's idea, and she was going to play the Mrs. Alving part, and then she died, unfortunately. I went ahead; Phyllis and I went ahead, and we did this thing as a memorial to Siobhan. So that in each of those cases, and right now I've just recently, in the last month, signed a commission to do a new version of another Pirandello, *Enrico Cuatro*, for an American director whom I admire very much, a young American director. He wants to do it as an off-Broadway production in 2005. I've started work on that. Now, I've been asked many other times to do adaptations, and I've tried to do them and I haven't been able to do them, so that it's a question of being asked to do something, and then actually discovering that you can do it. It may sound very prosaic, but that's the way it happens. With *Enrico Cuatro*, it's going to be, I think it's going to be a totally new contemporary play called *Henry*, but as a dedication, or as a great tribute, or a small tribute to the great writer Pirandello. So it takes the Pirandello idea, and tries to make a new play out of it. I actually think that good adaptations, no matter how much they depart from the original, always send you back to the original. But they send you back to the original with a fresh eye, hopefully.

DUBOST: You mentioned Pirandello; what about the influence of Brecht on your work?

KILROY: I came upon the whole Brechtian theatre in the sixties, at the time when the Ensemble made its first visit to London, and you had a whole spate of Brechtian style theatre in England at the time, and indeed, in Dublin. I absorbed a great deal of his theatre, and I think that a lot of it has stayed with me, in particular the whole attempt to create a public theatre. To create a theatre which addresses public issues. So that the private and the public, the obsession with this means that I draw upon the Brechtian notion of delivery, of delivering ideas, delivering stories that have a resonance that go beyond the individual.

DUBOST: In 1959, in a famous article entitled "Groundwork for an Irish Theatre," you stated "too often the view from our modern Irish windows is cluttered up with distracting monuments to the dead and glorious past of politics and art." Did that mean you wanted to break away — and possibly reject — a prestigious dramatic heritage of Ireland?

KILROY: The curious thing about heritage, the heritage of Irish theatre, is that the tradition of Irish theatre is very recent. Before Yeats and his compatriots, or his contemporaries, rather, before Yeats, you had no real indigenous Irish theatre, so compared to France, it's a very short period. Having said that, it's a very heavy tradition. I mean there was so much created across the twentieth century that you do have a very prominent heritage for a young playwright starting out. I think a lot of very young contemporary playwrights today just ignore it and get on with it, which is a healthy thing, but in my generation, you had to address that tradition in some fashion. Certainly, my generation, which would have been a generation which came into the theatre in the late fifties, and early sixties, we tended to be dismissive of what had gone before. Largely because we came in at a point where for the preceding couple of decades, the theatre was not the most exciting in Irish culture. So there was a certain iconoclastic motive in the writing of first plays. If you look at those plays, those early plays of people like Brian Friel, or Tom Murphy, John B. Keane, or Hugh Leonard, they tend to be plays that actually question the established ideas prevalent in Irish culture. They tend to undermine them, they tend to be iconoclastic. So, I would say yes, I certainly started out that way. I think in more recent times, I've become less involved, and tended to go off in my own direction.

General Questions

DUBOST: I'd like to move on to general questions. The first one is about dedications. You have dedicated your plays to actors, stage-directors, and friends, to two of your sons and to your parents. You may focus on the general question of dedication, but I should like to know why you chose to dedicate *Talbot's Box* to your parents.

KILROY: I've said earlier that I wrote the play as an agnostic, but in fact I come from a very religious family. My mother and father would have been both very conventional, Catholic, and would have come from a very traditional Catholic, Irish Catholic upbringing. So I wanted them to — well they were actually dead at the time — but I wanted them to witness this play in a certain sense, which is a play that looks at the religious thing from another point of view. It was kind of a response. In fact, my parents were hugely supportive of me as a writer. Absolutely, and from the very beginning. My first play that caused a certain reverberation in Dublin was *The Death and Resurrection of Mr. Roche,* because it used this figure of the homosexual man who was beaten up in it. I was actually quite worried about my parents' going to see that. Not only did they have no problem with it, but my mother showed a great deal of sympathy for this figure. And my father proceeded to tell me stories which were far better than the story in the play. He was a policeman, and he matched the story of the play with some very good stories of himself, so we often laughed about that afterwards. So they were conventional in that sense, but they were also quite remarkable people.

DUBOST: I feel that bodies play a major part in your works. Is this true, or is it a casual feature of your plays, starting with *Talbot's Box*?

KILROY: For me, theatre is very physical. In a sense, theatre is all about the human body on a stage, and of the different languages of the human body, not just the verbal, but the language of physique, of the way in which the physical body speaks to us. With great performers, you have a total physical performance, and that, to me, is the essence of theatre. It is the uniqueness of theatre in the sense that getting that in a theatre, you're getting something which cannot be reproduced on a camera, which cannot be reproduced in any other medium. It can't be even reproduced in great paintings, because you have a living human body on the stage. So that I start with that sense of awe, and of astonishment, it's an amazing thing to me to see great performers perform. Whether it's in dance or in straight theatre or whatever. Inevitably then, it seems to me that following that, plays themselves have to have something of this corporeal quality. A quality of flesh and the portrayal of living, active human bodies, so that it is true then that in quite a number of my plays, the actuality of the body becomes an important ingredient.

DUBOST: So, this was for the bodies on stage. Now, what about the mind? In all your plays, your characters mention religion. Is religion a compulsory subject in Irish drama?

KILROY: It's such a dominant feature of the culture, that if you write something with an Irish background, if you'd do this as a writer. In the fifties, in the nineteen-sixties, nineteen-seventies, or the nineteen-eighties, this is an inescapable phenomenon. Now, as you know, this has changed completely. It's gone, and it has happened so quickly that, again, people of my generation are quite startled that all of the preoccupations that we had, growing up, are now totally irrelevant. It's an immense joy to see this, but there is the other thing then that I think a lot of contemporary, young contemporary plays are filled with a nihilism and an emptiness, a spiritual emptiness, that there is a great kind of loss. It's a loss which I associate with repression and with subjugation of people, particularly of women, but it having gone, you wonder what is left. A lot of young playwrights are now writing out of a void, just an emptiness, a hole, so I don't know what's going to happen in the future.

DUBOST: That question is in *The Shape of Metal*.

KILROY: Yes, indeed.
DUBOST: Would you, like Oscar, in *The Secret Fall of Constance Wilde*, say: "Everything I write is autobiographical. With the facts changed, of course"?
KILROY: I think actually that everything that a writer writes in some sense, if it has any kind of quality to it comes out of the inner person. No matter what you are writing about, you're feeding off something internal to yourself, and to that extent everything is autobiographical. Having said that, when you give a character a line in a play, and in this instance I was trying to imitate something of the great Wildian epigram, when you give a character an opinion, or a definition, or a statement in the play, then it is not your statement. Your relationship to that could be close, could be distant, you know, it's not identical. In this instance, I was being ironical, and ironical in relation to myself, and in relation to the whole problem of writers, anyway. But I do think that it has to come out of the inner person, and to that extent, it's autobiographical.
DUBOST: In the opening scenes of *Talbot's Box* and *The O'Neill*, you start your plays with challenging situations for an Irish public. Do you consider that being a playwright is being a challenger?
KILROY: I do actually. Because of its very nature, theatre is confrontational, and it's also social. It's a very social art form. You have a crowd of people go into a room, sit in front of a stage, and they share, communally, share something, and they are sharing it at that moment. They're sharing something which is unique, which will be totally different tomorrow night, or will at least be different, so that there is that social quality to it, and to that extent, I think it relates to the world of that audience, initially. If it has any kind of lasting quality, it will relate to other audiences outside, but it does have that kind of local thing to it. But I also think that theatre, of its nature is confrontational; it provides conflict. Not all playwrights, some playwrights are very celebratory, and they offer consolations to the audience. I'm not that kind of playwright. I'm a playwright who — I enjoy meeting my audiences at a level of challenge, yes.
DUBOST: Then, how do you explain that in your works sexuality appears if not as a threat, at least, once again, as a challenge?
KILROY: I don't know, probably, it may well come out of my Catholic background. I think there's less in the more recent work. In the more recent work, I'm becoming much more interested in writing about women. I think there's a freedom in that. You know, there's a freeing up, certainly of treating the whole subject of sexuality. So that in something like *The Shape of Metal*, my most recent play, to a large degree it's about a woman who has this complete sexually free life, a life almost independent of men, a life which almost uses men, and moves on. This does allow a degree of freedom to me, as a man, writing about sexuality. I suppose to some extent, you could say that it catches up with her in the end.
DUBOST: What about the challenge of love? It seems to me, reading and rereading your plays, and thinking of *Blake* for instance, I came to the conclu-

sion — and I think it might be one of the opening statements about the chapter I wrote about *Blake*— that like all of your plays, *Blake* is a love play, it's about love.

KILROY: Yes, I think *Blake* is a good example to pick because this is a play about an extraordinary genius, maybe a madman, who had this vision of life — a bizarre vision of life — but a vision of life, nevertheless, and it made him into a figure who is larger than life. He kind of grew inside himself with this importance, and he is forced in the process of the play to come back down to earth by his wife, through love. I think that this is a pattern which I've touched on before, and it's one that I find fascinating and then I find it particularly fascinating in that sense that she was illiterate — she couldn't read or write — at the same time, she was the only one who understood what he was about. I love that kind of irony. I think that love, actually.... First of all, it is hard earned, you have to earn love, which is another line from one of my plays.

DUBOST: Yes, *The Shape of Metal*.

KILROY: Yes, you have to earn it, and then it is a great litmus test of human behavior. It's the test which actually quantifies the value of most living. And really, that's the heart of the Blake play, because she actually subjects Blake to that test, and he comes through, I think.

DUBOST: Very few children appear on stage in the plays, and yet reading the plays, one feels that childhood is crucial in your works. Is that due to technical motives?

KILROY: Well, it is a problem. Children on a stage, and child actors in a play create endless problems. It's the old joke of theatre, children and dogs, you avoid them. I did introduce children into the Wilde play as puppets. That was partly to get around that problem, but also to catch the way in which those children were puppets in life, as I think they were. For me the actual business of having children is one of the great mysteries. It is something which is endlessly questioning in the process of watching these children develop and so on, so it is a crucial part of the life experience of many of the characters that I write about for that reason, even though they're not present.

DUBOST: Bearing in mind the importance of images in your plays, who are your favorite painters?

KILROY: Um, I was thinking a lot about this question, because I think my favorite painters have nothing to do with my plays.

DUBOST: Really?

KILROY: Yes, I love impressionist painting, for example, just to take a small example, but I would not see it as having anything to do with my work as such. But then, there are painters that I find fascinating, who are highly theatrical, like Caravaggio, or a more contemporary, or neocontemporary painter like Francis Bacon, who actually paint events. They very often paint events at a highly dramatic point of crisis. I do think of those painters when I'm thinking of images for the stage. Again, there's a contemporary painter, well, he just recently died, an Irish painter called Tony O'Malley. I love Tony's work. I was a good friend of his, when he was alive, but I could never see his work as impinging upon anything I would do on the stage. But then, there are other Irish painters, contemporary Irish painters like Brian Burke, or whatever, whose work has this dramatic intensity, and they are certainly stimulating to the theatre-making side of my mentality.

Social Commitment and Theatre

DUBOST: In your adaptation of *Six Characters in Search of an Author*, an actor declares: "Theatre doesn't have to prove anything. Never has. Never will." This sounds like an authorial voice refusing any kind of assertion, and yet in *The Madame MacAdam Travelling Theatre*, *The O'Neill* or *Double Cross*, questioning becomes a way — if not of bringing proof — at least of asserting your vision of the world. In *Double Cross*, for instance, you subvert the ideology of nationalism, and doing so, I feel that you committed yourself. Is this true, or...?

KILROY: I think that it's virtually impossible to have definite statements in any art form. Because art of its nature is process, so that when you come across definitive statements or definitions in a novel, or a play, or a poem or whatever, you have to take them as provisional, because the context could in fact dispute the definition, as I think the context probably does in the Pirandello. But it's a way of, as it were, alerting the audience to an issue, so that a very definite statement like that, or a definite definition or denunciation or whatever, I would see those kinds of statements as having the same provenance as questions. I love questions. Questions too, in my work, don't necessarily seek answers. They're a stimulant, they're part of the engagement of the play itself. Having said that, I do have strong feelings about certain issues. I have very strong feelings about extreme forms of nationalism, and undoubtedly *Double Cross* was an attempt to subvert the kind of nationalism which creates monsters, human monsters. In that particular play, one had to have at the same time a sense of the humanity of those monsters.

DUBOST: How do you explain the concern for the denial of the self in your plays? This seems to be a major issue in your different works.

KILROY: In the sense of?

DUBOST: In various plays, there is this idea of the self not corresponding to a fixed image.

KILROY: Yes.

DUBOST: And also, thinking for instance of *Talbot's Box*, and of the character saying "No one can die for me!" this notion of being oneself, and being denied this existence by society. How do you explain this concern for the denial of the self in your plays?

KILROY: I suppose it's a preoccupation with the sense that the individual and one's individualism is threatened by a lot of what goes on in the world, whether it's politics, or institutions or whatever. There's a point at which the individual has to fight for survival, has to fight for the personal integrity, and personal authenticity, and that particular struggle is of great interest to me. I love the kind of moment when the individual with a sense of his or her own personal authenticity comes up against other forces, and that is part of the drama, of what I try to theatricalize.

DUBOST: In *The Shape of Metal*, the major character declares: "the young gather bits and scraps nowadays and call it sculpture. Bloody rubbish, that's what it is. Anyone can do it." Could one understand this as an indirect condemnation of contemporary forms of art?

KILROY: Well, for me this catches the kind of predicament of a sculptor who would have come out of a certain kind of classical training and classical tradition, as this woman would have. Faced with art forms today, which get away from the artifact, situational art, or art which employs a lack of fixed objects, whether it's through videos or whatever, art forms that are trying to pick up on the debris of contemporary living. So, it's *her* immediate reaction, it's not necessarily my own. I think that the ferment of contemporary art is actually quite fascinating and exciting. It has perhaps too much sensation for me. It certainly allows in a lot of stuff which is rubbish, but then maybe that's its subject, maybe its subject is rubbish in the corner, or whatever, but as far as this play is concerned, this woman would have very strong opinions about what she sees around her, and manifesting itself as art. Her opinions, and she is a very opinionated creature, I would share some of her opinions. For example, I would agree with her that some of the most exciting things that are happening imaginatively at the moment are happening in science, through the scientist. The scientist is very often fulfilling the role traditionally held by art, and that is imaginatively reconstructing reality. Some scientists are also beautiful writers, so that they're writing with great flair about their work. Some of the most exciting books that I read nowadays are books about science. So I would share that aspect of Nell's work, but not everything.

Field Day

DUBOST: Could you give us an outline of what Field Day was, and then tell us how and why you came to join Field Day?

KILROY: Field Day was — I use the past tense although some members of the old Field Day group are still active and still doing things, doing very interesting things. It was a movement that came out of the North, an artistic movement, mainly theatrical, but other wings to it as well, to play a role I think, really, in the whole kind of revolutionary situation in Northern Ireland. My involvement, as you know the original group was completely composed of people from Northern Ireland, Brian Friel, Stephen Rea, Seamus Heaney, Seamus Deane, Tom Paulin and David Hammond, and they were Northern artists. They had a vision that something could be done in the arts, which would in some way integrate into the political process, which was taking place, or be an expression of it. My involvement came out of friendship in the first instance in that I was — and still am — a close personal friend of many of these people. I was approached at one point by Brian Friel and Stephen Rea to write a play for the group. It was out of that then, and the fact that I was very involved with them as friends, and talking to them, and discussing what they were up to, and going to their theatre productions, that they asked me to join. I think, possibly, I was asked to join as the only southerner, I was asked to join to help to advance the theatrical side of the thing itself, of the movement. So, that was my main involvement. I was also profoundly interested in what was happening in the North of Ireland, so that my involvement as it were shadowed their involvement.

DUBOST: In *The Madam MacAdam Travelling Theatre*, Rabe declares: "What I want, more than anything, is a theatre which can hold — danger. Where danger can detonate upon a stage. You see, I believe if theatre can do that, there will be less — danger left in the world. Our only hope is that art transform the human animal. Nothing else has worked." Was this what you were trying to achieve with Field Day?

KILROY: If I was, it was a tall order, a big order! I think I probably did share that notion that in some way, theatre could siphon off some of the negative energy, by expressing itself through plays. Whether I still believe that, I'm not sure, but that's possible, but certainly *Double Cross* was an attempt to meet head on the kind of issues which were circulating, and which were being circulated by the Field Day group. You couldn't think of anything more dangerous than fascism. It's how nationalism leads to fascism that is the narrative of that play. I think that by expressing that on the stage, you are in fact meeting head on something of the activity of the streets, so that there is that sense. I'm not too sure that art can quite achieve that kind of goal that Rabe talks about. It's very much a young vision, a young idealism, and worthy for that reason.

DUBOST: When *Double Cross* was first published, in the author's note, one read: "This play could not have been written without Field Day." In your new introduction, that is, eight years later, one reads "I wanted to write a play about nationalism and in a real sense, *Double Cross* derives from the whole debate about national identity which Field Day did so much to promote in the seventies and eighties." Could you explain this alteration, which I don't read as a rejection, but as a maturing process that sheds a different light on your writing and staging experiences?

KILROY: Well, it is a more mature reflection on the whole thing. I mean the play could not have been written without Stephen Rea. Here is a perfect example of a play written for a particular actor, and very much dedicated to the kind of energy which he brings to the stage, but it also touches on an issue which is no longer a vital issue in Irish life, and that is national identity. You don't have the same degree of investigation of this today. It doesn't have the same currency, the same power to engage that it did in the sixties and the seventies, when in fact it was very much to the fore and this group was attempting to address it, and attempting in the way in which Yeats and his contemporaries addressed it in a similar kind of situation at the beginning of the twentieth century. The play was an attempt to probe the excesses of this energy, and to catch something of it. Sometimes, the Field Day group used to be described by its enemies as the cultural wing of the IRA, as the intellectual wing of the IRA [Irish Republican Army], which is an absurd statement because the Field Day group, one of its virtues, and also one of its problems, was that it was a mixture of people with very different views about the political issues of the day. By and large, it was a group that was sympathetic, more sympathetic to republicanism than it was to anything else, but having said that, you then have to graduate the individual responses, and they were in fact very different, which I found actually quite frustrating.

DUBOST: You resigned from Field Day because you stated that you felt that you didn't have enough artistic freedom. What did you mean by this? What about *The Madame MacAdam Travelling Theatre*, and the notion of staging nakedness, for instance? Was this at the core of your decision?

KILROY: It was less a question of artistic freedom, I think, than.... Well, to put it quite bluntly, I felt that Field Day might take a very strong public stance on certain issues. When I realized that that wasn't what Field Day was about, that Field Day was about some kind of process, and working out in a painful and discordant fashion the issues, I felt I wasn't getting anywhere. The one issue which I thought Field Day might have come absolutely clearly out on is the issue of sectarianism. But sectarianism from the outside, from the southern point of view is one thing. Sectarianism from inside the North of Ireland is something else again. It is a kind of overly simplistic adjective to use sectarian, even though we know that sectarianism operates in the North of Ireland on both sides. There was no way in which Field Day was going to do such a thing. I also felt that as things developed that Field Day might actually have force outside its artistic presence if it intellectually engaged issues like sectarianism. So it was less an artistic thing than a kind of issue thing.

Performance

DUBOST: Do you think of the stage as a place for violence?

KILROY. I suppose that when you are a certain age, you respond to issues like violence with much more stimulation than later in life. I would certainly have come out of a generation — not just Irish — but European generally, a generation which found the theatre a place, a staging ground if you wish, for actions that had a quality of violence about them. For example, I was immensely stimulated by Artaud, and by Peter Brook and by Peter Brook's early productions which would have been influenced by Artaud, like *Marat-Sade*, and they left quite a mark upon my work. I think it's a mark that continues right up to something like *Blake*, where what's expressed upon the stage are actions and images that violate the ordinary tenor of life. I think that theatre can do that, and can do it in a way that is in some respects more powerful even than cinema.

DUBOST: You mentioned the body of the actor, I'm concerned here obviously with the body of the actor, but also about music, about lighting, about the stage as performance, as a place of performance.

KILROY: To some extent, it relates to the communal aspect of theatre. To this extent that I do not legislate with a kind of absolutism what music should be used in a play, largely because I would not have the knowledge of music, say that my friend Brian Friel would have, who would conceive the play with music as an in-built factor. I don't do that, but I would hope to write sufficiently evocatively in stage directions and the like, to stimulate a stage director to find the right music. This music would change from production to production, depending on what is happening, so that I write to allow a great deal of freedom in the execution of the text, in the execution of the play, and the same would be true for design. Sometimes I work very closely with the designer and we work out in some detail together as I did for the first productions of *Talbot's Box* and *The Secret Fall of Constance Wilde*. There I talked to the two designers at some length, and the director, who is the same director, Patrick Mason for both productions, so that it's a hugely important part of what I'm about as a playwright, but there is an allowance. There is something large left to the imagination of the individual director and of the individual designer to actually make it happen. If that makes sense.... *Blake* actually is waiting for a composer to set the whole thing, which I would very much welcome. There would be numerous settings of Blake, right up to somebody like Van Morrison, who set individual songs, or sections of the poetry, but I would love to work with a composer who would actually look at the whole play operatically, and who would attempt to set the whole play — rather than the individual singing portions — because I think it's moving towards that type of event, stage event, it's moving towards opera.

DUBOST: I'd like to come back to this communal aspect of theatre. I guess that you have experienced if not disappointments at least misunderstandings possibly, with the public, stage directors, or actors. Could you tell us about these times, when your vision of the theatre, or the play differed from theirs? The next question is a follow-up to this one, which is: to what extent are you willing to be an unpopular playwright?

KILROY: Well, it comes out of this thing that I believe in very firmly that theatre is a collective event. I mean, the way I describe it is that I'm always astonished on the first day of rehearsal to see so many people gathered together. It's a humbling thing, you know, when you see so many people who are gathered together to do one of your plays, and when the thing is finally up on that stage, there is something of these people up there. Sometimes to a greater or lesser extent, so that you are talking about a communal process, a communal happening. I would go further than that and say that I'm not the type of playwright who sits on the production, and forces the thing to an autocratic vision. I do have a vision, a very strong vision, but it's one that invites in people to work on it. For that reason, I don't think my plays are that particularly easy to do. For that reason, there is a great deal of disappointment, and it's something that I live with, but where things do not quite jell the way you want them to jell. On the other hand, I've had terrific experiences, both with directors and actors, and I like working with directors, both in

Ireland and in the UK, and in the States. The director who's going to work on my next work is American, and I get a great deal out of that. At the same time, it's part of the risk of theatre. I think the risk, in my case, the risk-taking may be bigger than usual, simply because I don't have the thing kind of graphed out, and you can do this, and you must do that, and you will do this and you won't do that. I don't map the thing out with that degree of precision. So, some of the most effective productions I've seen of my work have actually come long after the opening production, and have been a terrific surprise to me to see the way in which a kind of an interpretation of the work, even goes away from what I started out with.

DUBOST: So, what do you expect from an actor, or an actress?

KILROY: The same with actors. I mean you get interpretations from actors. If you work closely with an actor, you tend to see the way the actor is working out the detail. Therefore the end result is something that you have, you know, you've followed the path in rehearsal. When you see a new performance of the work, it's often quite shocking, quite surprising that the actor has developed a personal, a highly personal way of doing things.

DUBOST: What do you expect from an audience?

KILROY: Engagement. I think my plays do demand a certain degree of attention. I was reading recently an account, an interview, with an actor whom I admire very much, John Cusack, the American film actor, and he was talking about how he has no interest in doing work which simply has the audience as a passive presence. He said, more or less that he wanted them on the edges of their seats with attention, and if they're not there, then he has no interest in their presence. That's the kind of things that I look for in theatre. It's not always easy to get that. We're now getting very accustomed to having packaged experiences and — let's not deny it — easier experiences than what theatre can offer.

DUBOST: Who do you write your plays for?

KILROY: I've had audiences, very mixed audiences for my work over the years, and I've had audiences that were not necessarily bogged down in the detail of the plays, which just took the experience for what it was, and that pleases me very much. I don't have any kind of elitist notion of what an audience should be, but I love reaching unexpected responses to my work, where strangers come up and talk about what they have seen, often in surprising ways!

DUBOST: In general, you tend to favor distancing to total involvement, even for actors. In John Molloy's obituary in the *Irish Times*, you praised him and you wrote: "He brought identification to the part. He became the part. By the end of the run it was very difficult to tell the art from the reality." How do you reconcile this statement with your initial principles?

KILROY: Yes, there is something in me which reacts against easy effects and easy feeling. It's actually quite easy to create feeling in theatre. It's easy to create sentiment in an audience. I think it's easy. I personally find that a lesser activity for a writer than other activities, which is what I was trying to get at there, I think. It's what I tried to get at in talking about distancing. Sometimes you see Irish commentators talking about a certain kind of coldness in my work, you know, I've had that said, and a lack of feeling. I think that's to misunderstand the feeling that's in the work, and the kind of passionate involvement that's in the work. The thing I was talking about with John Molloy was different, in a sense, a kind of rare thing which you get in theatre now and again. John Molloy was a stand-up comic, and had a very bizarre presence on the Irish theatrical scene. He played very little straight theatre. He was a wonderful mimic and comic. He came to Paris and studied mime, so that he was part of that whole Barrault tradition of theatre, but in the service of comedy, white-faced comedy, almost. He was cast in this part, in a stroke of genius by Patrick Mason, who felt that this would be a conjunction of two different — maybe a violent conjunction — of two different things. He was also a reprobate, a man who had a legacy of womanizing and illegitimate children, and families all over the place, a complete scoundrel, but with a lot of charm, a very, very difficult man to work with, particularly in an ensemble cast situation so this is the man we had in *Talbot's Box*. He was also somebody who had I think had one lung and was kind of in the throes of dying, almost, though he lived much longer than that, but so this was the man who was cast in this part. What happened was this identification process took place which, yes indeed, would have been against my better judgment, but I just stood and watched it in amazement, when he became totally self-identified with this mystical person. To the degree that he was going around like a saint. It was bizarre, it was very funny. That play, when it was done originally in the Peacock Theatre, it's just round the corner from the church which is dedicated to Matt Talbot. People started coming in from the church, and I will never forget this, I stood at the back of the auditorium at the Peacock Theatre, and Molloy was upstage doing his thing, as the saintly figure, emaciated, Christ-like, and the people in the audience were holding up their rosary beads. It was like, the church had invaded the theatre, so it went totally against my sense of what should be going on, but it is an acknowledgment of what theatre is capable of.

DUBOST: In *The Shape of Metal*, one reads, "Giacometti said, to see things whole, one has to see them from a distance, a remove." Apparently, this artistic perspective seems close to your vision, and yet I feel that you would differ greatly from such a perspective because I am not sure you try to see and show "things whole," and even challenge such a vision as dangerous. Would you concur or disagree on that point?

KILROY: I think it's almost impossible to achieve that. At the same time, I was talking about a phenomenon which is not uncommon in fact, in sculpture. That is the way in which the eye, the perspective of the eye, that you almost have to have a fixed point of observation to get a sense of the total effect of the piece. I think that this is true, in particular of some of the smaller pieces of Giacommetti. When you are on top of them, looking at them, you have this mess, and when you go a certain distance from them, the image begins to realize itself. So, I mean I think there is something comparable in writing, actually. You know that you can have an effect on stage which may come across as confusion, but it's confusion that will stay with you. You live with it, I think your friend Eugene O'Neill is a very good example, where the effect on stage is often one of confusion, incoherence, all the things that you would argue against in an art work, but it stays with you, with a truth of its own, and in many ways, a truth that is more persuasive than something simpler.

DUBOST: Have you ever acted in a play or directed one?

KILROY: Yes, as a student, I acted and I wrote sketches, more or less, and I directed and I also took part in a local amateur dramatic group in the town that I grew up in. So that I had a sense of theatre from a very early age. I also had a sense of something of the compositional quality that a director requires to bring together all the different elements, even before I started to produce plays myself. I really think that playwrights are *acteurs manqués*.

DUBOST: The last question is about your second introduction to *The Seagull*, and you wrote that age changed "the shape of thinking as well as that of the body." Conversely, what has remained unchanged in your dramatic outlook from *The O'Neill* to *The Shape of Metal*?

KILROY: I think the fact that so much is provisional, and exploratory, in a way denying a kind of finality. I mean there is a finality in representation, the thing begins and the thing ends on a stage, but what is actually happening at the inner core of the work, there is something about that which is — as I said — provisional, it's an attempt at something. I think my work embodies this process, including the failure of so much human endeavor. I hope, in that way, it is more truthful, more accurate, in its representation of life.

DUBOST: Thank you very much.

KILROY: Thank you very much.

13

An Interview with Lynne Parker, Dublin, October 30, 2003: On The Shape of Metal

THIERRY DUBOST: Could you introduce yourself as a director, as a stage director, possibly giving an outline of your career, your artistic approach to the play and to theatre?

LYNNE PARKER: Principally, I am the artistic director of Rough Magic Theatre Company, which was set up nearly twenty years ago. I am also an associate director of the Abbey Theatre. A lot of the work I've done with my own company has been premières of British, American and European plays, contemporary plays, and also new Irish plays. I've done quite a lot of new Irish writing. That's something that's a very important corner stone of our work. The first play we ever produced — Rough Magic that is — was Tom Kilroy's *Talbot's Box*. That was back in 1984. It wasn't the first production, but that was a very good one. I didn't direct it; in fact, my colleague did, I designed the set. I've known Tom for that length of time. This is the first time I've actually worked with him. But as I said, I've done quite a bit of new writing, some of it for the Abbey Theatre as well.

DUBOST: Why did you choose to stage *The Shape of Metal*?

PARKER: Well, one answer to that is that I didn't choose to stage it. It was the choice of the artistic director of the Abbey to do the play. They had been talking to Tom about this for some time, and Ben [Barnes] really wanted a new play by a major Irish writer to go into the Dublin Theatre Festival this year. So he scheduled it. It had been Tom's idea that it would be done in The Peacock, which is a small studio theatre, and Ben was quite keen that it be done on the main stage, and be given that kind of prominence, and what have you. That choice, I think, did place certain conditions on the production. But I'll come back to that, later. I chose to do it because I just thought it was a really wonderful play. And an astonishing role for a major actress; and they don't come along every day. I was very interested in the idea of the creative artist and the question of — about the behavior of such a person — what kind of behavior is excused by genius, and what is encouraged by genius — and by the notion of the creative artist as somehow special and set apart, and what that means for the people closest to them, principally their family.

DUBOST: In the plays, you mentioned *Talbot's Box*, and as you know, the plays of Tom Kilroy are very closely connected to the staging process of the play. To what extent did this involvement in performance of the playwright hinder you work or the assertion of your own creative process? Did it help it? How did it work?

PARKER: I suppose I've never felt that to be a hindrance, because I need the writer to give me the map for the journey. And, particularly with Tom, who is a very generous man, we worked very collaboratively on the ideas for the production. And also with Sara [Kestelman] who's playing Nell. He was quite keen, I think because his last play, *Constance Wilde* had been done in a very abstract set, very highly stylized, I think he was interested in exploring something closer to naturalism. I also felt that there was a surreal element in the play, in terms of the appearance of Grace and the haunting of Grace. And I felt that that would be most effective set against naturalism, surreal painting needs almost sort of photorealism to work, frequently. And so, that's the path we took. We also felt we wanted to represent and suggest to the audience the life and work of this woman. Now, there's quite a lot to do in this play. I mean, it's technically very difficult because you have things like smashing sculptures and you have appearances of a ghost, you have whole transformation scenes, all this kind of stuff. So, it was quite a challenge to the designers. And I think they rose wonderfully to it. But we wanted to create an environment that really felt like we were in a studio, so we did quite a bit of research into it.

DUBOST: That's a turning point from Tom's perspective. You mentioned the highly stylized performance of *The Secret Fall*. When watching the play, I couldn't help remembering *Tea and Sex and Shakespeare*, and the idea of these surrealistic moments taking place within the play. You mentioned *Talbot's Box*, and obviously each play has, or each play by any playwright, has its specificity. How would you characterize the kilroyan specificities from your perspective as a stage director?

PARKER: I think Tom is the most unashamedly intellectual writer I've come across in that he likes to rehearse the big ideas on stage. And he isn't afraid to put characters on stage who are fantastically articulate, in a way that, I suppose, ordinary people can't quite measure up to. But, hey, it's theatre. And, what's wonderful is the richness of his dialogue, and the complexity, and the contradictions and all of those things that make it very human as well as elevating it in such a way that the ideas can take flight. And hopefully, that's what we manage to achieve.
But it's a really tough thing for actors to negotiate. In order to present the ideas as real speech, he actually lairs in some *non sequiturs*, some contradictions within speeches. Not all questions have replies directly. Sometimes, the answer to one question will come a whole page later. So the thought processes are as complicated and labyrinthine as normal people's. Except that it's all done in this fantastically intelligent play.

DUBOST: And so would you view that as the challenging part — you know —
I read a couple of reviews, and I found that the word "challenging" was
coming in these reviews. So, would you see the intellectual process
that is being staged as the challenging factor? Especially in Ireland. I am
thinking in terms of audience reception, and what is being said by the
actress.

PARKER: Yes, well I think that the central idea of the play, the notion of
failure, is one that is terrifying. To put it on stage is very brave. You are
inviting a kind of fear in response. But within challenging on many levels;
challenging technically, challenging for the audience to assimilate the
idea at the moment, and then also to see the bigger picture and contain
that, contain a complicated story line, not one which is always done in a
linear way. I suppose also that these are difficult people, that Nell is not a
nice woman. She is a fascinating woman actually, but she has very unpleasant sides to her.

DUBOST: How did you use comedy in the play?

PARKER: I don't think you consciously use comedy in this kind of play. I think
it's funny because it is accurate, because it's a comedy of recognition,
simply that. Beside the intellectual conceptual side of the writing, there's
very basically a family drama, which everybody can relate to, and in this
country it's a very strong motif.

DUBOST: Yes, now you worked with Tom, and staging a play is making choices.
So did you make choices with which Tom didn't agree, or.... How did you
work together?

PARKER: We simply worked very closely. And from the work of — right at
the beginning of the year, we'd had many meetings, where we discussed
possible casting, possible staging, and all this kind of things. We actually
did a workshop, I think in May, where we got together two of the
actresses and did a couple of days, simply discussion. And Tom did a little
bit of rewriting, redrafting after that, and that was very useful because
the designers were also involved in that. So they were able to start thinking
of ways to put the whole thing together. So, it's been a long, slow, and
very enjoyable process, and we were fortunate in having the play cast quite
early. Sara agreed to do it quite a long time ago, and was able herself to
start putting ideas together.

DUBOST: What did you find difficult to represent when you staged the
play?

PARKER: I suppose the character of Judith is the most difficult to represent
because you have very little information about her other life. She's
something of a cipher. I think Eleanor found that quite hard because she
was having to balance, and in some ways, invent a whole back-story.
And Tom is curious in that he doesn't necessarily supply that. And you
have to do a lot of detective work, which he's very happy to do with you,
but it's not something that he has prescribed — a lot of writers would be
able to tell you what kind of job Judith has — and he hadn't worked
that one out. And we came up with the notion of her as a publisher,
someone who was involved in the arts, but not in a creative way, more
in an editorial, or a facilitating way. So, he was very happy with that.
That's a decision that he left it to us to make. That's quite fun, actually.

The Shape of Metal. Photograph by Tom Lawlor. From left to right, Justine Mitchell, Sara Kestelman, Eleanor Methuen. Abbey Theatre, Dublin, 2003 (courtesy of The Abbey Theatre Archive).

It was rather good. You asked actually if there was anything he wasn't happy with. I think initially he was a bit taken aback that I decided to use Miles Davis rather than the Schnittke that had been a huge influence on the writing of the play. This was very dark, and highly dramatic cello music, which I felt would set such a tone for the start of the play that it would be very hard then to take it any further. I felt it would scare the audience, I felt it would frighten the audience. I wanted something that would ease us into the telling of the story, that had some relevance to it. So, I wanted some Parisian jazz and Miles Davis had done this wonderful film score — and I've forgotten the name of the film. It was jazz, it was music that he'd written when he was living in Paris. And I thought, you know, however tangentially that's a nice connection. It also set a mood that was somber but not heavy.

DUBOST: Now, I have a question about the setting of the play. I was wondering whether you would set the play on a large or smaller stage, because I felt that there is some kind of intimate vision within the play, and I was wondering whether it might not have been easier for the audience to get into the play in the Peacock, for instance.

13. An Interview with Lynn Parker

PARKER: Well, I think it might have been. And certainly you could stage it in the Peacock. Again, the transformation and all of that stuff might be harder to achieve in a smaller space, but when we knew that, I mean, obviously from the beginning that it would happen in the Abbey, and the Abbey is a notoriously difficult stage, especially for a play which has such concentrated action, such stillness, and that's why we decided to thrust the stage as far forward as possible to bring the action as close to the audience as we could. The whole angle and design of the space was just that, that we cut into the auditorium of the Abbey in a way I haven't seen done before, and simply reduced the distance as much as possible.

DUBOST: OK. Regarding your choice of actresses, were there particular aspects in the play that made you look for one type of actress or another?

PARKER: Well, I knew the minute I read it that this was for Sara Kestelman, whom I'd known but not worked with for some years. She has a particular interest in this because her father was a painter and she spent a lot of time in his studio, and knows the territory of the creative visual artist very well. And also she is at a position in her life where she's looking at her own achievements as a creative artist and questioning them. That was very interesting and rich territory for her. I also felt that she obviously has the stature and intellectual caliber to take on this part, which is pretty huge. As to Eleanor, I've worked with her many times before, she's a highly intelligent actress, but has a very pragmatic and commonsensible approach to her work, and I felt that was good for Judith. That she wanted to feel that Judith came from the world I suppose of the common place, having experienced this extraordinary exotic and bizarre childhood that what she actually had gravitated towards was the world of ordinary people. And that, ironically, that's exactly what Grace always wanted, although Grace probably could never have achieved it, because Grace in a way is more like her mother than Judith. As to Justine, she is just one of our very exciting young talents, so I was keen to work with her, and I thought she was perfect for Grace. She has that fertile energy and vulnerability.

DUBOST: Now, to conclude, I'd like to know if you could tell us what your staging experience has brought to you in terms of your collaboration with Tom Kilroy. What are the significant features — I know this is very fresh — so it might be difficult for you to analyze something which is still in the process of being...

PARKER: Yes, well it is hard because the play is still running. I mean, maybe in a month or a year, I might have a different perspective. I don't know, when you're doing it, you're not conscious of bringing techniques as such to something, because you're simply trying to find the best way. I suppose I felt that there was a need for stillness because the text is so dense, because what the audience is having to receive and assimilate is so complicated that I felt that any extraneous movement would have been confusing and unnecessary. So, the physical presentation is quite controlled, quite simple in a way. And the physicality, for instance, in Sara's performance, where she moves from her eighty-two-year-old self to her fifty-two-year-old self is something that simply she worked out in relation to her own characterization. That wasn't a conscious thing. You just felt that, I mean, you just took it instinctively, I suppose. And that's part of the effect, the dramatic effect of the play is the build of tension and that had to be very carefully controlled. The surprises that the play throws up have to be very skillfully, I suppose, managed — if you tried to get too clever with it, I think it would probably work against you. And as I say, it's hard for me to know how successful that is because I can only see it as it is now, if I came back to it, I might see another way of doing it. But I think, I mean it was such an interesting job for me, because as a director you're having to make choices that preclude other things, all the way along, and sometimes you're wondering if you took exactly the right path. But in all these things I was very much guided by Tom.

DUBOST: Well, thank you very much.

PARKER: Thank you.

14

A Telephone Interview with Max Stafford-Clark, June 3, 2004: *On* Tea and Sex and Shakespeare *and* The Seagull

THIERRY DUBOST: Could you introduce yourself as a stage director (both when you first met Tom Kilroy and now)?
MAX STAFFORD-CLARK: When I first met Tom Kilroy, I was a freelance director. I had just left the Traverse Theatre in Edinburgh. I ran a theatre in Edinburgh called the Traverse Theatre, then I ran the Traverse Workshop Company, then I was a freelance director, and then I became the Director of the Royal Court Theatre in 1979. I ran it for fourteen years. When I left in 1993, I started my own company, which I called Out of Joint, and that's the company I still run. We're a touring company, but it's mostly text-based theatre, of a quite diverse kind. I first met Tom when I was asked if I wanted to direct *The Death and Resurrection of Mr. Roche*. Then, we were in contact, and I was asked to direct *Tea and Sex and Shakespeare* at the Abbey. It was a passive position for me, that is to say the Abbey rang, and said: "would you like to direct this play?" I answered that I was available, and they sent me the play. So, you read the play, talk to the writer, and respond to that. I remember the play being one of a number of Irish plays in which I would number *Faith Healer* by Brian Friel, and *The Gigli Concert* by Tom Murphy. They were, in a way, about writers' block, or about the inability of Irish writers to write directly about the things that were going on in their country: the Troubles. So that was the realistic starting point to a kind of surreal play; Donal McCann was in it, and I had a terrific time doing that play.

Then I got to the Royal Court. The whole ethos of the Royal Court is to do new work, but at the same time, occasionally, there is a classic, and the famous phrase is "the Royal Court does new plays like classics and classics like new plays." I had never done a Chekhov, and was keen to find a particular reason for doing it. I was eager to bring the Chekhovian experience nearer to our own culture and, by setting it in Ireland, I was able to make it both familiar and foreign. Tom's own knowledge of the Irish movement that gave birth to the Abbey informed the play that Constantine is writing. It seemed to me that relocating the play to Ireland would be both examining Chekhov in a new light and would enable us to look at a particular period of Irish history. I approached Tom with that idea, and he responded to it with a terrific enthusiasm and that's how the version of *The Seagull* came to be written.

DUBOST: That's the way you came to work with Tom. What about the staging process itself? How did you work with Tom? As a stage director, what kind of relationship did you have with the author?

STAFFORD-CLARK: Well, I am a Royal Court director, and the Royal Court director is brought up to believe that the writer is the senior partner, the senior creative partner of the relationship. So, you do try and serve the play, whereas the French and German and Russian tradition is a bit more like Hollywood, and that the writer simply provides the opportunity for the director to display his genius. That's not the tradition in which I was brought up. So, our relationship — as far as I recall — was an extremely cordial one. He would have been present all the time in rehearsal, although I think at that point he was living in the West of Ireland, and probably wasn't able to be; but I would certainly have encouraged him to be in rehearsal as much as he chose to be.

DUBOST: How did it work? Did you think it was a learning process for him? Did he talk to the actors...

STAFFORD-CLARK: Yes, hopefully any play is a learning process for both author and director. I mean you should go in not knowing the answers to every question, not having a totally rigid concept. It's hard for me to recall with any accuracy, but certainly I would have invited him to talk to the actors directly or to interpolate any feelings that he had.

DUBOST: I feel that *Tea and Sex and Shakespeare* is a difficult play, not in itself, but for the audience of the time it must have been quite hard to follow.

STAFFORD-CLARK: Well, it was quite coded, wasn't it? I think that was, possibly, a difficulty. I think that was both the point of the play and what was hard about it. It was at a time when I think Irish writers were finding some difficulty in coping with their own situation.

DUBOST: Yes, I wonder how an audience would react today.

STAFFORD-CLARK: I don't think the play has been revived, has it?

DUBOST: No.[1]

STAFFORD-CLARK: That's interesting in itself.

DUBOST: How did you use comedy in the play?

STAFFORD-CLARK: I can't honestly remember. I mean Donal McCann was a very accomplished actor. He certainly would have been keen to have got the laughs that were there, and Tom would have been keen to point them out, but it's difficult to do that in rehearsal. What you do is try and play the situation as loyally as you can, and trust that the laughs come from that.

DUBOST: Well, I guess you have kept an eye on Tom's works...

STAFFORD-CLARK: Yes, I saw his latest play, *The Shape of Metal*. I thought it was another coded message about the writer. You could parallel that with *Tea and Sex and Shakespeare*. In a way, there are similarities. They are both about the life of a creative artist. The message I got from *The Shape of Metal* is the damage you do to the people you love, your family, if you are an obsessive writer. Maybe that's an oversimplified condensation of what he is saying, but that's one of the things anyway. I found *The Shape of Metal* quite hard. Quite hard work to distill.

DUBOST: How would you, as a stage director, characterize Tom as a playwright?

STAFFORD-CLARK: I have not read all his plays, but he is an intellectual. In France, that's a polite term; in Ireland and England, it tends to be a term of abuse. We suspect intellectuals, while I think you respect them in France. He is part of the intelligentsia, and his contributions to the debate, what he feels about Irish theatre, what he feels about the position of the theatre in Ireland is always worth hearing. I have followed the plays at some distance. I think he is an awkward playwright, that is to say the business of staging the play is often quite hard, quite difficult for him. I remember *The Big Chapel*, his novel, and the feeling that it was a fluent novel and that he was a master of that medium, whereas sometimes in the theatre, the form is quite difficult, that's my feeling. But I think that what he says in his plays, and his relation to Irish history is always incredibly interesting. He's also a very witty writer.

DUBOST: Well, what you say is very surprising, because I would see him as a very stage-concerned playwright, so you would see him more as a writer of novels, is that what you...

STAFFORD-CLARK: No. It's not that I see him more as a novelist. It's that the flow of his ideas sometimes makes it quite hard to find the right structure for him in the theatre, that's what I am saying.

DUBOST: I see. Well, thank you very much for answering my questions and providing an interesting insight into the dramatic works of Tom Kilroy.

STAFFORD-CLARK: My pleasure.

15

A Telephone Interview with Patrick Mason, September 27, 2004: On Talbot's Box *and* The Secret Fall of Constance Wilde, *and the First Irish Production of* The Seagull

Self-Portrait

THIERRY DUBOST: Could you introduce yourself as a stage director, giving an outline of your career, your artistic approach to theatre?
PATRICK MASON: I started directing in the Abbey[1] in the late seventies, and I suppose the Abbey is my Alma Mater. It also defines in some ways who I am as a director, because it is a writer's theatre. The first work I did there was a new play by Tom MacIntyre. I am very involved with writers, with the use of language in theatre, but I am also known to have a very strong visual sense. My contribution to the Abbey over the years has been not only the sensitivity towards language, the dramatic potential of language both in terms of meaning and music, but also the importance of the visual, the gestural and the importance of image. That's a very brief sketch. Although I have obviously worked on classic repertoire, over the years someone pointed out to me that I have directed over a hundred and fifty new plays between one theatre and another. I suppose that's my thing.
DUBOST: You have staged two of Thomas Kilroy's plays *Talbot's Box* and *The Secret Fall of Constance Wilde,* as well as his adaptation of *The Seagull.* Before dealing with each play, could you tell us what attracts you in the theatre of Thomas Kilroy?
MASON: I think it is about the theatrical. One thing Tom has said about his work, and indeed work for the theatre, is that if it can be done in any other medium, then it's not for the stage. He is very keenly aware of the things that can only be done on stage, the way you can play around with time and space. The way you can compress action, meanings, locations, periods, the way in which theatre conventions call for play and playfulness,

the engagement between an audience's imagination and the actor's, writer's, director's imagination. All these things are done in real time, and yet, of course, have this intense imaginal dimension. That's what attracts me to him, because he is someone who has this great sense of theatre, but also overridingly a sense of the importance of the visual in theatre, the use of puppets, or banners, or lighting or whatever, he has a great sense of that.

DUBOST: Would you, as a stage director, say that there is such a thing as a "Kilroyan" specificity?

MASON: Yes, but also what has interested me, Kilroy is one of the most accomplished of writers, both as a novelist, as an essayist and a playwright. He has this extraordinary sensitivity to language, and the possibilities of language. Very often, I am afraid, in the theatre these days, you tend to get a divide between the wordsmith — the expert with words — and the image maker. It's very rare to come across a playwright who is both — the nearest may be Tom Stoppard — but Stoppard is less daring in conventional senses than Kilroy in some ways. Tom stands out particularly in Irish theatre because he also has a very demanding intellectual background. There is an intellectual rigor to his plays, whatever their theatrical richness and imagination.

DUBOST: I feel that Tom Kilroy's plays relate very strongly to staging processes. Did this involvement in performance hinder the assertion of your own creative process?

MASON: No, because I think in some ways it was a liberation for Tom that I was able to understand what he was getting at, and maybe also slightly improve, or achieve what he wanted in a slightly different way, but maybe more effectively. It was a kind of marriage of strength to strength. Again, starting back in the seventies or eighties, you know the idea of the director in Irish theatre was someone who simply told the actors where to stand. The play itself was a matter for the playwright. You just did what the playwright said. I suppose I put forward a slightly more dynamic process and the involvement of the director to achieve the playwright's vision, to make that world real. This meant that you did not take everything literally, that there might be ways in which the aspirations of the playwright could be more fully realized if certain things were done, certain things were pursued. I think what is interesting about playwriting is — whatever the comprehensive vision of the individual — there are always aspects of the work which are actually mysterious to the playwright himself. It's one of the many functions of a director to reconnect the playwright to his own work, to that world, in ways which are only potential in the script.

Talbot's Box

DUBOST: Why did you choose to stage *Talbot's Box*?

MASON: I suppose I was absolutely fascinated by the theme. Remember this was the late seventies. I think it was one of the first serious inquiries about the whole force of the Catholic Church in Ireland, in Irish society, in Irish history, its psychological force, all the topics that it raised about the sort of archetypal mother fixation of Catholicism to this extraordinary confusion of gender and sexuality in Irish life. As well as this intriguing man. It was funny, it was tragic. It was disturbing and inquiring. I thought, you rarely get a piece that operates on so many levels. All those were very good reasons for doing it. Also, I felt strongly it lent itself to a very physical kind of presentation with basically a small group of actors using a number of props, reconfiguring space, creating images out of nothing, a stretcher and a chair used as a street barricade, or whatever. It was good fun. It was playful with a group of young actors who could create images and locations out of body language, and I liked the non naturalistic basis of it. It was very unusual for its time in Irish theatre.

DUBOST: There is a culturally challenging religious ceremony. What kind of a reaction did you expect and get from the audience?

MASON: There always has been a rather rich vein of blasphemy in Irish life. It goes with a society that is repressed and particularly a Catholic society, and paradoxically, you get a great taste for blasphemy and for bawdy. As you know yourself, no one blasphemes as well as an Irishman. There was of course an element of outrage, this was mocking the Holy man, and the rest of it. At the same time, there was a lot of recognition and a lot of enjoyment of the satire, the humour of the piece. There is a particular enjoyment of the absurdities if you like of the sort of Catholic ethos in Irish history. That, I think, won over the amount of opposition. I mean there was quite a lot, and offense was taken at various levels.

DUBOST: Did you fear that it might have negative consequences on your career?

MASON: (*Laughter.*) No, I was too young to think about it. What was interesting about it actually was because, as you may know, I was actually born in England and educated in England, although I was educated in Catholic schools. When I came to Ireland, I was very much regarded as being English, although my mother being Irish I had Irish nationality. But you know that old nationalist thing in Ireland that somehow being born outside of the country, you couldn't really be truly be Irish. But, of course, I was a Catholic, even a lapsed one. And it meant that I recognized, I knew all the references, just as a French Catholic would recognize things in Irish plays which an English Protestant would not see. You know the references, you know what is being said, what is being undermined, or being alluded to. *Talbot's Box* was interesting because the assumption was in many quarters that because I was from England, I was Protestant, and how could I do this play? (*Laughter.*) It was an interesting personal sidelight. I suppose in many ways, for the Irish theatre, it made me more accepted: I could do this play and understand this play, even if it was blasphemous.

DUBOST: We have talked about your connection and your relationship with the author, would you like to add something specific on *Talbot's Box*, if not we are going to move on to actors and actresses.

MASON: No, it was a highly enjoyable and very stimulating collaboration with Tom. As I said, the texts are demanding. They bring out the best of everyone, actors, directors, and designers. We had a very good cast and a

Talbot's Box. Photograph by Fergus Bourke. From left to right, Clive Geraghty, Eileen Colgan, John Molloy, Ingrid Craigie, Stephen Brennan. Abbey Theatre, Dublin, 1977 (courtesy of The Abbey Theatre Archive).

very happy time. Of course, what is important is that Tom and I became great friends. That friendship has lasted over the years.

DUBOST What about actors and actresses? Were there particular aspects in *Talbot's Box* that made you look for a specific type of actor?

MASON: Matt Talbot was such an extraordinary creature that we wanted someone who had to be absolutely steeped in that old Dublin working class culture, and be a very charismatic performer. That's why we were so fortunate to get John Molloy. John was the epitome of that particular kind of Dublin working class figure. He just *was* Dublin in some extraordinary way, and he was a very charismatic performer. Dangerous too, with drink and that sort of stuff. We had our problems, but in a strange way, all that fed into the characterization of Matt Talbot and his struggle with alcohol. So there was a huge level of personal, almost autobiographical energy in John's performance, which made it something very unique, very moving.

DUBOST: What about the priest figure, was it a problem that the priest figure should be played by a woman?

MASON: Well, there were a lot of mutterings about it, but there was no problem in casting it at all. We went for a very pleasant character actress, maternal, and very kind of matter of fact. We took the line that she should play it as a benevolent parish priest and let the gender thing just work for itself, and it worked extremely well.

DUBOST: Tom mentions the idiom of the Dublin streets. How did you work on that aspect with the actors?

MASON: Irish theatre is very small. We are a very small country and we have really a very small theatre. So there is a very small pool of people, a lot of whom are Dublin-based, and we had a group of young actors and actresses who were all from the city. This is the sort of thing you get in Dublin. You do not get that in France or in the United States, where you have this heterogeneous mix of actors from different backgrounds, different towns, different states. I think every one in the play was actually a Dubliner. The identification with place, and indeed with history, the knowledge of history, the knowledge of references, I think every single one of them was a Catholic. In fact, you might not get that now in Ireland. It's slightly more mixed up but, at the time, that was the case. So, there was a terrific enjoyment of the Dublin idiom, and a thorough knowledge of it. Every one was alert to that, and able to follow it, and to do so without exaggerating it. That was the key thing, that it arose very naturally from everyone.

DUBOST: Did you choose to set up the play in a large or small theatre, with a small or large stage, and what did you find difficult to represent when you staged the play?

MASON: The choice was clearly to do it in the smaller theatre, both for economic and artistic reasons. There is always a larger risk involved in a new play at the box office. It is one way of safeguarding the risk for the theatre, but also for the playwright. The play was potentially troublesome, politically and culturally. It was not an obviously popular play, therefore there is a certain protection for it in a smaller theatre than in a larger one. But equally, the scale of the scenes, although there are street scenes, actually the scale is very intimate. As you know, one thing about the Abbey is, although it is a 610-seat theatre, it is anything but intimate. It is like a football pitch [soccer field]. Finally, artistically, I felt it would be much better for the actors, for the play itself, to have the intimacy of a smaller theatre. I think a lot of Tom's plays involve these intimacies. One of the problems we had when we did *Constance Wilde* in the big theatre was how to create — on an epic scale — how to create moments of great intimacy. I think we were only partly successful in that.

DUBOST: You chose the music for *Talbot's Box*. What did you choose?

MASON: It was a kind of mosaic of sounds. We decided to use snatches of religious music, very passionate, very strong, and we mixed them with street sounds, sound effects and so on. It was quite disjointed, quite deliberately broken up. It was very much impressionistic, but not looking for any composed music. It was the bits and pieces of Matt Talbot's world and of the religious-psychological world around him.

DUBOST Thomas Kilroy dedicated *The Secret Fall of Constance Wilde* to you. Could you shed some light on your artistic collaboration for this play?

MASON: I was then artistic director of the Abbey, and I asked Tom to do a play for the bicentenary of Wilde's imprisonment in Reading jail. I asked him if he would look at *The Picture of Dorian Gray*, maybe to adapt it for the stage. He said he would, and he had some idea about using Dorian Gray to reflect the sort of biographical situation of Oscar, and Lord Alfred Douglas and Constance. In researching that, he got more and more fascinated by Constance Wilde. Six months afterwards, he telephoned me, and said "I think I have got something about Constance. Can I forget about Dorian Gray?" I said, "Of course you can, follow wherever it is going to lead you." That was the beginning of *The Secret Fall*. From the start, he was sending me scenes, he was sending me drafts, he was sending me scenarios and we were kind of batting them back and forwards, but when the Constance thing came clear to him, he very quickly completed a draft of the play. We discussed a lot, and then he went on to write a second draft. So, I suppose it arose from a commission that I gave him, but also the way it developed may have had something to do with our discussions. I was very pleased and honored to have it dedicated in that way.

DUBOST: What did you find difficult to represent when you staged the play, which is an extraordinary play in a way?

MASON: It is absolutely an extraordinary play. I mean the whole presentation, the use of the puppets and the attendants, and how to avoid something like "figures of fate," as they are described at one point, becoming very pretentious. They can become self-consciously arty in the wrong way. I worked with Joe Vanek, the designer, to try and find a style of presentation that would have a very clean aesthetic. Because it seemed to me that if you are dealing with anything to do with Oscar Wilde, all the arguments about the aesthetics, the purity, the importance of "line," you needed something that visually was very clean, very pure, and yet could also generate these moments of extraordinary passionate ritual. I suppose that was the hardest thing. I think, maybe on balance, we were too refined. If I

Robert O'Mahoney in *The Secret Fall of Constance Wilde*. Photograph by Amelia Stein. Abbey Theatre, Dublin, 1997 (courtesy of The Abbey Theatre Archive).

were to do it again, I would go for a much rougher kind of aesthetic. Much more rough and ready. Which in fact, to be fair, Tom would have liked it to be rougher. That was the hardest thing to calibrate in terms of the visual style.

DUBOST: Yes. The statue "rises, poses, naked, arm aloft in front of the great white disk." Was nakedness on stage a problem?

MASON: Yes, it was. Male nakedness was. More with the actor than the audience, I think. The year before we had done *Angels in America*, and we had male nudity, the actor was not troubled at all. Andrew was a bit troubled. He was self-conscious about it. So, in fact what we did, we suggested nakedness without having him entirely naked. He was in fact naked, but you never saw him naked completely. There was one particular sequence which is in the script, when it becomes very sexually explicit, with Alfred kissing Oscar.

DUBOST: Yes, I was coming to that. It seems to me that puppets bring a form of distance with the story that is presented to the audience, but sometimes the play can become very realistic when, for instance, the two men kiss with what is described as a "full-tongued kiss."

MASON: Yes, in the end, we felt the tension between realism and expressionism. We tried the kiss in rehearsal, and we felt that it became too literal for its own good. So, we created the tension of it about to happen for an audience, and yet it never did quite happen. In other words, we tried to create a suggestion of it, without actually having to do it. Simply because the minute you start doing it, the audience sort of switches off. It's the same with a straight couple kissing as well. I mean, what are you supposed to do as an audience while two actors kiss each other? The play stops, doesn't it? Interestingly, with the Oscar/Bosie relationship, every one knows that they were lovers, so it became less important to spell it out physically.

DUBOST: It would have been a redundant image.

MASON: In a strange way, yes.

DUBOST: Andrew Scott played the part of Lord Alfred Douglas. Tom indicated that "the parts of Douglas and the Androgyne may be played by the same actor (male or female)." Why did you choose a man?

MASON: Because we had Andrew. It was very much specific to the actor. He was a very exciting young actor. He has a sort of febrile energy and has a kind of boyish androgynous thing about him, actually. We both decided that given we had that actor that that was the way to go. The androgynous idea is a nice idea, but again to find the actress who could play that... We did not feel we had an actress who had that quality, but we did have an actor.

DUBOST: A critic — Tim Richards — stated that there was "something strangely unemotional about *The Secret Fall of Constance Wilde*." Do you agree with him?

MASON: (*Laughter.*) No, I am completely mystified about that because I thought it was extremely passionate. I cannot see a sequence like the jailing of Oscar, at the end of the first act, Oscar in his cage, the appearance of the father, the extraordinary scene after that with Oscar and Constance when she rejects him, without being moved. I just don't get it. Unemotional? It was the most passionate theatre I have seen in a long time. I don't know. I think I'll go back to this thing about — maybe the visual aesthetic was overrefined. Often people get slightly put off by that, and maybe that's what it was. That it slightly put them at a slight distance. But then, I would argue that there is a thing that Tom is doing, that he wants moments to be very distant *and* he wants moments to be absolutely passionate. I think the key, what we got absolutely right, was the children, the puppet children. There were moments when they were just very cool distant figures, and there were moments when they were absolutely real, quite extraordinarily, powerfully so. So, what do you say? For instance, I used the St. John Passion at the end of the first act when he is imprisoned. Now, for me that is enormously emotional music. It is very clear, very

The Secret Fall of Constance Wilde. Photograph by Amelia Stein. Left to right: Robert O'Mahoney, unidentified actor, Andrew Scott. Abbey Theatre, Dublin, 1997 (courtesy of The Abbey Theatre Archive).

obvious, it is the moment of his passion, of his calvary. That's all clear and that's all set, but there are people who find classical music very distancing. I don't. I find it has an incredible impact, but there are those who say, well, you know, classical music ... that's high culture. So, I don't agree with Tim Richards.

DUBOST: My last question is about *Talbot's Box*, *The Secret Fall of Constance Wilde*, and *The Seagull*. What have your staging experiences with Tom Kilroy brought to you?

MASON: He poses these immense challenges. Both stylistic, in that he wants so many different colors, he wants to speak in so many different languages, and yet he also wants a great sort of unity to the piece itself, an integrity to the piece. These challenges are posed on all kinds of different levels. It is a challenge for the actors because they have to discover different registers of language, of behavior, and different ways of presentation. There are moments when they have to be passionately naturalistic, and other moments when they have to be very cool and almost expressionistic in their behavior. It's the same problem for the designer and for the lighting designer, and for the director. So, you are constantly being challenged in what you might call an area of taste. I mean that in the big sense, in the way Nietzsche says "taste is everything." In many ways, it is. Every moment has to be calibrated, every moment has to be precisely presented. This is the great challenge of Tom's work. It's work of enormous detail, where he is pushing all kinds of boundaries. It's a work of great subtlety. It is often a thing that people miss, because we live in a culture that does not know what subtlety is. We live in a purely sensationalist culture. If it's not loud, violent, or heavily underlined, no one understands what is going on, because our sensibilites are so blunted. Tom is exactly the opposite. Enormously subtle, highly calibrated moments, language, gesture, image, and that is a huge challenge. It's very exciting, because there are very few writers who really push you to respond in all those ways. It is a discussion I often had with Tom — increasingly over the last ten years — about the blunting of sensibilities, this dominant mass culture of the loud, the fast, the obvious, the sensational. There is an appetite to the point of addiction for sensationalism now. It's deeply worrying. Also it makes it actually harder to find people who can tune in anymore. People who listen, people who watch, people who discern, who can actually discriminate between different registers, different colors, different levels of energy.

DUBOST: In an interview, I asked Tom how he felt about being an unpopular writer, because it seems to me he will be a major playwright in forty years time.

MASON: Oh, yes.

DUBOST: I think it is going to take time for him to be recognized.

MASON: I think that's true. I think he is acutely aware of that. You know, what is always wonderful about Tom is his absolute integrity. He is such a generous mentor to other writers, to directors, and actors. He gives of his time unstintingly. He has a great sense of responsibility towards his art, which extends to other talents, anyone who comes to him looking for advice, or opinion, or help, he is always there. He is a most generous man in that way.

DUBOST: Thank you very much.

MASON: Thank you.

16

An Email Interview with Andrew S. Paul, December 2005: On The Seagull *and* Henry

THIERRY DUBOST: Could you introduce yourself as a stage director, giving an outline of your career and your artistic approach to theatre?

ANDREW S. PAUL: Like many directors, I started out as an actor, training at the Guildford School of Acting in England. It is here I gained my appreciation for smart, literate theatre. I would describe myself as an actors' director, as I am extremely collaborative and actively seek the input of my collaborators at every stage of the process. I founded the Pittsburgh Irish and Classical Theatre (PICT) in 1996. My early work focused on style comedy (17th- and 18th-century plays), but I soon developed a passion for the comic drama or tragicomedy so common in Irish and Russian theatres, plays that make us laugh and cry (often simultaneously). My work has evolved more recently towards a grander, more visual aesthetic, and this is exemplified by my work on *Henry*.

DUBOST: You have staged two of Thomas Kilroy's adaptations: *The Seagull* after Chekhov and, more recently, *Henry* after Pirandello. You actually commissioned Tom Kilroy to make the adaptation. What were you expecting from him?

PAUL: Tom is one of the smartest theatre minds I know — I knew he would deliver a modernist reinterpretation of what remains a difficult, enigmatic play.
Tom has a strong understanding of the world of Pirandello and shares many of his fascinations; reality and illusion, sanity and madness, the past and its effect upon the present and the future. He also shares Pirandello's interest in the medium of film. We began our process by reviewing the numerous Englishlanguage translations and adaptations currently extant and quickly agreed that our version would depart radically from these earlier versions. To begin with, Pirandello's play has one of the great, glowing roles of the theatre in the first half of the twentieth century. Yet, the character Henry doesn't appear until an hour into the play. This may have worked in the Italian theatre of the nineteen twenties, but we felt that this does not work

with contemporary audiences so, in our version, he haunts the stage space from the very beginning. This reflects something in the original where there is the supposition that Henry, Prospero-like, conjures up everything that happens upon the stage. We have also shortened the play considerably, reducing exposition and replacing it wherever possible with visual representation. For example, the vision of Henry kneeling in the snow and seeking redemption at Canossa is, for us, the key to the entire play. This is described at length in the original, but never actually shown. In our version, we see it twice — at the beginning of each act; the first comedic, as a sort of parody, and the second as a moment of pure theatrical magic.

DUBOST: Would you, as a stage director, say that there is such a thing as a "Kilroyan" specificity? How would you characterize it?

PAUL: Tom Kilroy is a playwright of ideas, rejecting naturalism in favor of an open, expressionistic and often cinematic style. A good production of a Kilroy play will have a strong visual esthetic and leave an audience with much to think about.

DUBOST: The name of your company is the Pittsburgh Irish and Classical Theatre. I should like to focus on the "Irish" link between your company and the plays. What Irish features do you see in Tom Kilroy's works?

PAUL: Tom comes from a very long and distinguished line of Anglo-Irish playwrights hearkening back to Farquhar, Goldsmith and Sheridan. His love of language, great as this is, however, is perhaps transcended by his interest in theatre as a forum for the expression of ideas. It is no coincidence that he was an active participant in the Field Day Theatre Company, renowned for connecting classic myths with modern realities (the "Troubles" in Northern Ireland), which premiered two of his plays.

DUBOST: I take it that you think highly of Tom as a playwright. If I am right in this, why did not you stage one of his plays, *Blake* for instance, instead of focusing on adaptations?

PAUL: We performed *Double Cross* in our reading series. Tom and I had discussed doing an entirely original work, but our mutual interest in the Pirandello play led to the commissioned adaptation. I believe his adaptations to be among the very best available, always retaining the essence of the original authors' intent, while illuminating key themes and ideas for contemporary audiences. Having said this, I am also a huge proponent of his original works for the stage, and have every intention of tackling *Talbot's Box* and the revised *Death and Resurrection of Mr. Roche* at some point in the near future. *Blake*, like *Henry*, is an imaginative and largely visual meditation on art and madness. I am saddened that it has not yet received a full production and must revisit the script.

DUBOST: Did you set up *Henry* on a small or a large stage?

PAUL: *Henry* was set up on a large proscenium stage, the Charity Randall Theatre, a church-like, Gothic-influenced stone building with high vaulted ceiling. This natural environment, so conducive to a staging of the piece, allowed scenic designer Frank Conway and me to eschew the traditional setting (the medieval throne room at Goslar) in favor of a modernist, technology-inspired world more in keeping with Tom's deconstruction of the play.

DUBOST: At different levels, depending on the plays — one may think for instance of *Tea and Sex and Shakespeare, Talbot's Box, Blake,* or *Henry* — Tom Kilroy addresses the issue of madness. He never provides an easy way out for the audience, in that a character would obviously be mad, or society wrong in its judgment of his sanity. Madness becomes disturbing because of its dark complexities, and the reader — or the audience — never knows where to stand. How did you stage madness in *Henry*?

PAUL: Designer Frank Conway came up with a brilliantly simple conceptualization, utilizing a large golden box to represent Henry's brain and his place of safety. The interior of the box was painted to provide a serene, Zen-like atmosphere of peace and tranquility, a safe harbor. We chose to introduce Henry's madness at the outset through an elaborate series of projected and filmed images, many of them extremely disturbing, filling the stage and representing the inner workings of his mind. This disconcerted the audience, establishing a tone which enabled Henry's later moments of cogency and "normality" to truly disturb.

DUBOST: Because of its theatricality, I feel that *Henry* deeply corresponds to Tom Kilroy's dramatic scope. Sartorial aspects and their staging prove essential; what costumes did you use?

PAUL: Costumier Cletus Anderson brilliantly echoed the modernist text and scenic conceptualization with modern costuming that fused Henry's 11th-century world with the present. His sackcloth, for example, resembled haute couture. Henry throughout wore a stylish European designer striped suit and tie.

DUBOST: Ciara Moore and Buzz Miller were in charge of video design and projection. How did you include this in your stage work?

PAUL: Ciara and Buzz took what they felt were the central characteristics of Henry's inner mind and worked with them to come up with some symbolic images representing obsession, narcissism, religion, royalty, lust, betrayal, penance, isolation, repetition, power, spirit, hatred, jealousy and incest. They used images from classical paintings to illustrate some of these themes, for instance the story of "Roman Charity," which is about a woman who breast-feeds her father to keep him alive in prison, and projected them, at least two at a time, creating a dichotomy between both content and style. For instance there is a very medieval painting of the wounds in Jesus' feet which can flash up on a screen or surface at the same time as Dorothy's ruby slippers. The cumulative effect combines pain and suffering with Hollywood fantasy and escape. It's difficult to articulate, but looked quite nutty, darkly comic, subliminal, and open to numerous interpretations. The juxtaposition of images created enormous tension.

DUBOST: What music did you choose?

PAUL: When Sound Designer Liz Atkinson and I first read the script, we immediately thought of edgy, contemporary music to landscape the sounds of Henry's insanity. This impulse was further impressed upon us when we began to incorporate the use of video and other modernist design elements. From early design meetings it was clear that the designers would not be afraid to flaunt, Brechtian-style, whatever cool technology we had available to us. So we needed to get that same feel in the choices and use of music, finding a genre that the general public was not very familiar with and not very comfort-

Henry. Photograph by Suellen Fitzsimmons. From left to right, Sam Tsoutsouvas, Ben Hersey, Robin Walsh, Patrick Jordan, Richard McMillan, Martin Giles, Joseph Schulz, Larry John Myers. Pittsburgh Irish and Classical Theatre, Pittsburgh, PA, USA, 2005 (courtesy of Suellen Fitzsimmons).

    able with. We used music to set the audience, and the cast, on edge a little, get their hearts pumping and energized. Liz spent a lot of time watching Richard McMillan (Henry) in rehearsal, getting to know and understand his energy flow through the piece, and scoring Henry's peaks and troughs with German-inspired industrial music.

DUBOST: In a seminal article entitled "Groundwork for an Irish Theatre," Tom Kilroy wrote: 'the serious dramatist should fulfil the role of commentator on current values, practising espionage for everyman." The context is different: his adaptation of a play written by an Italian playwright was first staged in the United States. Still, I feel that his initial social concerns remain. What social connection did *you* see (and express) between *Henry* and contemporary American and Irish societies? Did you talk about this with Tom?

PAUL: Ireland has become an affluent society — the Irish used to leave the island in droves, but now multiculturalism is on the rise, with vast numbers of Eastern European, African and Asian immigrants arriving annually. Ireland has also become the center for the European communications and technology industries, and this high-tech globalization is precisely

Henry. Photograph by Phil Pavely. From left to right, Martin Giles, Ben Hersey, Patrick Jordan, Richard McMillan (front), Joseph Schulz. Pittsburgh Irish and Classical Theatre, Pittsburgh, PA, USA, 2005 (courtesy of Phil Pavely).

what Henry comments upon. "Everywhere surfaces, surfaces, flickering images, no depth, and that is why we must constantly invent love." The production purposefully utilized state-of-the-art lighting, projection, live camera and digital effects to present a modern world increasingly disconnected from itself and humanity. We are becoming increasingly isolated. The technology is exciting, but does it truly free us? Tom and I saw Henry's retreat into the 11th-century world as a direct comment upon the perils of technology and globalization.

DUBOST: Tom Kilroy's plays relate very strongly to staging processes. Did this involvement in performance hinder the assertion of your own creative process? How did you work with Tom?

PAUL: Tom and I are, in many ways, ideal collaborators. He used our prelimi-

16. An Interview with Andrew S. Paul

nary discussions about Henry to create a vision for the piece, including text and elaborate visual and staging descriptions. I then took this blueprint and worked with the creative team to bring his vision to life on stage. Tom is extremely collaborative and always open to the input of his director, designers, and actors. In the case of *Henry*, we worked through a visualization of the piece step by step, with a production style evolving gradually and organically. Frank Conway's scenic conceptualization, for example, was transformative. Many of Tom's original visual and staging descriptions were further altered during the rehearsals, with changes arising directly out of the collaborative process.

DUBOST: What have your two staging experiences with Tom Kilroy brought to you?

PAUL: Infinite joy! Tom's is a restless mind, always seeking new ways to tell stories and provoke intelligent response from his audience. I always enjoy discussing life and theatre with him, and look forward to many more fruitful collaborations.

Appendix:
Premières of Thomas Kilroy's Plays and Adaptations

The Death and Resurrection of Mr. Roche was first produced at the Olympia Theatre, Dublin, in October 1968. Kelly: Niall Toibin. Seamus: Kevin McHugh. Myles: Clive Geraghty. Medical student: Derry Power. Kevin: Chris O'Neill. Mr. Roche: Ronnie Walsh. Director: Jim Fitzgerald. Design: John Behan.

The O'Neill was first produced at the Peacock Theatre, Dublin, in May 1969. Hugh O'Neill: Joseph O'Connor. Cormac: John Kavanagh. Art: Frank Grimes. Mabel Bagenal: Bernadette McKenna. Roisin: Joan O'Hara. Poet: Alan Delvin. Patrick M'Art Moyle: Edward Byrne. Thadie Mahon: Dermot Kelly. Gillaboy O'Flannigan: Tom McGreevy. Sir Robert Cecil: Patrick Duggan. Lord Mountjoy: Aiden Grennell. Master Mountfort: Joseph Pilkington. Secretary: Patrick Dawson. Harpist: Marese Dolan. Others: Seamus Newham, Desmond Ellis, Louis McCracken, Eddie Lynch, Michele Lohan, Deidre Lawless, Barry O'Kelly, Seamus Brennan, Jack Kelly, Catherine O'Rourke, Marcella O'Riordan. Director: Vincent Dowling. Design: John Ryan. Music: Gerard Victory.

Tea and Sex and Shakespeare was first produced in the Abbey Theatre, Dublin, in October 1976. Brien: Donal McCann. Elmina: Aideen O'Kelly. Mummy: Kathleen Barrington. Daddy: Des Perry. Mrs. O: May Cluskey. Deidre: Angela Harding. Sylvester: Kevin McHugh. Director: Max Stafford-Clark. Design: Bronwell Casson.

Talbot's Box was first produced in the Peacock Theatre, Dublin, in October 1977. Matt Talbot: John Molloy. First Man: Stephen Brennan. Second Man: Clive Geraghty. Woman: Ingrid Craigie. Priest figure: Eileen Colgan. Director: Patrick Mason. Design: Wendy Shea. Lighting Design: Tony Wakefield.

The Seagull was first produced at the Royal Court Theatre, London, in April 1981. Mary: Veronica Duffy. James: Tony Rohr. Constantine: Anton Lesser. Peter:

Stuart Burge. Lilly: Harriet Walter. Pauline: Maggie McCarthy. Dr. Hickey: T. P. McKenna. Cousin Gregory. Alan Delvin. Isobel Desmond. Anna Massey. Mr. Aston. Alan Rickman. Director: Max Stafford-Clark. Design: Gemma Jackson.

Double Cross was first produced by Field Day Theatre Company, in Derry, in February 1986. William Joyce: Stephen Rea. Brendan Bracken: Stephen Rea. Narrator, Popsie, Margaret Joyce, a Lady Journalist: Kate O'Toole. Narrator, fire warden, Lord Castlerosse, Lord Beaverbrook, Erich: Richard Howard. Director: Jim Sheridan. Design: Consolata Boyle. Lighting: Rory Dempster. Film: Thaddeus O'Sullivan.

Ghosts was first produced by the Abbey Theatre, Dublin, (Peacock), in October 1989. Mrs. Aylward: Doreen Hepburn. Oliver: Conor Mullen. Father Manning: David Kelly. Jacko English: Kevin Flood. Regina: Noelle Brown. Director: Michael Scott. Designer: Geraldine O'Malley. Lighting Designer : Leslie Scott. Sound: Nuala Golden.

The Madame MacAdam Travelling Theatre was first produced by Field Day Theatre Company, in Derry, in September 1991. Madame MacAdam: Helen Ryan. Lyle Jones: Julian Curry. Sally: Amanda Hurwitz. Rabe: Tom Radcliffe. Simon: Donagh Deeney. The Sergeant: Kevin Flood. Marie Thérèse: Tina Kelleher. Jo: Fionnuala Murphy. Bun Bourke: Conor McDermottroe. Chamberlain: Conor McDermottroe. Young Maher: Donagh Deeney. Slipper: Donagh Deeney. Director: Jim Nolan. Design: Monica Frawley. Lighting Design: Conleth White.

Six Characters in Search of an Author was first produced in the Abbey Theatre, Dublin, in 1996. Mother: Barbara Brennan. First Actress: Susan Fitzgerald. Madame Pace: Olwen Fouere. Young Son: Rory Keenan. Scenic Painter: Michael McCabe. First Actor: Brian McGrath. Step Daughter: Alison McKenna. Father: Gerard McSorley. Daughter: Katie Monelly ASM: Fionnuala Murphy. Second Actress: Mary O'Driscoll. Director: Owen Roe. Son: Andrew Scott. Scenic Painter: Renée Weldon. Second Actor: David Wilmot. Director: John Crowley. Designer: Tom Piper. Lighting: Nick McCall.

The Secret Fall of Constance Wilde was first produced in the Abbey Theatre, Dublin, October 1997. Constance Wilde: Jane Brennan. Oscar Wilde: Robert O'Mahoney. Lord Alfred Douglas: Andrew Scott. Mute parts: Muirne Bloomer, Eric Lacey, Kevin Murphy, Ciar O'Callaghan, Jonathan Shankey, Jack Walsh. Director: Patrick Mason Design: Joe Vanek Lighting: Nick Chelton. Stage Director: Finola Eustace. Assistant Stage Directors: Brendan McLoughlin, Stephen Dempsey. Sound: Dave O'Brien. Movement Director: David Bolger.

My Scandalous Life. A rehearsed reading of the play (commissioned by The Oscar Wilde Centre for Irish Writing, Trinity College Dublin) was given at the Peacock Theatre in December 2000. Lord Alfred Douglas: Mark Lambert. Stage directions: Jane Brennan. Voices (off-stage): Michael J. Forde. Director: David

Parnell. Lighting Design: Mick Doyle. Lighting operator: Kevin Mc Fadden. Sound: David Nolan. Stage director: Catriona Behan. Slides: Sinead O'Hanlon.

The Shape of Metal was first produced in the Abbey Theatre, Dublin, in September 2003. Nell: Sara Kestelman. Grace: Justine Mitchell. Judith: Eleanor Methuen. Director: Lynne Parker. Design: John Comiskey and Alan Farquharson. Lighting Design: John Comiskey. Sound: Gareth Fry.

Henry was first produced at the Pittsburgh Irish and Classical Theatre, Pittsburgh, PA (USA), in September 2005. Henry: Richard McMillan. Landolf: Joe Schulz. Ordulph: Martin Giles. Harold: Patrick Jordan. Bertold: Ben Hersey. Carl: Joel Ripka. Frieda: Erin Krom. Margaret: Robin Walsh. Doctor: Larry John Meyers. Thomas: Sam Tsoutsouvas. Director: Andrew S. Paul. Scenic Designer: Frank Conway. Lighting Designer: Cindy Limauro. Costume Designer: Cletus Anderson. Sound Designer: Elizabeth Atkinson. Video Designer: Ciara Moore. Video Design and Implementation: Buzz Miller.

Chapter Notes

Chapter 1

1. Christopher Murray sees the playwright's ambition as "seriously revisionist." Christopher Murray, "The State of Play: Irish Theatre in the Nineties," *State of Play: Irish Theatre in the Nineties,* Eberhard Bort, ed. (Trier: Wissenschaftlichter Verlag Trier, 1996): 17.

2. But in various plays, the playwright has shown his interest for the tensions between the two sides of an individual: "I have always been fascinated by the way in which private qualities, maybe even private weaknesses, become hugely important when the figure is a figure of authority." Gerry Dukes, "Tom Kilroy in Conversation with Gerry Dukes," *Theatre Talk: Voices of the Irish Theatre Practitioners,* Lilian Chambers, Ger FitzGibbon, and Eamonn Jordan, eds. (Dublin: Carysfort Press, 2001): 241.

3. To which Anne Fogarty rightly adds that of gender: "*The O'Neill* and *Making History* contest preconceived views of the Irish past and confront us with the ongoing necessity of re-evaluating the function of ideology and of gender roles in the formation of identity and the political arenas of contemporary Ireland." Anne Fogarty, "The Romance of History: Renegotiating the Past in Thomas Kilroy's *The O'Neill* and Brian Friel's *Making History,*" *Irish University Review* 32:1, Special Issue: *Thomas Kilroy,* Anthony Roche, ed. (Spring/Summer 2002): 32.

Chapter 2

1. A point which Christopher Murray rightly underlines, focusing on the emptiness of the ritual: "Tradition, which O'Faolain defined as 'the ritual of life,' is something rapidly slipping outside Kelly's grasp. An aging bachelor, he lives a nightly round of distraction found in drink among companions who care nothing for him." Christopher Murray, "Kilroy's World Elsewhere," *Irish Writers and Their Creative Process,* Jacqueline Genet and Wynne Hellegouarc'h, eds. (Gerrards Cross: Colin Smythe, 1996): 69.

2. As well as on other aspects linked to representation, in general. See, for instance, Barbara Hayley's perspectives on that point: "So many of the characters playact by stepping out of their own or usual selves that we question the whole nature of representation, particularly, theatrical representation. As in Jacobean drama, our consciousness of theatricality, imposed on us by the playwright, forces us to question not just representation but reality." Barbara Hayley, "Self-Denial and Self-Assertion in Some Plays of Thomas Kilroy: *The Madame MacAdam Travelling Theatre,*" *Studies on the Contemporary Irish Theatre: Actes du colloque de Caen,* Wynne Hellegouarc'h, ed. (Caen: Presses Universitaires de Caen, 1991): 50; or Godeleine Logez-Carpentier, "Kilroy oblige le spectateur à reconsidérer la nature de la représentation de la réalité." Godeleine Logez-Carpentier, "Thomas Kilroy." *Anthologie du théâtre irlandais d'Oscar Wilde à nos jour,* Jacqueline Genet and Wynne Hellegouarc'h, eds. (Caen: Presses Universitaires de Caen, 1998): 300.

3. "*The Death and Resurrection of Mr. Roche* took a resolutely contemporary look at the Ireland of the 1960s, not only through tackling the subject of homosexuality..." Anthony Roche, "Thomas Kilroy," *Post-War Literatures in English: A Lexicon* (Groningen: Wolters-

Noordhoff, 1989): 5. Anthony Roche's outlook on the play (corroborated in private conversations with Tom Kilroy) implies that staging homosexuality was a challenge at the time, but thinking, for instance, of *The Secret Fall of Constance Wilde*, one can measure how much has changed in the staging of such relations.

Chapter 3

1. It is interesting to note that the gender issue may not be as neutral as it might seem at first sight, as Anna McMullan aptly noted in an article written before *The Shape of Metal* was published: "Kilroy's work is a radical refusal of realism, and an exploration of the masks of gender and authority. Yet, it is primarily the male figures who are irresponsible and creative, leaving the women to 'pick up the pieces.' There is a tendency therefore to produce a binary opposition between (male) creativity and (female) reality, (male) invention and (female) responsibility." Anna McMullan, "Masculinity and Masquerade in Thomas Kilroy's *Double Cross* and *The Secret Fall of Constance Wilde*," *Irish University Review* 32:1, Special Issue: *Thomas Kilroy*, Anthony Roche, ed. (Spring/Summer 2002): 136.

2. That she should not succeed in dissipating mutual incomprehension should come as no surprise, as Anthony Roche explains: "Part of Brien's neurosis, and a reason for Shakespeare's presence in the title, is the attempt to keep rewriting his own life as a version of *Othello*. He casts himself in the role of the jealous husband, with Elmina as his Desdemona, and the Anglo-Irish Sylvester as a psychologically and culturally intimidating Iago." Anthony Roche, "Kilroy's Doubles," *Contemporary Irish Drama: From Beckett to McGuinness* (Dublin: Gill and Macmillan, 1994): 200.

Chapter 4

1. Which has a significant impact on the audience, as explained by Christopher Morash: "Within the box are five actors, four of whom take on a variety of roles, usually overplayed with an edge of self-caricature; and a fifth, John Molloy, who played Matt Talbot with seamless realism. By juxtaposing these two theatrical styles, Kilroy stages both Talbot's strength and his inaccessibility." Christopher Morash, *A History of Irish Theatre* (Cambridge: Cambridge University Press, 2002): 250.

2. Fintan O'Toole admirably analyzes the consequences of multifaceted personalities: "In *Talbot's Box*, as in other Kilroy plays, even the most fixed and obvious human relationships — father, son, brother — become confused and threaten to melt into each other. Matt Talbot's struggle is to stop himself becoming, through drink, his father or his brother, and this struggle is embodied before our eyes as the boundaries of character slip and slide. It is this business of embodiment which makes Kilroy, in spite of his considerable stature as a novelist and critic and the cinematic elements in some of his plays, so inescapably a playwright." Fintan O'Toole, "*Talbot's Box*, by Thomas Kilroy," *Critical Moments: Fintan O'Toole on Modern Irish Theatre*, Julia Murray and Redmond O'Hanlon, eds. (Dublin: Carysfort Press, 2003): 207.

3. For the other characters, Anthony Roche showed that the playwright's mode of questioning was different: "The doubling-up of roles, usually a fact of economic necessity, is acknowledged and utilized within the stage-narrative itself for several reasons: metamorphosis is one of the chief properties of drama and so it is entirely 'natural' within its privileged frame that people should assume a number of identities; there is also a social truth to this role-changing about which the play has some satiric points to make; and finally it admits to the deep kinship between the stage and the act of dreaming, whereby the normal boundaries that separate and define human beings no longer operate and one identity or setting blurs readily into another." Anthony Roche, "The Fortunate Fall: Two Plays by Thomas Kilroy," *The Irish Writer and the City*, Maurice Harmon, ed. (Gerrards Cross: Colin Smythe, 1984): 163.

4. Bearing in mind that Kilroy constantly relies on ambivalent images, his challenging vision also implies that orthodox perspectives are taken into account, as is shown by the illustration of a pieta scene which was staged by Patrick Mason in the first production of the play in 1977. See Christopher Fitz-Simmon, "The Abbey Theatre," *Ireland's National Theatre: The First Hundred Years* (London: Thames and Hudson, 2003): 142.

5. "Kilroy's treatment of Talbot's story, cleverly told in the manner of Brecht's epic theatre, with much use of comedy and alienation devices (such as woman as priest) concentrates less on the idea of sanctity than on Talbot's fight to preserve a personal vision and with it his integrity. He is obsessive about this

personal vision to a degree which relates him to the artist in modern society." Christopher Murray, *Twentieth Century Irish Drama: Mirror Up to a Nation* (Manchester: Manchester University Press, 1997): 178. Regarding the break between the saint and society, and the connection with artists, Christopher Murray's analysis seems to have been confirmed by the portrait of Nell in *The Shape of Metal*.

6. Emile-Jean Dumay insists on the seriousness of the playwright's intent: "The double image of the church and the mortuary appears as the theatre, so to speak, breaks into the church. The play is the wild rehearsal of a performance, a critical version of the mystery play. I feel it as a new approach to man and saint through and thanks to the medium of drama inside drama." Emile-Jean Dumay, "The Church on Stage in Contemporary Irish Drama: Tom Kilroy's *Talbot's Box* and Tom Murphy's *The Sanctuary Lamp*," *Etudes Irlandaises* 19:2 (1994): 71.

Chapter 5

1. An intellectual perspective which Denis Sampson summarized very efficiently, when referring to Kilroy's comments on the play. "This ... explains Kilroy's affiliation with the Field Day project to affirm a sense of Irish identity free from racial or geographical boundaries, beyond the incoherence of the colonial psyche, beyond inherited myths of Irishness and Englishness." Denis Sampson, "The Theatre of Thomas Kilroy: Boxes of Words," *Perspectives of Irish Drama and Theatre*, Jacqueline Genet and Alan Cave, eds. (Gerrards Cross: Colin Smythe, 1990): 130.

2. This is the reason why one should be cautious before equating *Double Cross* with a pamphlet: "Another result of the association between Field Day's pamphleteering and its plays was just discernible by 1985. Tom Paulin's *The Riot Act* had been the first Field Day play to be written with the pamphlets in mind. This influence became more pronounced after the production of Thomas Kilroy's *Double Cross* in 1986, which had been written, as the author explained, in lieu of a pamphlet promised but never delivered." Marilynn J. Richtarik, *Acting between the Lines: The Field Day Theatre Company and Irish Cultural Politics, 1980–84* (Oxford: Clarendon Press, 1994): 242.

3. Kilroy is a demanding playwright, not merely for the audience or directors; actors too have to face challenges, a point stressed by Marilynn Richtarik: "These two men (both played by Rea in the Field Day production in a theatrical tour de force) achieved what Kilroy in an author's note to the play describes as 'one kind of mobility, one kind of action across the barriers, the restrictive codes which separate countries from one another.'" Marilynn Richtarik, "The Field Day Theatre Company," *The Cambridge Companion to Twentieth Century Irish Drama*, Shaun Richards, ed. (Cambridge: Cambridge University Press, 2004): 199.

4. Martine Pelletier rightly shows that this process does not merely concern individuals: "Self-denial and self-assertion, service and rebellion appear as the two alternative ways of responding to a colonial situation, the two sides of the same worthless coin Kilroy suggests. The play deconstructs and teases out the process of mutual recreation at the heart of colonization: through Joyce's and Bracken's re-inventions of themselves as loyal or disloyal British subjects, Ireland is reinventing herself according to British rules while Britain too becomes altered by her role in the colonial process." Martine Pelletier, "'Against Mindlessness': Thomas Kilroy and Field Day," *Irish University Review* 32:1, Special Issue: *Thomas Kilroy*, Anthony Roche, ed. (Spring/Summer 2002): 118.

5. Nicholas Grene, connecting Field Day and history, writes: "The Irish in their obsession with history are often said, like the Bourbons, to have learned nothing and forgotten nothing. Modern Irish dramatists have tried to belie this reputation by a recourse to history which will enlighten and illuminate the present. This was always a major objective of the Field Day Theatre Company..., from Thomas Kilroy's evocation of the paired Irish lives of Brendan Bracken and William Joyce in *Double Cross* to Steward Parker's use of the 1974 background of the Ulster worker's strike in *Pentecost*." Nicholas Grene, *The Politics of Irish Drama* (Cambridge: Cambridge University Press, 2000): 235. If one bears in mind "a basic tenet of [Nicholas Grene's] argument that Irish drama is outward-directed, created as much to be viewed from outside as from inside Ireland" [3], one may face a paradox with *Double Cross* in that, as this chapter tries to show, the reference to dark pages of European history might prevent spectators from accepting Tom Kilroy's attempt at insisting on the common point between the two main protagonists.

6. Available *in extenso* in an article published in Chapter 11, p. 127.

7. A process which is doomed to fail, as noted by Fintan O'Toole: "the invented, fictional self of Tom Kilroy's Brendan Bracken in *Double Cross* gives way under extreme pressure to another self of his past life." Fintan O'Toole, "Irish Theatre: The State of the Art," *Theatre Stuff: Critical Essays on Contemporary Irish Drama*, Eamonn Jordan, ed. (Dublin: Carysfort Press, 2000): 53.

Chapter 6

1. As for the staging of the play, the main influence is undoubtedly *Bunraku*. On this, see Nicholas Grene's penetrating analysis in: Nicholas Grene, "Staging the Self: Person and Persona in Kilroy's Plays." *Irish University Review* 32:1, Special Issue: *Thomas Kilroy*, Anthony Roche, ed. (Spring/Summer 2002): 78–82.
2. A photo of another scene in Patrick Mason's staging of *The Secret Fall of Constance Wilde* in 1997 — with the help of David Bolger as puppet director — illustrates the specific impact of puppets on stage. See Christopher Fitz-Simmon, "The Abbey Theatre," *Ireland's National Theatre: The First Hundred Years* (London: Thames and Hudson, 2003): 49.
3. Robert Welch rightly insists on the political side of the play: "This play about Wilde is a visitation into the psyche of an Ireland at the end of the 1990s, in which many of the forms that protected and imprisoned Irish people were breaking up, not least among which was that form of radical separation of the different lives of the country evident in the line drawn across the province of Ulster, the border." Robert Welch, *The Abbey Theatre 1899–1999* (Oxford: Oxford University Press, 1999): 233.
4. In this respect, it is interesting to note that Kilroy's perspective in *The Secret Fall of Constance Wilde* shows that he does not quite correspond to Emilie Fitzgibbon's views regarding the political involvement of Irish playwrights: "Irish playwrights live under the shadow of a gunman forced by his constant presence to consider politics as those of a civil war state. Broader concerns, world politics are kept at bay by the shadow, and it tends to keep political drama in Ireland in the country's major venues at the level of history analysis while it ignores other aspects of the socio-political debate. That such a focus has produced and continues to produce fine drama is undeniable — the success of the Field Day Company whose artistic program is confined to plays which analyze aspects of the northern situation is a case in point, having staged excellent political works by Friel, Mahon, Kilroy, Parker — but it tends to perpetuate the notion that Irish political theatre must deal with tradition, violence and identity rather than with the subjects which might otherwise constitute political theatre." Emelie Fitzgibbon, "Theatre with Its Sleeves Rolled Up," *Irish Writers and Politics. Irish Literary Studies 36*, Komesu Okifumi and Masaru Sekine, eds. (Gerrards Cross: Colin Smythe, 1990): 311.

Chapter 7

1. Thomas Kilroy, "Theatrical Text and Literary Text," *The Achievement of Brian Friel*. Alan J. Peacock, ed. (Gerrards Cross: Colin Smythe, 1993): 91.
2. Both forms of writings illustrate his meditation on the theater, as well as his deliberative quest for renewed dramatic techniques and perspectives to correspond to his ever-changing needs.
3. Kilroy, Thomas. "Groundwork for an Irish Theatre," *Studies: An Irish Quarterly Review of Letters, Philosophy and Science* 48 (Summer 1959): 192–198.
4. While vision is at the core of Kilroy's dramatic perspectives, music is also given a prominent part, and its future interaction during the performance would certainly be worth studying, especially in its connection to scenic images. Indeed, the use of music in *Blake* shows Kilroy's commitment to evolving forms of theater, but while this chapter will only focus on vision, the reader should bear in mind that music is also very important. In *Blake*, one notes that the development of his skills as a playwright enables Kilroy to head toward a more complete form of performance: "While there have been numerous musical settings of Blake's poetry over the years, including some of the lyrics used in the play, I would want to work with new compositions. I have a composer in mind. Obviously, the choral passages in the play will undergo transformations when a composer is in place. The singing should be unaccompanied" [Thomas Kilroy, *Blake*, Introduction, p. 3].
5. Speaking of influence — which, for obvious reasons, cannot be restricted to the notion of scenic images — the playwright himself mentioned Peter Weiss's *Marat-Sade*.
6. This may not be perceived as comic by the audience. All will depend on the performance of the group of actors.

7. The common points are not merely formal; they also concern the subject of the play, which, like many others, is a love story. By love story (should one say, love query?) one understands the staging of individuals whose relationship makes the audience wonder about the essence and nature of love between individuals.

8. Literally, the sole converging point between Blake and Kilroy lies in the combination of one scenic image, which establishes the link between the two creators (image fifty-seven), when the stage direction coincides with one of Blake's images.

9. Although there are no characters on stage at that time, it is important to take into account the spatial division between the two levels, which the playwright himself defines as significant.

10. "As far as we know, Blake was never confined in a lunatic asylum. The story of the play, then, is a fiction. Finchley Grange Asylum never existed. However, Blake was widely regarded as mad (but harmless) by friend and enemy alike.

"From about 1806 to about 1815 Blake and his wife Catherine withdrew into isolation ('I am hid') and the play is set towards the latter part of that period of withdrawal" [Thomas Kilroy, *Blake*, Introduction, p. 3].

11. And to do so, Kilroy creates a gender dichotomy, which Christopher Innes — sharing Anna McMullan's perspectives — defines as follows: "The self-immolating drive to spiritual apotheosis is a specifically male quality; humanity and the demands of social responsibility are feminine." Christopher Innes, "Immortal Eyes and Fearful Symmetry: Towards a Drama of Vision," *Irish University Review* 32:1, Special Issue: *Thomas Kilroy*, Anthony Roche, ed. (Spring/Summer 2002): 171.

12. By ordinary, one understands a banal and realistic — albeit horrifying — vision of what could take place in an asylum.

13. In others, like image 12, what takes place results from particular circumstances, and refers to a general context. The characters' gestures reveal that decisions are being made, and through this, summarize the situation.

14. In *Blake,* the characters on the gallery are reminiscent of the parts given to the attendants in *The Secret Fall of Constance Wilde.* "The attendants lead Oscar and Constance to either side of the stage, downstage and there, facing the audience, they communicate with one another across a distance, without looking at one another. As they speak, they are transformed by the attendants into their youthful selves" [Thomas Kilroy, *The Secret Fall of Constance Wilde*, p. 18].

15. Scenic image 20. The potential of a ritual for these actions is reinforced by a comparable situation depicted in interesting terms in *The Secret Fall of Constance Wilde:*

The attendants suddenly seize her and she screams. They drag her to the staircase and she struggles against them as they push her up the steps to the landing.

No! Please! Don't! I can't go up there! I can't. Can't do it. Not on my own! Please! Where is Oscar? Where is Oscar?

She is now on the landing, crouched, facing the audience, drinking. The attendants retreat to the foot of the steps where they raise their white-gloved hands to receive her [Thomas Kilroy, *The Secret Fall of Constance Wilde*, p. 35].

16. BLAKE: Half of London proclaims my madness. Am I as mad as the king? That is the question? Am I as mad as the old men who send our youth to die in red uniforms so that Commerce and Religion may join hands in profit? Am I as mad as those who would ensnare a child in a mill or a black woman in Surinam? These are the questions they should answer [Thomas Kilroy, *Blake*, p. 35].

17. CATHERINE also says: "(*Loudly*) All you need is to pretend! Pretend! For but a little while!" [*Blake*, p. 35]. This tension between husband and wife is most interesting as it is the exact mirror image of what Oscar Wilde's wife had said in the beginning of *The Secret Fall of Constance Wilde.*

CONSTANCE: Playacting!
OSCAR: Not playacting!
CONSTANCE: You never face the situation as it really is. Never [Thomas Kilroy, *The Secret Fall of Constance Wilde*, p. 11].

18. As often in the case of writers, *Blake* is probably also a form of self-portrait, an inquiry into the workings of the mind of an artist.

19. He too suffers from a particular form of blindness:

"CATHERINE: You're so puffed up with your greatness, Mr. Blake, that you can't see what's in front of you. Head in the sky and tripping over stones, you are" (36).

This rather unflattering portrait of the poet characterizes him as an individual who may associate his life with vision, but proves unable to cope with the basic reality of sight.

20. Blake insists on the divine aspect of

his visions, perception amounting to a form of belonging, an acknowledgment that he deserves to see them.

BLAKE: Nor are these visions my own, no, I am but the secretary and the author dictates to me from Eternity — catherine. All this I know, William — blake. *(Transfixed by his vision)*. Satan is risen, the Beast stirs and the Whore of Babylon is crowned in dominion over the world of vegetative Nature! [Thomas Kilroy, *Blake*, p. 37].

21. BLAKE: At first I thought I saw Antichrist splayed against the wall there but it was only this poor madman. It is a lesson [Thomas Kilroy, *Blake*, p. 45].

22. In view of the obsessive invasion of Shakespearean images in the playwright's mind, in *Tea and Sex and Shakespeare*, the Ophelian vision appears natural, almost expected.

23. Both Blake ("Raphael and Michelangelo and Albert Durer knew this line to the finest point. Reynolds blurs and blotches" [29]) and Catherine ("Even when he's in the worst mood he'll become peaceful again when he talks about pictures that he loves. Italians, mostly. Though there's this German man too that he's very fond of. Durer they call him" [49]) mention painters and thus enlarge the scope of reference concerning images.

Chapter 8

1. A point which Adrian Frazier summarizes in his powerful presentation of the play: "Kilroy's new play grapples with the significance of art, but not in its folk or even Irish dimension; this play is about the fate of the 20th century modernist ambition to confront chaos, failure, and meaninglessness with form alone, not with God, or nation, or the dignity of man." Adrian Frazier, "The Body of Life," Abbey Theatre brochure for *The Shape of Metal* (2003).

2. "We write plays, I feel, in order to populate a stage." Thomas Kilroy, "Theatrical Text and Literary Text," *The Achievement of Brian Friel*, Alan J. Peacock, ed. (Gerrards Cross: Colin Smythe, 1993): 91.

Chapter 9

1. Whether they live in the free State (Cf. "Do you know, I believe we simply reached a crossroads somewhere in Ulster. Someone mentioned the Free State. The name beckoned. So here we are!" [Thomas Kilroy, *The Madame MacAdam Travelling Theatre* (London: Methuen, 1991): 2]) or in Ulster, Irish people's outlook on their connection with the former colonial power plays an essential part in the way they define themselves. Living in the South or in the North also has consequences in the way individuals claim or reject their Irish identity. While some define themselves as citizens of a free state — a former colony of the British Empire — others, in Ulster, often have conflicting visions of who they are.

2. Thomas Kilroy, *The Seagull: An Adaptation*, *The Cambridge Companion to Chekhov*, V. Gottlieb and P. Allain, eds. (Cambridge: Cambridge University Press, 2000): 80. Other critics have commented on Kilroy's adaptation of Chekhov: see, for instance, Frank McGuinness, "A Voice from the Trees: Thomas Kilroy's Version of Chekhov's *The Seagul*," *Irish University Review: A Journal of Irish Studies* 21.1 (Spring/Summer 1992): 3–14; and also, Joseph Long "An Irish Seagull: Chekhov and the New Irish Theatre," *Revue de Littérature Comparée* 4 (Oct.–Dec. 1995): 419–426.

3. Thomas Kilroy, *The Seagull (after Chekhov)* (Loughcrew: Gallery Press, 1993): Introduction to *The Seagull*, p. 12.

4. See, for instance, Brian Friel's adaptations of *Three Sisters* and *Uncle Vanya* (after Chekhov), and Frank McGuinness' adaptations of Ibsen's *Rosmersholm*, *Peer Gynt*, *Hedda Gabler*, *A Doll's House*; Chekhov's *Three Sisters*, *Uncle Vanya*; Lorca's *Yerma*; Brecht's *The Caucasian Chalk Circle*; Sophocles' *Electra*; and Ostrovsky's *The Storm*.

5. Kilroy's adaptation of *Six Characters in Search of an Author* was first staged at the Abbey Theatre, Dublin, in May 1996. His adaptation of *Ghosts* was first produced at the Abbey Theatre in October 1989.

6. The Big House itself possibly symbolizes Ireland.

7. Anton Chekhov, *The Seagull*, E. K. Bristow, trans. (New York: Norton): 6. Other similarly discreet elements are mentioned as part of everyday life, and thus contribute to the creation of this colonial atmosphere. Compare the following two lines, for instance:

MEDVEDENKO: We must have tea and sugar, don't you think? [Anton Chekhov, *The Seagull*, p. 6].

JAMES: ...duty on the tea. I'm telling you, ya don't know the half of it" [Kilroy, *The Seagull*].

8. Brian Friel, *Translations* (London: Faber and Faber, 1981).

9. And this corresponds to Field Day's

objectives as stated in *Ireland's Field Day*: "All the directors are northerners; they believed that Field Day could and should contribute to the solution of the present crisis by producing analyses of the established opinions, myths and stereotypes which had become both a symptom and a cause of the current situation" [Field Day Theatre Company Ireland's Field Day (London: Hutchinson, 1985): vii.] In brief, all the directors felt that the political crisis in the North and its reverberation in the Republic had made the necessity of a reappraisal of Ireland's political and cultural situation explicit and urgent.

10. Anton Chekhov, *The Seagull*, p. 22.

11. The excerpt below further corroborates this:

PETER: The tenants are in revolt. This man Parnell. Indeed, it has just occurred to me, quite clearly, that we may have to sell [Thomas Kilroy *The Seagull*, p. 59].

This extract, which does not correspond to any political allusion in Chekhov's *Seagull*, does underline the idea of a conflict with Parnell, but one feels that Kilroy is wary of creating clear-cut oppositions.

12. *Ibid.*, p. 63.

13. By contrast, Mary has no illusions about the perception that James' family has of their future marriage:

MARY: My James isn't the brightest of creatures and he hasn't a shilling to his name and he's a Roman Catholic and he has all that awful family of his down in that awful cottage but I believe he truly loves me. His family look on me as a kind of loot rifled from the Big House [*Ibid.*, p. 56].

This situation reminds one of *The O'Neill*, in which Hugh and Mabel, who belonged to opposite clans, could not agree on a *modus vivendi*.

14. One should note that in his three adaptations (*The Seagull, Ghosts*, and *Six Characters in Search of an Author*), the question of identity — posed in terms of insiders and outsiders — is raised.

15. For instance, compare:

DORN: That's true, there are very few actors gifted with brilliance nowadays, but the average actor is much, much better than he used to be.

SHAMRAEV: I just can't agree with you [Anton Chekhov, *The Seagull*, p. 12].

DR. HICKEY: We may not have the acting, perhaps, on the old scale but there is more reality on the stage nowadays...

ISOBEL: Reality. Fiddlesticks! What on earth has theatre got to do with reality? [Thomas Kilroy, *The Seagull*, p. 26].

16. For instance, "a poor man" becomes "the tinkers out on the road," as exemplified below:

MEDVEDENKO: Even a poor man can be happy [Anton Chekhov, *The Seagull*, p. 6].

MARY. Even the tinkers out on the road can be happy [Thomas Kilroy, *The Seagull*, p. 17].

Sentences like "Your father won't give me the lend of a horse" [Thomas Kilroy, *The Seagull*, p. 70] further contribute to the staging of an Irish identity built on common expressions.

17. Compare this quote with the one below:

MASHA: My leg's gone to sleep ... (*Goes out*).

DORN: She'll go and soak up a couple of glasses before lunch.

SORIN: She has no personal happiness, poor thing.

DORN: Nonsense, your Excellency [Anton Chekhov, *The Seagull*, p. 21].

18. This passage parallels the following one in the Russian original:

NINA: I open my lips to speak once in a hundred years, and my voice resounds despondently in this barren, desolate place, and no one hears ... [Anton Chekhov, *The Seagull*, p. 13].

19. But, as Joseph Long shows, he is bound to fail: "In this group without a centre, it is the dynamics of failure that hold the community together, and the failure is not only of the heart, but also of the creative imagination. In varying degrees, each of the characters in the grip of frustrated artistic ambition, to write or to perform." Joseph Long, "An Irish Seagull: Chekhov and the New Irish Theatre," *Revue de Littérature Comparée* 4 (Oct.–Dec. 1995): p. 421.

Chapter 10

1. p. 192.
2. p. 192. While today the concept of community theater might be rejected by the playwright, he has repeatedly stated that he viewed theater as collaborative work.
3. p. 194.
4. p. 195.

Chapter 14

1. In fact, the rewritten version of the play was staged by Rough Magic in 1988, director Declan Hughes.

Chapter 15

1. The Abbey Theatre, Dublin.

Bibliography

Primary Sources

Kilroy, Thomas. *The Death and Resurrection of Mr. Roche*. London: Faber and Faber, 1969.
_____. *Talbot's Box*. Loughcrew: Gallery Press, 1979.
_____. *Double Cross*. London: Faber and Faber, 1986.
_____. *Double Cross*. *Field Day Anthology of Irish Writing*. Ed. Seamus Deane. Derry: Field Day Theatre Company, 1990. 1274–305.
_____. *The Madame MacAdam Travelling Theatre*. London: Methuen, 1991.
_____. *Double Cross*. Loughcrew: Gallery Press, 1994.
_____. *The O'Neill*. Loughcrew: Gallery Press, 1995.
_____. *The Secret Fall of Constance Wilde*. Loughcrew: Gallery Press, 1997.
_____. *Tea and Sex and Shakespeare*. Loughcrew: Gallery Press, 1998.
_____. "The Secret Fall of Constance Wilde." *New Plays from the Abbey Theatre*. Eds. Judy Friel and Sanford Sternlicht. Syracuse, NY: Syracuse University Press, 2001. 59–110.
_____. *The Death and Resurrection of Mr. Roche*. (Revised Edition) Loughcrew: Gallery Press, 2002.
_____. *The Shape of Metal*. Loughcrew: Gallery Press, 2003.
_____. *My Scandalous Life*. Loughcrew: Gallery Press, 2004.

Unpublished Plays

Kilroy, Thomas. *Blake*.
_____. *Dreaming House*.

Novel

Kilroy, Thomas. *The Big Chapel*. London: Faber and Faber, 1986.

Adaptations

AFTER CHEKHOV
The Seagull. Loughcrew: London: Methuen, 1981.
_____. Loughcrew: Gallery Press, 1993.

AFTER IBSEN
Ghosts. Loughcrew: Gallery Press, 2002.

AFTER PIRANDELLO
Henry. (Unpublished).
Six Characters in Search of an Author. (Unpublished).

AFTER WEDEKIND
Christ Deliver Us! (Unpublished)

Radio Plays (Unpublished)

Kilroy, Thomas. *The Door.* BBC Radio 4, 27 October 1967.
_____. *That Man Bracken.* BBC Radio 3, 20 June 1986.
_____. *The Colleen and the Cowboy.* RTE Radio, September 11, 2005.

Television Plays (Unpublished)

Kilroy, Thomas. *Farmers.* TV Broadcast in 1978, Radio Telefis Eireann.
_____. *The Black Joker.* 1981.
_____. *Gold in the Streets.* 1996.

Excerpts from Novels and Plays

Kilroy, Thomas. "Young Magdalen and the Pharisee." *Threshold* 17, 66–74.
_____. "Her Whiteness Attracts a Blackness." *The Writers: A Sense of Place.* Dublin: O'Brien Press, 1980. 92–6.
_____. "Angela Falling from Grace." *Krino 1.* Spring 1986. 16–23.
_____. "Poulatinna." *The Flight Path: Writings by the Winners of the American Ireland Fund Literary Award 1972–96.* Maurice Hayes, ed. Oldcastle, County Meath: Gallery, 1996. 19–24.
_____. "From *Blake*: A play." *Irish University Review* 32:1, Special Issue: Thomas Kilroy, Spring/Summer 2002. 159–63.

Author's Notes and Introductions

Kilroy, Thomas. "Author's Note." *Talbot's Box.* By Kilroy. Loughcrew: Gallery Press, 1979. 5–6.
_____. "Introduction." *The Enemy Within.* By Brian Friel. Loughcrew: Gallery Press, 1979. 8–9.
_____. "Author's Note." *Double Cross.* By Kilroy. London: Faber and Faber, 1986. 6–7.
_____. "Introduction." *The House by the Churchyard.* By Sheridan Le Fanu. Belfast: Appletree Press, 1992. XI-XIV.
_____. "Introduction." *The Seagull.* By Kilroy. Loughcrew: Gallery Press, 1993. 11–4.
_____. "Introduction." *Double Cross.* By Kilroy. Loughcrew: Gallery Press, 1994. 11–5.

Critical Study

_____. Ed. *Sean O'Casey: A Collection of Critical Essays.* Englewood Cliffs, N.J.: Prentice-Hall, 1976.

Contributions to Books and Periodicals

_____. "Mervyn Wall: The Demands of Satire." *Studies* 47, Spring 1958. 83–9.
_____. "Groundwork for an Irish Theatre." *Studies* 48, Summer 1959. 192–8.

_____. "Reading and Teaching the Novel." *Studies* 56, Winter 1967. 356–67.
_____. "The Playboy as Poet." *PMLA* 83, 1968. 439–42.
_____. "The Outsider." *The Irish Times*, April 16, 1971. 8.
_____. "Synge and Modernism." *J. M. Synge Centenary Papers*. Ed. Maurice Harmon. Dublin: Dolmen Press, 1972. 167–79.
_____. "Synge the Dramatist." *Mosaic* 5.1, 1972. 9–16.
_____. "Tellers of Tales." *Times Literary Supplement*, March 17, 1972. 301–2.
_____. "The Writers' Group in Galway." *The Irish Times*, April 8, 1976. 10.
_____. "Two Playwrights: Yeats and Beckett." *Myth and Reality in Irish Literature*. Ed. Joseph Ronsley. Toronto: Wilfrid Laurier University Press, 1977. 183–95.
_____. "Anglo-Irish Playwrights and Comic Tradition." *The Crane Bag* 3.2, 1979. 19–27.
_____. "The Moon in the Yellow River: Denis Johnson's Shavianism." *Denis Johnson: A Retrospective*. Ed. J. Ronsley. Gerrards Cross: Colin Smythe, 1981. 49–58.
_____. "The Irish Writer: Self and Society, 1950–1980." *Literature and the Changing Ireland. Irish Literary Studies 9*. Ed. Peter. Connolly. Gerrards Cross: Colin Smythe, 1982. 175–87.
_____. "The Anglo-Irish." *The Irish Times*, December 7, 1983.
_____. "Brecht, Beckett, and Williams." *Sagetrieb* 3.2, Fall 1984. 81–7.
_____. "Goldsmith the Playwright." *Goldsmith, the Gentle Master*. Ed. Sean Lucy. Cork: Cork University Press, 1984. 66–77.
_____. "The Autobiographical Novel." Ed. A. Martin. *The Genius of Irish Prose*. Dublin: Mercier, 1985. 67–75.
_____. "Ireland's Pseudo Englishman." *Magill* 11.5, January 1988. 52–4.
_____. "Reassessment. Thomas Kilroy on J. M. Synge: Synge, the Complex Creator of a Closed World." *The Irish Times*, Saturday, April 29, 1989. Weekend section, 9.
_____. "Secularized Ireland." *Culture in Ireland: Division or Diversity?* Ed. E. Longley. Belfast: Queen's University Belfast, 1991. 135–41.
_____. "A Generation of Playwrights." *Irish University Review* 22:1, Spring 1992. 135–41.
_____. "Theatrical Text and Literary Text." *The Achievement of Brian Friel*. Ed. Alan J. Peacock. Gerrards Cross: Colin Smythe, 1993. 91–102.
_____. "Chekhov and the Irish." Program Note, *Uncle Vanya* adaptation, Frank McGuinness. Field Day Theatre Company, 1995.
_____. "*John Bull's Other Island*: Shaw's Irish Play." *Banado ShoKenkyu*, Vol. 3, 1995, 11-1, 1–20.
_____. "The Literary Tradition of Irish Drama." Anglistentag Proceedings, Vol. XVI. Eds. W. Riehle and H. Kieper. Tübingen: Max Niemeyer Verlag, 1995. 7–15.
_____. "From Page to Stage." *Irish Writers and Their Creative Process*. Eds. Jacqueline Genet and Wynne Hellegouarc'h. Gerrards Cross: Colin Smythe, 1996. 55–62.
_____. "The Anglo-Irish Theatrical Imagination." *Bullan* 3.2, Winter 1997/Spring 1998. 5–12.
_____. "Friendship." *Irish University Review*, 29:1, Spring/Summer 1999. 83–9.
_____. "*The Seagull*: An Adaptation." *The Cambridge Companion to Chekhov*. Eds. Vera Gottlieg and Paul Allain. Cambridge: Cambridge University Press, 2000. 80–90.
_____. "Master of Re-Invention." *The Irish Times*, September 17, 2001.
_____. "The Wildean Triangle." *What Revels Are in Hand? Assessments of Contemporary Drama in English in Honour of Wofgang Lippke*. Eds. B. Reitz, H. Stahl. *Contemporary Drama in English 8*. Trier: WVT Wissenschaftlicher Verlag, 2001. 47–55.

Interviews

Battersby, Eileen. "Kilroy Is Here." *The Irish Times* / Features. Thursday, October 2, 1997.
Brennan, Paul, and Thierry Dubost. "New Voices in Irish Theatre: an Interview with Thomas Kilroy." *Etudes Irlandaises* 26.1, Spring 2001. 7–20. (Reprinted in this book.)
Dawe, Gerald. "An Interview with Thomas Kilroy." *Krino 1976–96: An Anthology of Modern Irish Writing.* Eds. Gerald Dawe, Jonathan Williams. Dublin: Gill and Macmillan, 1996. 230–35.
Dukes, Gerry. "Tom Kilroy in Conversation with Gerry Dukes." *Theatre Talk: Voices of the Irish Theatre Practitioners.* Eds. Lilian Chambers, Fitzgibbon Ger, and Eamonn Jordan. Dublin: Carysfort Press, 2001. 240–51.
Edwards, Jane. "Identity Crises." Interview with Thomas Kilroy. *Time Out*, May 7–13, 1986. 32.
Kilroy, Thomas. Interview in *Education and the Arts: A Research Report.* Ed. David Murphy. Published on behalf of the School of Education by the Department of Higher Education and Educational Research, Trinity College, 1987. 189–97.
Kurdi, Maria. "The Whole Idea of Writing Historical Fictions Is Paradoxical." An interview with Thomas Kilroy. *Hungarian Journal of English and American Studies* 8.1, Spring 2002. 259–68.
Roche, Anthony. "Thomas Kilroy: An Interview." Ed. Anthony Roche. *Irish University Review* 32:1, Special Issue: Thomas Kilroy, Spring/Summer 2002. 150–8.

Published Translations

Kilroy, Thomas. *La Vraie vie de Mathieu Talbot.* Trans. Denis Rigal. Bédée: Ed. Folle Avoine, 1997.
———. *Illusions Comiques à l'irlandaise.* (Includes *Tea and Sex and Shakespeare* and *The Madame MacAdam Travelling Theatre.*) Trans. Godeleine Logez-Carpentier, Emile-Jean Dumay. Lille: Presses Universitaires du Septentrion, 1998.

Secondary Sources

Full Length Studies

Dubost, Thierry. *Le théâtre de Thomas Kilroy.* Caen: Presses Universitaires de Caen, 2001.
Roche, Anthony ed. *Irish University Review* 32:1, Special Issue: Thomas Kilroy, Spring/Summer 2002.

Articles about the Plays

Barnett, Gene A. "Thomas Kilroy." *Contemporary Dramatists.* Ed. K. A. Berney. London: St. James Press, 1993. 354–7.
Burke, Patrick. "Thomas Kilroy's Latest and Rough Magic." *Irish Literary Supplement* 7:2, Fall 1988. 15.
Dawe, Gerald. "Thomas Kilroy." *Theatre Ireland* 3, 1983. 117–9.
———. "A Life of Our Own: *Double Cross* by Thomas Kilroy." *Theatre Ireland* 15, 1988. 24–6.
———. "Thomas Kilroy." Ed. Anthony Roche. *Irish University Review* 32:1, Special Issue: Thomas Kilroy, Spring/Summer 2002. 33–8.
———. "Kilroy's Wilde: on *The Secret Fall of Constance Wilde.*" *The Importance of Being*

Misunderstood: Homage to Oscar Wilde. Ed. Giovanna Franci, Giovanna Silvana. Bologna: Patron Editore, 2003. 135 — 41.

Dubost, Thierry. "Irish Disconnections with the Former British Empire: Thomas Kilroy's Adaptation of *The Seagull*." *Crucible of Cultures: Anglophone Drama at the Dawn of the New Millenium*. Eds. Marc Maufort, Franca Bellarsi. Brussels: Peter Lang, 2002. 151–62.

———. "Kilroy's Theatre of the Conflicted Self." Ed. Anthony Roche. *Irish University Review* 32:1, Special Issue: Thomas Kilroy, Spring/Summer 2002. 10–7.

———. "Boucicault, Friel et Kilroy: Etude en Do bémol majeur." *Etudes Irlandaises*, no. 30-1, Spring 2005. 67–81.

Dumay, Emile-Jean. "The Church on Stage in Contemporary Irish Drama: Tom Kilroy's *Talbot's Box* and Tom Murphy's *The Sanctuary Lamp*." *Etudes Irlandaises* 19.2, 1994. 65–72.

Dunne, Phil. "An Uncluttered Window on Irish Life: The Work of Thomas Kilroy." *Studies*, Summer 2000. 140–7.

Eamonn, Jordan. "Thomas Kilroy's *Double Cross*: Mediatized Realities and Sites of Multiple, Projected Selves." *Focus: Studies in English Literature*, Winter 2004 (special issue devoted to multi-media and theatre). 101–115.

Etherton, Michael. "Dublin: Thomas Kilroy, *Talbot's Box; Double Cross*." *Contemporary Irish Dramatists*. Basingstoke: Macmillan, 1989. 51–62.

Fallon, Gabriel. "All This and the Abbey Too." *Studies*, Winter 1959. 432–42.

Fallon, Peter, and Sean Golden, eds. "Thomas Kilroy." *Soft Day: A Miscellany of Contemporary Irish Writing*. Portmarnock: Wolfhound Press; Notre Dame, IN: University of Notre Dame Press, 1980, 98–102.

Fitzgibbon, Emelie. "Theatre with Its Sleeves Rolled Up." *Irish Writers and Politics*. Eds. Komesu Okifumi and Masaru Sekine. *Irish Literary Studies* 36. Gerrards Cross: Colin Smythe, 1990. 306–15.

Fogarty, Anne. "The Romance of History: Renegotiating the Past in Thomas Kilroy's *The O'Neill* and Brian Friel's *Making History*." *Irish University Review* 32:1, Special Issue: Thomas Kilroy, Spring/Summer 2002. 18–32.

Frazier, Adrian. "The Body of Life." Abbey Theatre brochure for *The Shape of Metal*. 2003.

Genet, Jacqueline. "Thomas Kilroy." *La Littérature irlandaise*. Eds. Jacqueline Genet and Claude Fierobe. Paris: Armand Colin, 1997. 175–9.

Grene, Nicholas. "Staging the Self: Person and Persona in Kilroy's Plays." Ed. Anthony Roche. *Irish University Review* 32:1, Special Issue: Thomas Kilroy, Spring/Summer 2002. 70–82.

Harmon, Maurice. "By Memory Inspired: Themes and Forces in Recent Irish Writing." *Eire Ireland*, VII, 2, Summer 1973. 3 —16.

Hayley, Barbara. "Self-Denial and Self-Assertion in Some Plays of Thomas Kilroy: *The Madame MacAdam Travelling Theatre.*" *Studies on the Contemporary Irish Theatre: Actes du colloque de Caen*. Wynne Hellegouarc'h. Caen: Presses Universitaires de Caen, 1991. 47–56.

Hogan, Robert, ed. "Kilroy, Thomas." *Dictionary of Irish Literature*. Westport CT: Greenwood Press, 1996. 670–3.

Hunt Mahony, Christina. *Contemporary Irish Literature*. New York: St. Martin's Press, 1998. 146–55.

Hunter, Charles. "Thomas Kilroy: A Private Subversive." *The Irish Times*, July 2, 1988. Weekend section, 11.

Imhof, Rudiger. "Thomas Kilroy." Eds. A. Jochen, I. Rudiger. *Irische Dramatiker der Gegenwart*. Darmstadt: Wissenschaftliche Buchgesellschaft, 1996. 56–70.

Innes, Christopher. "Immortal Eyes and Fearful Symmetry: Towards a Drama of Vision."

Irish University Review 32:1, Special Issue: Thomas Kilroy, Spring/Summer 2002. 164–75.

Logez-Carpentier, Goldeleine. "Introduction." *Illusions Comiques à l'irlandaise*. Trans. Godeleine Logez-Carpentier, Emile-Jean Dumay. Lille : Presses Universitaires du Septentrion, 1998. 7–10.

———. "Shakespeare Revisited : théâtre et métathéâtre dans les comédies de Thomas Kilroy." *Irlande : Vision (s) / Révision (s)*. Ed. Martine Pelletier. Tours: Graat, 1998. 75–88.

———. "Thomas Kilroy." *Anthologie du théâtre irlandais d'Oscar Wilde à nos jours*. Eds. Jacqueline Genet and Wynne Hellegouarc'h. Caen: Presses Universitaires de Caen, 1998. 297–323.

Long, Joseph. "An Irish Seagull: Chekhov and the New Irish Theatre." *Revue de Littérature Comparée* 4 Oct.–Dec. 1995. 419–26.

———. "Diction and Ideology: Chekhov's Irish Voice." *Double Vision: Studies in Literary Translation*. Ed. Jane Taylor. Durham: University of Durham Press, 2002, 163–73.

Mangan, Michael. "Thomas Kilroy." *British and Irish Dramatists Since World War II*. Ed. J. Bull. Detroit: Bruccoli Clark Layman, 2001. 188–95.

Mason, Patrick. "Acting Out." *Irish University Review* 32:1, Special Issue: Thomas Kilroy, Spring/Summer 2002. 137–47.

Maxwell, Des. *A Critical History of Modern Irish Drama 1891–1980*. Cambridge: Cambridge University Press, 1984. 171–75.

McGuinness, Frank. "A Haunted House: The Theatre of Thomas Kilroy." *Irish Theatre Today*. Ed. Barbara Hayley and Walter Rix. Würzburg: Königshausen and Neumann, 1985.

———. "A Voice from the Trees: Thomas Kilroy's Version of Chekhov's *The Seagull*." *Irish University Review: A Journal of Irish Studies* 21.1, Spring/Summer 1992. 3–14.

McMullan, Anna. "Masculinity and Masquerade in Thomas Kilroy's *Double Cross* and *The Secret Fall of Constance Wilde*." *Irish University Review* 32:1, Special Issue: Thomas Kilroy, Spring/Summer 2002. 126–36.

Mikami, Hiroko. "Kilroy's Vision of Doubleness: the Question of National Identity and Theatricality in *Double Cross*." *Irish University Review* 32:1, Special Issue: Thomas Kilroy, Spring/Summer 2002. 100–9.

Murray, Christopher. "Thomas Kilroy." Contemporary Irish Writers: series 5. *Ireland Today, Bulletin of the Department of Foreign Affairs* 993, November/December 1982. 11–4.

———. "Kilroy's World Elsewhere." *Irish Writers and Their Creative Process*. Eds. Jacqueline Genet and Wynne Hellegouarc'h. Gerrards Cross: Colin Smythe, 1996. 63–77.

———. "The State of Play: Irish Theatre in the Nineties." *State of Play: Irish Theatre in the Nineties*. Ed. Eberhard Bort. Trier: Wissenschaftlichter Verlag Trier, 1996. 9–23.

———. "A Generation of Playwrights, Playing the North." *Twentieth Century Irish Drama: Mirror Up to a Nation*. Manchester: Manchester University Press, 1997. 162–222.

———. "The Artist and the Critic." *Irish University Review* 32:1, Special Issue: Thomas Kilroy, Spring/Summer 2002. 83–94.

O'Toole, Fintan. "Double Vision: the Ambivalences of Thomas Kilroy." *Magill* 11, 1988. 57–9.

———. "Mr. Roche Earns His Place in the Repertoire." *The Irish Times*, June 3, 1989. Weekend, 5.

———. "No Resting Place in Kilroy's Plays." *The Irish Times*, May 10, 1990. 8.

———. "Irish Theatre: The State of the Art." *Theatre Stuff: Critical Essays on Contemporary Irish Drama*. Ed. Eamonn Jordan. Dublin: Carysfort Press, 2000. 47–58.

———. "*Double Cross*, by Thomas Kilroy." *Critical Moments: Fintan O'Toole on Modern*

Irish Theatre. Eds. Julia Murray and Redmond O'Hanlon. Dublin: Carysfort Press, 2003. 50–3.

———. "*Talbot's Box*, by Thomas Kilroy." *Critical Moments: Fintan O'Toole on Modern Irish Theatre*. Eds. Julia Murray and Redmond O'Hanlon. Dublin: Carysfort Press, 2003. 206–8.

———. "Thomas Kilroy." *Critical Moments: Fintan O'Toole on Modern Irish Theatre*. Eds. Julia Murray and Redmond O'Hanlon. Dublin: Carysfort Press, 2003. 310–3.

Pelletier, Martine. "'Against Mindlessness': Thomas Kilroy and Field Day." *Irish University Review* 32:1, Special Issue: Thomas Kilroy, Spring/Summer 2002. 110–125.

Rabey, David Ian. "The Bite of Exiled Love: Abjective Protagonists in Some Contemporary Anglo-Irish Dramas." *Essays in Theatre/Etudes Théâtrales* 13(1), 1994. 29–43.

Randaccio, Monica. *Il Teatro irlandese contemporaneo: Soggettività e comunità in Friel, Murphy e Kilroy*. Trieste: Parnaso, 2001.

Richtarik, Marilynn. "The Field Day Theatre Company." *The Cambridge Companion to Twentieth Century Irish Drama*. Ed. Shaun Richards. Cambridge: Cambridge University Press, 2004. 191–203.

Roche, Anthony. "The Fortunate Fall: Two Plays by Thomas Kilroy." *The Irish Writer and the City*. Ed. Maurice Harmon. Gerrards Cross: Colin Smythe, 1984. 159–68.

———. "Thomas Kilroy." *Post-War Literatures in English: A Lexicon*. Groningen: Wolters-Noordhoff, 1989. 1–13.

———. "Kilroy's Doubles." *Contemporary Irish Drama: From Beckett to McGuinness*. Dublin: Gill and Macmillan, 1994. 189–215.

Sampson, Denis. "The Theatre of Thomas Kilroy: Boxes of Words." *Perspectives of Irish Drama and Theatre*. Eds. Jacqueline Genet and Alan Cave. Gerrards Cross: Colin Smythe, 1990. 130–9.

Trotter, Mary. "Double Crossing Irish Borders: The Field Day Production of Tom Kilroy's *Double Cross*." *New Hibernia Review* 1, Spring 1997. 31–43.

Welch, Robert, ed. "Thomas Kilroy." *The Oxford Companion to Irish Literature*. Oxford: Clarendon Press, 1996. 290.

Other Works

Byrne, Ophelia. "Thomas Kilroy: A Bibliography." *Irish University Review* 32:1, Special Issue: Thomas Kilroy, Spring/Summer 2002. 176–90.

Fitz-Simon, Christopher. *The Abbey Theatre: Ireland's National Theatre: The First Hundred Years*. London: Thames and Hudson, 2003.

Grene, Nicholas. *The Politics of Irish Drama*. Cambridge: Cambridge University Press, 2000.

King, Kimball. "Thomas Kilroy." *Ten Modern Irish Playwrights: A Comprehensive Annotated Bibliography*. New York: Garland, 1979. 65–9.

Morash, Christopher. *A History of Irish Theatre*. Cambridge: Cambridge University Press, 2002.

Murray, Christopher. *Twentieth Century Irish Drama: Mirror Up to a Nation*. Manchester: Manchester University Press, 1997.

Princess Grace Irish Library (Monaco): EIRData, Electronic Irish records Dataset: *http://www.pgil-eirdata.org/html.pgil_datasets/authors/k/Kilroy,T/life/htm*

Richtarik, Marilynn J. *Acting Between the Lines: The Field Day Theatre Company and Irish Cultural Politics, 1980–84*. Oxford: Clarendon Press, 1994.

Welch, Robert. *The Abbey Theatre 1899–1999*. Oxford: Oxford University Press, 1999.

Index

Abbey Theatre 2, 25, 26, 55, 98, 104, 142, 155, 158, 159, 161, 162, 164, 167, 169, 170, 172, 181, 182, 183, 186, 188, 190, 191
Albee, Edward 131
Anderson, Cletus 176, 183
Angels in America 170
Artaud, Antonin 94–96, 150
Artifice 47, 59, 68, 70, 71, 78, 115, 125, 138
Aston 114
Atkinson, Liz 176, 183

Bacon, Francis 146
Banville, John 135
Barnes, Ben 155
Barrault, Jean-Louis 128, 153
Barrington, Kathleen 181
Bates, Jessica 117
Baudelaire, Charles 43
Beckett, Samuel 33, 40, 80, 101, 106, 128–133
Behan, John 181, 183
Béjart, Maurice 128
Bertinazzi, Carlo Antonio 82
The Big Chapel 1, 137, 142, 163
Blake ix, 3, 81–96, 98, 99, 136, 138, 145, 146, 150, 151, 175, 176, 188, 189, 190
Bloomer, Muirne 182
Bolger, David 182, 188
Botticelli, Sandro 103
Le Bourgeois Gentilhomme 35
Bourke, Fergus 26, 29, 55, 167
Boyle, Consolata 182
Bracken 2, 57–68, 187
Brecht, Bertolt 10, 34, 82, 122, 142, 186, 190
Brennan, Barbara 111, 182
Brennan, Jane 72, 182
Brennan, Paul 125–136
Brennan, Seamus 181
Brennan, Stephen 55, 167, 181
Brien 34–40, 42, 43, 186

Brook, Peter 82, 150
Brown, Noelle 182
Bunraku 82, 129, 138, 188
Burge, Stuart 182
Burke, Brian 147
Byrne, Edward 181

Caravaggio, Michelangelo Merisi da 146
Casson, Bronwell 181
Catherine 50, 85–87, 89, 90–93, 189, 190
Cecil 10–13
Charity Randall Theatre 175
Chekhov, Anton ix, 2, 98, 108–110, 112, 114–116, 121, 142, 162, 174, 190, 191
Chelton, Nick 182
Churchill, Winston 57, 62, 68, 127
Claudel, Paul 71, 128
Cluskey, May 181
Coleman, Alex 117
Colgan, Eileen 55, 167, 181
Comiskey, John 183
Constance 2, 69, 70–80, 132, 133, 156, 169, 171, 189
Constantine 114–116, 162
Conway, Frank 175, 179, 183
The Cowboy and the Colleen 140
Craigie, Ingrid 55, 167, 181
Crowley, John 142, 182
Curry, Julian 182
Cyril 71

Davis, Miles 158
Dawson, Patrick 181
Deane, Seamus 148
The Death and Resurrection of Mr. Roche ix, 1, 4, 20, 21, 24–26, 28, 82, 99, 144, 161, 175, 181
Deeney, Donagh 182
Delvin, Alan 181, 182
Dempsey, Stephen 182

201

Dempster, Rory 182
Desdemona 186
Diderot, Denis 82
Dr. Hibbel 85–89, 92, 93
Dr. Hickey 114, 115, 191
Dolan, Marese 181
Double Cross ix, 2, 57, 58–60, 64, 68, 125, 127, 128, 132, 138, 147, 149, 175, 182
Douglas 71, 74, 75, 132, 169, 171
Dowling, Joe 26, 181
Doyle, Mick 183
Doyle, Roddy 135
Duffy, Veronica 181
Duggan, Patrick 181
Dukes, Gerry 185
Durer, Albert 190

Eliker, Darren 117
Ellis, Desmond 181
Elmina 39, 40, 42, 82, 186
Endgame 131
Enrico Cuatro ix, 142
Eustace, Finola 182

Faith Healer 161
Farquhar, George 175
Farquharson, Alan 183
Field Day 1, 2, 23, 57, 60, 148–150, 175, 182, 187, 190
Fitzgerald, Jim 181
Fitzgerald, Susan 182
Fitzgibbon, Ger 188
Fitz-Simmon, Christopher 186, 188
Fitzsimmons, Suellen 117, 177
Flaubert, Gustave 128
Flood, Kevin 182
Fogarty, Anne 185
Ford, John 140
Forde, Michael J. 182
Fouere, Olwen 182
Frawley, Monica 182
Frazier, Adrian 190
Friel, Brian 81, 99, 110, 112, 126, 143, 148, 151, 161, 188, 190
Fry, Jarrod 117, 183

Genet, Jean 31
Geraghty, Clive 25, 55, 167, 181
Ghosts 2, 3, 110, 142, 182, 190, 191
Giacometti, Alberto 101, 106, 153
Gigli Concert 161
Giles, Martin 117, 177, 178, 183
Goebbels, Joseph 57, 60, 62, 127
Gogol, Nicholaï 82
Golden, Nuala 182
Goldsmith, Oliver 175
Grace 102, 103, 106, 156, 159
Grene, Nicholas 187, 188
Grennell, Aiden 181
Grimes, Frank 181

Hamlet 38
Hammond, David 148
Harding, Angela 181
Heaney, Seamus 148
Henry ix, 3, 174–179, 183
Hepburn, Doreen 182
The Herne's Egg 130, 131
Hersey, Ben 177, 183
History 1, 2, 4, 7–11, 16–18, 27, 31, 58, 59, 65, 78, 93, 101, 108–110, 112, 113, 121, 133, 134, 137–140, 162, 163, 166, 168, 185, 187, 188
Hitler, Adolf 62, 68, 106, 127
Howard, Richard 182
Hugh 1, 7–19, 143, 191
Hughes, Declan 191
Hurwitz, Amanda 182

Iago 186
Ibsen, Henrik ix, 2, 72, 110, 121, 142, 190
Identity 2, 7, 11–19, 30, 32, 45, 46, 48, 52, 59, 60, 63–67, 71, 96, 114–116, 121, 134, 149, 185–188, 190, 191
Innes, Christopher 189
IRA 149
Irish Academy of Letters 1

Jackson, Gemma 182
Jerusalem 50, 83, 88, 90, 93, 96
Jo 24, 27, 29, 30
John Bull's Other Island 115
Jones 28
Jordan, Patrick 177, 183
Joyce 2, 57–68, 130, 187
Judith 3, 98, 100, 102, 103, 105–107, 157, 159

Kabuki 70, 129
Kavanagh, John 181
Keane, John B. 143
Keenan, Rory 111, 182
Kelleher, Tina 182
Kelly 24, 27, 29, 30, 181, 182
Kestelman, Sara 104, 106, 158, 159, 183
King George V 62
Krom, Erin 183

Lacey, Eric 182
Lady Fetchcroft 85, 87, 88, 93, 95
Lambert, Mark 182
Lawless, Deidre 181
Lawlor, Tom 158
Lawrence, Ben 117
Leonard, Hugh 143
Lesser, Anton 181
Lily 90, 116
Limauro, Cindy 183
Logez-Carpentier, Godeleine 185
Lohan, Michele 181
Long, Joseph 191
Lorca, Frederico-Garcia 190
Lynch, Eddie 181

Mabel 8, 13–15, 17, 191
MacGahern, John 128, 129
MacIntyre, Tom 125, 164
Madame MacAdam 21
The Madame MacAdam Travelling Theatre ix, 2, 4, 20, 21, 23, 24, 27, 28, 98, 119, 147, 150, 182, 190
Making History 185
Marat-Sade 150, 188
Marie-Thérèse 24, 29
Mary 114, 115, 191
Mason, Patrick 142, 151, 153, 164–166, 168–173, 181, 182, 186, 188
Massey, Anna 182
Mauriac, François 128, 129
McCabe, Michael 182
McCall, Nick 182
McCann, Donal 161, 162, 181
McCarthy, Maggie 182
McCracken, Louis 181
McDermottroe, Conor 182
McFadden, Kevin 183
McGrath, Brian 182
McGreevy, Tom 181
McGuinness, Frank 110, 125, 141, 190
McHugh, Kevin 181
McKenna, Bernadette 182
McLoughlin, Brendan 182
McMillan, Richard 177, 183
McMullan, Anna 186, 189
McSorley, Gerard 182
Medea 103
Methuen, Eleanor 158, 183
Meyers, Larry-John 177, 183
Michelangelo 190
Miller, Arthur 131, 176, 183
Mr. Roche 1, 24
Mitchell, Justine 104, 158, 183
Molloy, John 55, 152, 153, 167, 168, 181, 186
Monelli, Katie 111, 182
Montague, Hélène 41
Moore, Catherine 117, 176, 183
Morash, Christopher 186
Morrison, Van 151
Mosley 62, 63, 127
Mountfort 9, 10
Mountjoy 10
Mrs. O 34, 38–40
Mullen, Conor 182
Murphy, Fionula 182
Murphy, Tom 143, 161
Murray, Christopher 185
Murray, Julia 186, 187
Music 3, 53, 96, 97, 120, 122, 139, 151, 158, 164, 169, 172, 176, 177, 181, 188
My Scandalous Life ix, 182

Nell 3, 98–107, 148, 156, 157, 187
Newham, Seamus 181
Nietzsche, Friedrich 173

Noh 82, 129
Nolan, David 183
Nolan, Jim 182

O'Brien, Dave 182
O'Callaghan, Ciar 182
O'Carrigan, Mairtin 117
O'Casey, Sean 139
O'Connor, Joseph 181
Odéon 128
O'Driscoll, Mary 182
O'Hanlon, Sinead 183, 186
O'hAonghusa, Michael 26
O'Hara, Joan 181
O'Kelly, Barry 181
O'Leary, Hal 117
Olympia Theatre 181
O'Mahoney, Robert 170, 172, 182
O'Malley, Tony 146, 182
O'Neill 1, 7–19, 120, 126, 131, 134, 135, 154
The O'Neill ix, 1, 7, 8, 11, 14, 91, 138, 145, 147, 154, 181, 191
O'Neill, Chris 181
O'Riordan, Marcella 181
O'Rourke, Catherine 181
Oscar 2, 70, 71, 73–80, 132, 135, 145, 169, 171, 189
Ostrovsky, Alexander 190
O'Sullivan, Thaddeus 182
Othello 186
O'Toole, Fintan 182, 186, 188
Out of Joint 161

Parker, Lynne vii, 155–157, 159, 160, 183, 187
Parnell, David 182, 183
Paul, Andrew S. vii, 174–178, 183
Paulin, Tom 148, 187
Pauline 112
Pavely, Phil 178
Peacock 153, 159, 181, 182
Pelletier, Martine 187
Pentecost 187
Perry, Des 181
Peter 36, 82, 112, 114, 115, 191
The Picture of Dorian Gray 169
Pilkington, Joseph 181
Piper, Tom 182
Pirandello, Luigi ix, 2, 110, 121, 142, 147, 174
Pittsburgh Irish and Classical Theatre 117, 174, 175, 177, 178
The Playboy of the Western World 1, 130, 131
Polina Andreevna 112
Power, Derry 181
Priest Figure 47
Prospero 175
Puppets 18, 59, 66, 69–72, 79, 83, 129, 138, 146, 165, 169, 171, 188
Purgatory 131

The Quiet Man 140

Rabe 29, 30, 31, 149
Radcliffe, Tom 182
Ramsay, Michael 117
Raphael (Sanzio) 190
Rawson, Mary 117
Rea, Stephen 60, 148, 149, 182
Religion 9, 17, 47, 49, 50, 52, 53, 73, 84, 93, 114, 116, 121, 139, 143, 144, 166, 169, 176, 189
Richtarik, Marilynn 187
Rickman, Alan 182
The Riot Act 187
Ripka, Joel 183
Roche, Anthony 186
Roe 182
Rohr, Tony 181
Roisin 15
A Room of One's Own 42
Rough Magic 41, 155, 191
Royal Court 1, 109, 128, 142, 161, 162, 181
Royal Society for Literature 1
Ruoti, Helena 117
Ryan, Jonathan 25, 142, 181, 182

Sampson, Denis 187
Schnittke, Alfred 158
Schopenhauer, Arthur 53
Schulz, Joseph 177, 183
Scott, Andrew 171, 172, 182
The Seagull ix, 2, 3, 98, 108–110, 116, 117, 142, 154, 161, 162, 164, 172, 174, 181, 190, 191
Seamus 29, 30
The Secret Fall of Constance Wilde ix, 2, 69, 70, 74, 76–78, 98, 101, 133, 138, 140, 145, 151, 164, 169–172, 182, 186, 188, 189
Sexuality 29–31, 68, 74, 145, 166, 185, 186
Shakespeare, William 36, 39, 94, 99, 110, 186
Shankey, Jonathan 182
The Shape of Metal ix, 3, 98, 99, 101, 103, 104, 106, 107, 144, 145, 146, 148, 153–155, 158, 162, 163, 183, 186, 187
Shaw, George-Bernard 115
Shea, Wendy 181
Sheridan, Jim 182
Sheridan, Richard 175
Six Characters in Search of an Author ix, 2, 3, 110, 111, 142, 147, 182, 190, 191

Sophocles 190
Sorin 112, 191
Spring Awakening ix
Stafford-Clark, Max vii, 109, 142, 161–163, 181, 182
Stein, Amelia 72, 111, 170, 172
Stoppard, Tom 165
Style 33, 76, 91, 121, 125, 138, 143, 169–171, 174–177, 179, 186
Susan 49, 50
Sylvester 39, 40, 186
Synge, John Millington 127, 131

Talbot 45–47, 49–55, 120, 139, 153, 168, 169, 186
Talbot's Box ix, 2, 44, 45, 52, 55, 56, 84, 91, 138, 139, 143–145, 147, 151, 153, 155, 156, 164–169, 172, 175, 176, 181
Tea and Sex and Shakespeare ix, 2, 33, 35, 41–43, 82, 94, 98, 99, 106, 107, 110, 140, 141, 156, 161–163, 176, 181, 190
La Tentation 128
Le Théâtre et son double 96
Toibin, Niall 181
Townsend, Stanley 41
Translations 112
Traverse Theatre 161
Tsoutsouvas, Sam 177, 183

Vanek, Jo 182
Virgin Mary 47, 84
Vivyan 71

Wakefield, Tony 181
Walsh, Robin 177, 181–183
Walter, Harriet 182
Wayne, John 35, 36, 140
Weiss, Peter 188
Welch, Robert 188
Weldon, Renée 182
White, Conleth 182
Wilde 2, 64, 69, 70, 74, 77, 78, 120, 129, 132–135, 138, 146, 156, 169, 189
Williams, Tennessee 131
Wilmot, David 182
Woolf, Virginia 42

Yeats, W.B. 69, 82, 129–131, 143, 149

www.ingramcontent.com/pod-product-compliance
Lightning Source LLC
Chambersburg PA
CBHW032056300426
44116CB00007B/770